The Law of the Land

The Law of the Land

Two Hundred Years of American Farmland Policy

John Opie

University of Nebraska Press
Lincoln and London

This book was made possible in part by a research grant from the Duquesne University Faculty Development Fund.

The paper in this book meets the minimum requirements of American National Standard for Information Sciences—Permanence of Paper for Printed Library Materials, ANSI Z39.48–1984

Library of Congress Cataloging-in-Publication Data

Opie, John, 1934–
  The law of the land.

  Includes index.
  1. Agriculture and state—United States—
History. I. Title.
HD1761.O65   1987   338.1'873   86-30860
ISBN 0-8032-3553-4 (alk. paper)

To Barbara and the Opie-Ray Six

Contents

Figures

Fig. 1. A graphic history of the public domain. Revised from *American Environmental History*, by Joseph M. Petulla. Copyright 1977 by Boyd and Fraser Publishing Co. Reprinted by permission of the publisher.

Timeline columns (left to right): 1770, 1780, 1790, 1800, 1810, 1820, 1830, 1840, 1850, 1860, 1870, 1880, 1890, 1900, 1910, 1920, 1930, 1940, 1950, 1960, 1970, 1980, 1990

Category	Entries (earliest → latest)
Administration	Cadastral Surveys; District land offices; Lead mines; General land office; Interior Department; Geological survey; Forest Service; Park Service; Mineral leasing; Grazing Service; Bureau of Land Management; Nat'l. Agricultural Land Study
Land for cash policy	First sales; First patent; Sale on credit; End of credit; $1.25 minimum; Price graduation; Three-year homestead; $1.25 minimum abandoned
Settlement policy	Advance settlement forbidden; General preemption; Five-year homestead; End of preemption; Enlarged homestead; Stockraising homestead; Advance settlement forbidden in states; Recreation and Public Purposes Act; Lands for school construction and recreation $2.50/acre
Land grants	First school grant; Zane's Trace; First road grant; First canal; 1st river grant; General purpose grants; Swamp grants; Railroad grants; A&M college grants; Desert grants; timber and stone; timber culture; Desert land acts; Reclamation homestead; Forest homestead; Landlaws applied to Alaska; Mineral Leasing Act; End of Indian land allotment
Other laws	Indian rights proclaimed; 1st allotment of Indian lands; Sale of mineral lands; Yellowstone; Forest reserves; National monuments; Reclamation projects; Taylor Grazing Act; Small tracts O&C lands
Public land states	OH; LA, IN, MS, IL; AL, MO; AK, MI; IA, WI, FL; CA; KS, MN, OR; NV, NE; CO; MT, ND, SD, WA; ID, WY, UT; AZ, NM; OK; Alaska statehood; HI
Water	Powell's Arid Lands Report; Carey Act; Reclamation Act; Colorado River Compact; Soil & Water Conservation Act; Colorado-Big Thompson Project; Imperial Valley Project; Soil & Water Conservation Act; 2nd Nat'l Water Assessment; 6 States Ogallala Report; Reclamation Reform Act; AZ Central Water Project
Transportation	National Road; Canal Fever; Railroad Land Grants; Interstate Highway System
External events	Northwest Ordinance; Louisiana Purchase; Post-War Land Boom; Panic of 1819; Specie Circular of 1837; Panic of 1837; Post-War Land Boom; Panic of 1893; Farmer Depression; Federal Subsidies

Preface

This history argues that a cherished American tradition is in large part unfounded. Americans have long been committed to the proposition that the checkerboard land pattern so agreeably laid out over the public domain since 1785 was an ideal instrument to secure ownership of private farmland for the typical American as frontier settlement moved westward. Until the early twentieth century, independent citizen-farmers on their own land made up most of the nation's population. But despite this apparent success story, there is evidence that the policy originally set out by the Land Survey Ordinance of 1785 mismanaged the nation's primary natural resource (chap. 1). Yet the survey seemed so promising an instrument that two years later the new Constitution did not tamper with it. But the process by which the public domain became private property often did not secure the promised fertile garden spot that was to guarantee permanent security for the American farmer. There is evidence that independent family farmers at home on their surveyed tracts—so often eulogized even today as representative (and necessary) Americans—rarely enjoyed prosperity equal to American life off the farm.

This book also argues that land laws and farm policies were based entirely upon the principle of unrestricted ownership of private property for personal profit, another fundamental American tradition (chap. 2). At several critical points, this dedication to private property distorted the stated goals of farmland policy. The real beneficiary of the extraordinary transfer of the nation's sovereign territory was speculative private enterprise. This book is unlike most farmland histories because it emphasizes the great power of private ownership to galvanize Americans of all kinds into a land frenzy (chap. 3). In fact, the inability of today's family farmers to save themselves is based in large part on their continued dedication to the myth that they are the bulwark of private enterprise because they still work their own property. Instead, today's independent farmers find little safety in owning land; they have become trapped by its ever-greater costs and debts whipsawed by uncontrollable global markets.

This book also argues that agricultural land use policies established long ago under different conditions continue to exist no matter how much they contradict their original intentions and are demonstrably harmful as well as irrelevant under new conditions (chaps. 4, 5, and 6). For example, two twentieth-century attempts to increase access to good land and improve farmers' well-being—the 1902 Reclamation Act and the 1936 Soil Conservation Act—still butt up against old constraints, such as unrestricted private property rights and geometric survey lines that have no relation to a workable agricultural geography.

I emphasize the agricultural region between the Appalachians and the Rocky Mountains—Turner's Old West, today's romanticized Middle West, and the bountiful and troubled Great Plains (chaps. 1, 3, and 7). This is the historic American heartland, now dogged by misfortune from global, national, and natural forces. Just as it was once believed American farmers could weather any hardship as long as they owned their land, so Americans still believe that the nation will prevail as long as the heartland holds true. No doubt critics of this book will find fault with my exclusion of anything but a glance at farmland and farming in California. Conditions there admittedly have set many precedents that are now observed nationally, but chapter 9 argues that California is more an exception than the rule. The great middle region—midwestern prairies and high plains—is undeniably the breadbasket of the nation and the world.

I also emphasize the unexpectedly chronic vulnerability of independent family farmers throughout American history; they were repeatedly placed in harm's way (chaps. 7 and 8). The strange mixture of myths and truths that forms our national sense of loyalty to the farm family, and our supposed dependency upon its well-being, is a major question to be addressed here, particularly in chapters 10 and 12. Special attention is given to attempts to settle in dryland regions west of the 100th meridian that were so flawed they have always posed risk conditions that typically belonged to frontier life.

The book concludes on two controversial notes. One is the argument that the venerable survey gridiron landscape, harking back to 1785 and only imperfectly laid upon the public domain, is long overdue for replacement by more appropriate agricultural districts, zones, conservancies, and other rigorous protection plans (chap. 11). As it stands, the nation is losing good farmland at unacceptable levels because it was never adequately identified or protected. A second argument is that the on-site independent farm family, partly because of its history, may be unable to guarantee the high-yield food production so many people depend on worldwide (chap. 12). Evidence is strong that the family farm is no longer a main actor in food production. There are irreconcilable policy differences between farming as a way of life, individualistic private enterprise, domestic demand and global markets, and environmental protection. The ferocious debates in Congress over the 1985 farm bill, and subsequent attempts to ignore the strictures of its legislation, demonstrate these differences.

In the pages that follow I argue that Americans have assigned "duties" and roles, even a moral imperative, to American farmland and American farmers that have persistently made both vulnerable. Many of these duties, such as producing both abundant *and* cheap food, must continue indefinitely into the future. Other duties, such as upholding the powerful agrarian ideal of the independent farmer, are being dramatically changed. The task of this book is to explore the historical forces that controlled our national capacity to mold an agricultural landscape, and our relative ability today to reshape that landscape into something more workable.

This history looks at repeated misconceptions that shaped American farm policy—badly. Two recent examples are typical: they reflect misjudgments in federal agricultural planning in the 1970s and 1980s that did much to fuel the current agricultural paradox of farmer failure amid abundance. Both planning errors seriously distorted land values and farmers' incomes.[1]

The United States entered the world grain market on a massive scale when it began to supply Soviet deficiencies in 1972–73. American farmers were patriotically urged to plant their own farmland "fencepost to fencepost" and build up production on marginal-quality land as well. Large food surpluses would give the United States important foreign policy leverage and help resolve a growing international trade deficit. Far more than ever before, the American farmer became responsible for a strategic national resource traded in a global marketplace. Under these incentives—duty to the nation and the promise of higher profits—the price of good farmland multiplied spectacularly, rising three to four times higher during the 1970s. Where in 1970 less than one acre out of every five served international markets, by 1980 foreign demand accounted for one of every three.

The classic laws of supply and demand for once served the farmer well: foreign demand grew at the satisfying rate of over 8 percent a year while total domestic output grew less than 3 percent a year.[2] Hence the marketplace promised higher prices. In fact, overseas volume in grain and grain products alone multiplied tenfold between 1950 and 1980, and dollar value rose a dramatic seventeenfold.

The future for efficient private American farmers seemed more bountiful than ever. But farm policy could not tolerate significantly higher food prices for domestic consumers—Washington's ultimate farm policy sin. Unlike earlier days, when farmers were a significant population—over 50 percent in 1900, 20 percent in the 1930s, and still 10 percent following World War II—by the 1970s 96 percent of the population were consumers and only 4 percent were farmers, and by 1985 the figure had declined to 2.2 percent. The die was cast; agricultural interests were losing their political leverage. But it appeared that American farmers could once again shoulder their responsibility to produce cheap and abundant food. They were participating in agriculture's technological revolution: greater efficiency kept production costs down while offering a decent return. Real net farm income in 1973 was the best since World War II. Growing global markets encouraged projections of permanent prosperity. Impelled by inflation, patriotic fervor, and even greed, farmers went into unprecedented debt (high interest rates seemed no problem) to expand their landholdings, buy sophisticated and expensive equipment, and expand their productivity. These actions would also hold down domestic prices and expand American participation in international markets. As late as 1981 a major Department of Agriculture policy report looked at the new equation and concluded that "our future focus will be meeting a growing demand, fueled in large measure by exports."[3]

Land values were projected to go up indefinitely. Wheat and rice acreage was expected to rise to 84 million acres in 1985 compared with 51 million in 1970, oilseed to 79 million acres from 41 million. It was expected that American farmland would be working at almost 90 percent of capacity in 1985 compared with 75 percent in 1970.[4] Excess capacity had kept farm income low and farmland underpriced. No longer would the government spend valuable dollars, as it had in 1972, to support an unused 62 million acres—nearly a fifth of the nation's cropland. For the first time, forecasters talked about how to cope with the limits of American agricultural productivity.[5] America's chronic farm problem was over.

But farm policy still sought lower food prices to keep domestic consumers happy and to compete in global markets. But would descending prices stay above the farmers' break-even point, much less give them a "fair" profit? Planners optimistically noted that good farmland was soaring in value, with double-digit annual increases. Independent farmers would prevail despite low commodity prices because land made valuable by its demand was now their safety net rather than their annual production income. Contrary to the troubled record of the past fifty years, they could prosper even as crop prices stayed low to satisfy consumers. It was the best of all possible worlds until a combination of forces brought a disastrous collapse in the price of food and the price of land.[6] In the split second between 1980 and 1983, the rising dollar overseas pushed American farm prices out of international competition. The global Green Revolution raised international productivity and made Third World nations much less food dependent. Foreign-policy-oriented grain embargoes in the late 1970s undermined American credibility on international markets and allowed heavily subsidized European farmers to undercut American commodity prices. Brazil entered and captured much of the world soybean market. Domestically, farmers were compelled to borrow at high interest rates not seen for more than a century. As food prices and land values declined, American farmers could not protect themselves from all these forces simultaneously. They felt victimized by a multilayer collapse in which government farm policy was a major actor. Between 1981 and 1983 American wheat acreage dropped 20 percent, from 81 to 61 million acres, while yield per acre grew from 34.5 to 39.4 bushels. The cheerful 1980 estimates for 25 percent more exports by 1985 did not materialize. After peaking in 1981, exports declined to 1979 levels in 1983 and continued to fall.[7]

The second error compounded the first. In a 1980–81 agricultural planning misjudgment, Department of Agriculture officials argued that the capacity of American farmland had in fact reached its high point, even if better seeds, pesticides, fertilizers, and equipment became available. Hence more farmland would be needed to meet domestic and foreign needs. Normally cautious agricultural officials feared the nation had reached its peak capacity for food production, with little or no surplus farmland. The era of consistent agricultural growth, averaging 2 percent each year, which more than doubled productivity in fifty years, had come to a close. The United States, for the first time in its history, would be producing at capacity.[8] Perhaps 65 million marginal acres—a 25 percent increase—could be brought into production, but higher expenses to compensate for poorer conditions would demand a 70 percent rise in crop prices. But the period 1980 to 1985 did not save the American farmer by eliminating surpluses and putting all available land under the plow. Instead, between 1980 and 1985 food production reached new heights, the anticipated global market dwindled, and it appeared that crop prices would be chronically depressed. Instead of rising, land values—upon which farmers and farm planners depended—began to fall. The conditions predicted in 1980–81 did not materialize.

Such recent misjudgments and unanticipated changes were not the first to bring often-fatal costs to American farmers. The whipsawing of land values was not an isolated event. Much of the politics and plight of farmer and farmland results from two hundred years of mythology and history combined.

Introduction

There are 1,500 miles of fertile flat land between the Appalachians and the Rockies. To anyone looking out a plane window while flying at 30,000 feet over the vast sameness of middle America, the most obvious sights are man-made. A vast grid of rectangles and squares, ranging from 40 acres to the square mile of 640 acres, often alternating green or golden fields, brown or black soil, rich and humid or dry and barren areas, presents a landscape precisely divided and measured. The western half of this checkerboard vista features the geometric, aesthetically pleasing green circles inside brown squares that signal center-pivot irrigation across perennially rainless land.

On the ground, as anyone who was a midwestern farm youngster remembers, the grid also meant section roads that ran straight for miles in isolated country. You could get your old high-powered car up to top speed along the single narrow concrete strip and you might run off into a telephone pole if you were unlucky, or cut a wide swath across a cornfield if you were lucky. This was a side attraction of the peculiar but effective land revolution dating back to one of Congress's earliest public statutes, the Land Survey Ordinance of 1785. This law allowed a frontier settler west of Pennsylvania and north of Texas to walk up to a plat map on the wall of a regional land office and democratically shop for a tidy, right-angled square representing a standard tract of fertile farmland enclosing, for example, one-quarter of a square mile or 160 acres—the fabled quarter section.

One immediately apparent flaw was that the law allowed no space for public roads. Their sixty-six-foot width had to be expropriated from farmers' lands.[1] In the Dakotas, Kansas, and Nebraska, section lines were simply declared public roads with no look at the terrain they crossed. Roads did not skirt steep hills, bypass swampy land, or follow meandering streambeds. The same stream might be crossed many times to maintain the section line, taxing the assets and skills of counties and townships to grade, pave, and maintain the roads. Section roads connected towns, villages, railheads, or markets only by a bizarre zigzag line. One Wisconsin state geologist encountered section roads with forty-five-degree grades: "I have lived in hillier countries, but never had to climb such hills as where they lay roads on section lines."[2] A crop-laden horse-drawn wagon could not make the grade, nor could early automobiles or trucks. The system violated the dictum that straight roads are good but level roads are better.

The rational survey was indiscriminate. It might cut a farm on good soil off from needed water on a neighbor's claim across the section line. Or it might divide a valuable grove of trees into three rectangular woodlots; none could survive independently, and so the grove disappeared in a decade. If by some quirk of colonial history the French had persevered in the American heartland instead of the English, the land would have been developed by the logic of waterways and river basins, soil quality and terrain, instead of the checkerboard. Frenchmen moved along the river valleys, following the natural contours of the land, whereas the English forged west against the grain of the continent's north-south geography.

The law gave the grid an abstract reality that offered psychological security to settlers. Arbitrarily, like the English twelve inches to a foot, the Phoenician alphabet of twenty-six letters, or the Babylonian ninety degrees to a right angle, the checkerboard pattern, as it spread westward from the Pennsylvania-Ohio line and eventually covered 69 percent of the lower forty-eight states, became a preordained landscape. Even the newly arrived European immigrant, looking at the American vista with a fresh eye, did not question but took comfort in the regular, geometric arrangement. It is the received textbook design of the United States. And it profoundly affected both farmers and soil.

But from the first the gridiron survey overwhelmed both the natural terrain and alternative farmland patterns. By 1862 Abraham Lincoln, in his remarks on the new Homestead Act, observed that the only identifying markers and locating points on the vast inland prairie were visible rivers and invisible surveyor's lines.[3] On the plains the visible scene was reduced to a minimalist landscape of unbounded grasses, the flat surrounding horizon, and the infinite sky. The checkerboard became the sole orientation of this vast American space, and hence its true measure. The survey pattern took hold in large part because this level, uninterrupted land made a harmonious match with right-angled planning. It was as if the men of 1785 could see over the horizon to land they knew nothing of and did not dream of owning until the surprising French offer in 1803. One historian of the survey, Hildegard Binder Johnson, wrote about the plane geometry of farmland along the fertile and absolutely flat bonanza farmland of the Red River of the North: it was the "near-perfect realization of a design planned 200 years earlier."[4]

The survey created the most extensive cadastral land system in the world. In a remarkable way it could be expanded continuously and contiguously over thousands of square miles. The true geography of America—the fatness of the land or its barrenness—disappeared under the checkerboard, which smoothed out the varied terrain into a single recognizable pattern. No other nation made a more positive affirmation of the rationality, order, and passion for control of the eighteenth-century Enlightenment. One wonders what the plan would have been in another era with another people, perhaps the Chinese or the Vikings.

Across the midland plains, the survey is America's tour de force on the land, civilizing infinite vistas. The survey changed open fragmented space into an ordered geometry that could be enclosed by the human imagination and domesticated into the classic American farmstead. There is a human capacity to create geometric space, turn it into a mathematical abstraction, and contain it for convenient use. The plains, a nothingness to their first travelers, were given recognizable form by the mental construct of the survey. As in a schoolbook geometry, the lines and planes extended indefinitely beyond the immediate frame. The grid could be extended beyond the original vision of the 1785 ordinance.[5] The emotional center of infinity shifted from fear of the unknown land to the human capacity for unending conquest. The wonder of the survey was that it could reach into unknown regions, like over-the-horizon radar, to capture unmapped landscapes as far away as the Pacific Ocean. The survey landscape offered to newcomers an unexpected sense of security and safety not available elsewhere, replacing an amorphous and chaotic wilderness with the human world of rational familiarity. Plat maps predicted the existence and direction of furrow, fence, and road, creating a vertical-horizontal rhythm in the land.

The utility of the survey cannot be overestimated. Land became a standardized, interchangeable commodity, even though its quality varied widely. Individual ownership could be guaranteed by simple and accurate descriptions. Irregularly shaped holdings, burdened with uncertain boundaries and overlapping claims, began to disappear as the survey took hold in Ohio and Indiana. It gave previously

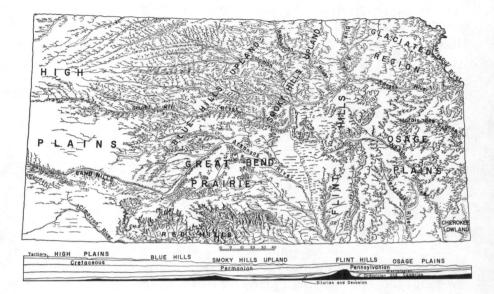

Fig. 2. Presurvey landforms of Kansas. The natural terrain of Kansas, particularly important river valleys and prime farmland, was ignored when the public domain was surveyed and sold to farmers and speculators.

unknown security to settlers. In America private land purchase and ownership are reliable and dependable as nowhere else. As a result, according to Roy M. Robbins, another historian of the survey, the great western migration after the War of 1812 must be called "a movement of peoples comparable to the barbarian invasions of Europe in the Fourth Century."[6] By 1860 the commissioner of the General Land Office could claim: "The system is perfect, the price moderate, and the settler is secured in his improvements."[7] Hildegard Binder Johnson has observed that the land survey facilitated the "greatest real estate deal in history" as it began the transfer of 1.3 billion acres (out of a total of 1.8 billion) from public trust into private ownership.[8]

The psychological impact of the survey also cannot be overstated. Few people can be persuaded to carve a farm out of primeval wilderness, but the survey gave the impression of orderly, controlled, legal land development under the umbrella of government regulation and management. The survey pattern transformed the strange wilderness into a familiar geometry. German immigrants to Nebraska, for example, arrived with preconceived notions that "nature" meant

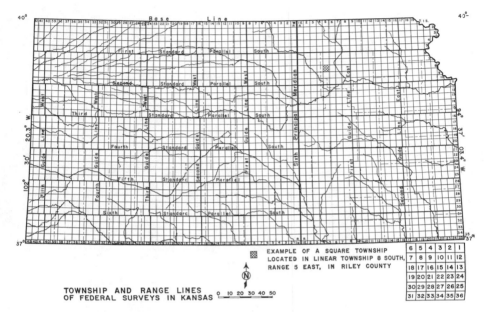

Fig. 3. Township and range lines in Kansas. The geometric pattern of the land survey system controlled Kansas settlement. The extreme contrast between physiography and geometric survey in Kansas was typical of land surveys in all the public domain states. From *Historical Atlas of Kansas,* by Homer E. Socolofsky and Huber Self. Copyright 1972 by the University of Oklahoma Press. Reprinted by permission of the publisher.

formal gardens and domesticated lands. Human orderliness, not wilderness, dominated the European landscape. Europe's remaining primeval wilderness existed as islands surrounded by centuries of culture and tradition. But immigrants to Middle America were stunned to find themselves living on islands of domestic settlement in a vast ocean of wilderness. They were skilled farmers, but they did not know how to clear or prepare wilderness. The survey simply removed "wilderness" from their view.

The survey did more to determine the nature, values, and qualities of American society than has usually been acknowledged. Never before had there been such an opportunity to create national policy afresh, to invent a national landscape, and hence to direct the course of an entire nation. Even the new federal Constitution when it was devised in 1787, did not interfere with the Land Survey Ordinance of 1785.

CHAPTER I

Order on the Land

Now when the Republic was young all Americans knew what to do when they got real money: If you gave an American a dollar, he would buy something costing ten. This was only good sense, the American knew, because soon the ten would, by the sheer magic of America, become a hundred. The instrument of this magic, the touchstone, was land.

Forrest McDonald,
The Formation of the American Republic, 1776–1790

When the Mississippi River reached flood crest in the spring of 1785, its turbulent muddy waters attacked the small French settlement of Ste. Genevieve on the Missouri side, across from Kaskaskia in Illinois. The unrelenting river literally wiped out the "long-lot" property lines that in French colonial tradition ran inland from the shoreline. On a ratio of one *arpent*, or 192 feet, along the shore, to ten or more inland, these *rangs* each included a riverfront floodplain, a house closely spaced with its neighbors on adjoining long lots, and room for a garden, stable or barn, and farmland. The appearance was very similar to long-lot forest villages in Germany, Bohemia, and Poland as well as in France.[1]

On 20 May 1785, a few weeks after the river washed away the long-lot lines on Ste. Genevieve's shore, the struggling Confederation Congress of the raw new United States laid out its own property-line system upon the entire national wilderness west of Pennsylvania. The legislators, like Olympian deities, infused with the hubris of the Age of Reason, took an overwhelmingly large and chaotic wild region and put it into order. The Land Survey Ordinance of 1785 changed the western United States from formless wilderness into a remarkable national geometry of gigantic squares and rectangles varying from 640-acre sections to 23,040-acre townships. Later the minimum tracts would go down to 320-acre half sections, to the famous 160-acre quarter sections, and even to 40-acre quarter-

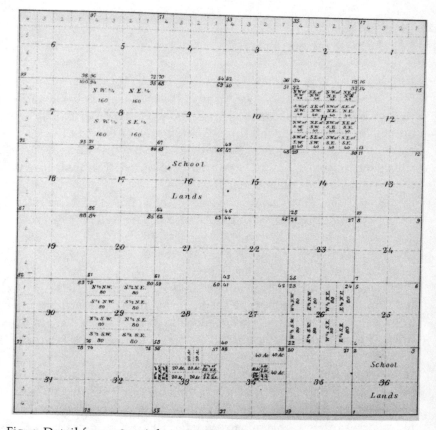

Fig. 4. Detail from 1875 Atlas, "Explanation of the Government Surveys," showing representative organization of a township, including section numbers, school lands (sections 16 and 36), half-, quarter-, and quarter-quarter sections, familiar to settlers on the public domain. From a typical late nineteenth-century farmer's vanity atlas, *Illustrated Historical Atlas of the State of Iowa*, by A. T. Andreas (Chicago: Lakeside Press, 1875).

quarter sections. A continuously expanding gridiron would eventually crisscross the western two-thirds of the emerging United States.

The ordinance brushed aside alternative landownership patterns based on tradition or geography. Exactly at the point where another river, the Ohio, flows across the border of western Pennsylvania, 350 miles west of the Atlantic coast and 600 miles from Ste. Genevieve, the landscape would shift dramatically from the irregular metes-and-bounds property lines taken from Old World practices into the characteristic American checkerboard landscape. With an extravagant bravado bordering on folly, Congress forced a geometry of squares and rectangles upon the naturally curving field shapes based on terrain, soil quality, and watercourses. Then, in an extraordinarily powerful act of human organization, the abstract geometric survey lines were extended into unknown regions over the horizon. The square and rectangular survey had no final boundary line. It measured and described public lands, known or unknown or imagined, as the new nation continuously expanded westward over unseen forests, plains, mountains, deserts, and gardens to the Pacific shore.

The 1780s were a yeasty decade for the new nation. Few people would have bet on the future of the United States as a lasting entity. The national land was so severely undermined by overlapping claims from the wrangling states, aggressive colonizing companies, profiteering speculators, and proudly independent settlers that the weak sovereignty of Congress was laughingly ignored. Who, for example, owned the new nation's grand prize, the vast empty zone north and west across the Ohio River, acquired under the terms of the 1783 Treaty of Paris?[2]

The original thirteen colonies were now landed states under a national jurisdiction, but little else was clear. All parties agreed that prior landholdings would remain binding and accepted British precedents for solving land disputes, claims, and charters. In 1834 Chief Justice John Marshall would say, "the people . . . may change their allegiance . . . but their relations to each other and their rights of property remain undisturbed."[3] The land rights of the states and of private parties did not have to be reinvented ex nihilo. Passions rose over the vast overlapping colonial charter claims of Massachusetts, New York, Connecticut, Virginia, the Carolinas, and Georgia. States with no claims—New Hampshire, Rhode Island, New Jersey, Delaware, Maryland—fought off potential second-class status in the land-grabbing struggle. One quickly approved solution was to make the unsettled lands from the Pennsylvania line west to the Mississippi into common national property. Such territory, it was effectively argued, had been "wrested from the common enemy by the blood and treasure of the thirteen states."[4] Even during the war, Maryland announced it would never ratify a central government unless the West was held in common. For months the angry debate over the western lands brought threats of state armies marching against each other and the speedy dissolution of a barely born nation.

Virginia broke the impasse, under Jefferson's egalitarian prodding, by ceding her trans-Ohio claims to Congress on 1 March 1784. Since Virginia was the largest and most powerful state, its cession induced the others to comply. All state claims were surrendered by 1786, aside from the craftily conceived Virginia and Connecticut military reserves.[5] Land-law historian Paul Gates rightly concludes that "the transfer of these territories probably did more than anything else at the time to give prestige to the [central] government."[6] The gargantuan public domain quickly became the national preoccupation between 1784 and 1786.

With surrender of claims outside their own boundaries, the states experienced a gradual decline in their land-ruling powers; sovereignty would instead become a national right.[7] Historians have made much of the equal standing between new states and old forged under the ordinances of 1784 and 1787. But the first new states, beginning with Ohio, found they could not prevent the central government, weak as it was, from controlling the physical landscape. The Articles of Confederation gave the central government the right of "disposal of the soil." This power carried over into the Constitution. True, a new state had a legal existence, but it stood as an abstraction unless a benevolent central government tendered it real property. While the states were fighting internecine battles to settle their boundaries, the central government won the war over territory in its ordinances of 1784, 1785, and 1787.

Land grabs were not limited to wrangling between the states and the central government. Most Americans went "land crazy." The profits were tantalizing. One backcountry Pennsylvania farmer-speculator, William Findley, piggybacked a personal fortune and political power on his dealings. A man could borrow £100 from the state on a tract he already owned, then exercise the right to buy state securities on the open market at a third of their face value. The law then allowed him to trade these public securities back to the state at par or full value for state lands, thus generating an instant paper profit of 200 percent. Findley called the procedure magical. The state also benefited, because it received 6 percent interest on the original £100 and sold off a £300 parcel of land to reduce its public debt. This Byzantine arrangement was typical of early American land speculation.[8] Two years before, in 1783, the people of North Carolina had made themselves rich by selling their public lands to themselves at outrageously low prices.[9] This self-delivered gift would become the state of Tennessee.

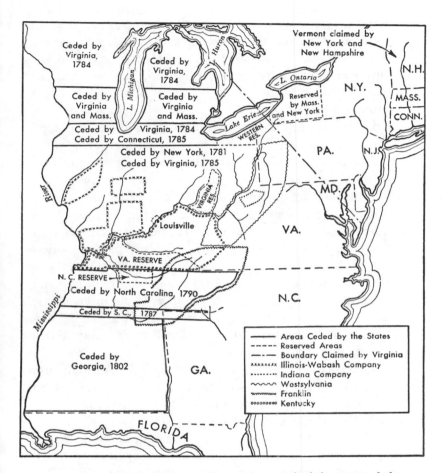

Fig. 5. Western land cessions, 1780–1802. Several of the original thirteen states, led by Virginia, surrendered their claims to western lands and created the original public domain, which then was surveyed and sold off according to the geometric system. Reprinted with permission of Macmillan Publishing Company from *Westward Expansion: A History of the American Frontier*, 4th ed, by Ray A. Billington and William L. Hedges. Copyright © 1974 by Macmillan Company.

George Washington, stiff and unemotional as war hero and as president, got visibly agitated over a good land deal. While a young militia officer, smarting under British disdain for colonial ineptness, he still kept an eye out for investment in the Forks of the Ohio country. He returned in 1784 to inspect his timely purchases: "Such is the rage of speculation . . . that scarce a valuable spot . . . is left without a claimant." Again, the amount of open land amazed speculators.

Washington wrote, "Men in these times talk with as much facility of fifty, a hundred, and even 500,000 acres as a gentleman formerly would do of 1000 acres. In defiance of the proclamation of Congress, they roam over the country on the Indian side of Ohio, mark out lands, survey, and even settlement."[10] Even at times of national crisis, Washington's agents scoured the countryside for advantageous deals, and he would drop almost anything to ride and see some opportunity. By 1796 he held 32,373 acres in the Ohio country. Washington wrote, "Any person, therefore, who neglects the present opportunity of hunting out good lands, and in some measure marking and distinguishing them for his own (in order to keep others from settling them), will never regain it."[11] Robert Morris, Pennsylvania financier and politician and the most determined speculator of the era, noted that backcountry or wilderness lands were exceptional acquisitions, since they could lie undisturbed as prices rose, with minimal taxation, until some squatter happened upon a good site, improved it, and then could be obliged to pay the improved-land price, "which fully repays [the owner's] original advance with interest."[12] Major land investors included Benjamin Franklin, Patrick Henry, George Morgan, and most other public figures.

Daniel Boone's romanticized wanderings over the Kentucky frontier were actually quasi-secret, well-financed searches for multimillion-acre tracts of fertile land for the archspeculator Judge Richard Henderson of North Carolina. Even while rushing over eight hundred miles in sixty days to warn settlers of an Indian uprising, Boone's own land hunger made him pause to stake out a wilderness claim for himself and guarantee it with a new cabin. Boone's Wilderness Road was built to exploit the Kentucky bluegrass country so that Henderson could build his own inland empire, the Transylvania Company. He petitioned the Continental Congress in 1775 to recognize it as a fourteenth colony. After setbacks, Henderson was compelled to settle for only 400,000 acres.[13] Other intense efforts to carve out feudal holdings in the west included 500,000 acres along the Ohio River by the Ohio Company, 800,000 acres along today's North Carolina–Tennessee–Virginia border for the Loyal Land Company, Benjamin Franklin's western Pennsylvania speculations, and George Washington's Mississippi Company. The prerevolutionary Illinois Company claimed 1.2 million acres. This was surpassed by the 1.8 million acres of the Indiana Company. George Washington had already been very visible in the attempt in 1769 by four major enterprises to capture for the Grand Ohio Company an extraordinary 20 million acres covering much of the Ohio valley. This was proposed as a new proprietary colony to be named Vandalia to honor the royal consort, descended from the Vandals. But political support in London collapsed, and overlapping claims clouded title to the lands.[14]

State and federal claims for the vast public domain were thus not the only ones. Nor were the intentions of public agencies clear. Most European monarchs held their power by armed control of their territory. In theory the English monarchs owned all of England and carefully granted rights to its use to deserving noblemen. But in the new United States, state constitutions, notably that of Virginia in 1784, opened the door to unknown new arrangements when they repudiated the great feudal traditions based on oaths of fealty, primogeniture, quitrents, and entail.[15] To discard the feudal land system, despite its European universality, was easy; to devise a fresh alternative taxed the inventive powers of Congress. Strong arguments can be made, from the perspective of two hundred years, that Congress failed. It faced enormous pressure for outright sale to the highest bidder. In the process it lost opportunities to devise a national commons, invent long-term leasing, and offer tracts more adapted to terrain, climate, and soil conditions.

Officials in early Virginia and Maryland did not conceive of selling land. But less prosperous farmers went into the distant wilderness as the first "squatters." Both colonies succumbed to cash sales by 1683 and 1705. By 1750 the Eastern Shore and the Piedmont were in private hands. Grants ranging from 10,000 to 40,000 acres created landlord estates in the Great Valley.[16] The rush to land, however, led to badly drawn boundaries, often marked only by tree slashes, entailing serious overlapping, expensive, lengthy litigation, and settlers who found that the land they had purchased had to be bought a second time from another claimant. To its credit, the Confederation Congress, despite its Virginia bias, would reject "indiscriminate location and subsequent survey." Claims were irregular and land titles in conflict. Although the Virginia system allowed easy possession of good land, prime farmland often languished on large plantations, contradicting the widely accepted public ethic favoring useful development of good land. The system encouraged speculation and absentee ownership, gave little attention to the establishment of schools, churches, and other signs of civilization, and seemed to promise more of Europe's inequities.[17]

Landscape historian John R. Stilgoe writes that William Penn tried to build his colony according to the vision of "an Old World order transplanted across the Atlantic, a landscape of baronies, manors, and tightly nucleated agricultural villages."[18] Pennsylvania and other middle colonies made large and small grants and sales to individuals and companies. These often were held off the market undeveloped and unsettled for decades, profoundly inhibiting western expansion, economic growth, and rising land values.[19] Such delays did not suit a spirit of enterprise. Pennsylvania soon found it useful to tolerate squatters, even communities of Palatine Germans and feisty Scotch-Irish, who had improved their lands despite dubious title.[20]

The Confederation Congress struggled to maintain control over its major asset, the public domain. Pressure to sell off the public lands was nearly irresistible. The weak and harried Congress deserves credit for its attempt to avoid the confusions of land speculation, uncertain ownership, and delayed development already rampant in the states. It turned to the controlled, orderly land sale and settlement patterns that had worked for more than a century in New England.[21] New England seemed the ideal national landscape: dotted with small farms and having well-developed communities with schools and churches, centralized control of land development, and few large speculators' tracts. Originally Massachusetts expanded its frontier by the planned movement of entire religious communities onto prepared sites in the wilderness. By the eighteenth century, gradual secularization of the religious impulse, and the lure of profits from land speculation, led to independent wilderness development. Speculators divided large tracts or "towns," sometimes covering 60 square miles, into regular geometric units instead of traditional village house lots surrounded by a ring of long fields. A common speculative tract was 6 miles square, conveniently divided into 640 acres in each square mile. The New England system avoided ownership conflicts, guaranteed title to readily identifiable tracts, and above all promised an organized and systematic means of locating and selling land instead of the usual chaotic rush and perpetual conflict. The settler was to buy a definite tract of land, based on an objective mathematical survey, with specific boundaries that could be located on a map. The geometric landscape was a physical manifestation of a universal order that appealed to both Puritan theology and Enlightenment rationalism. The momentum toward the geometric simplicity of the square tract took hold elsewhere: in Virginia's plantation survey laws after 1701, in North Carolina by 1715, in the survey precedents set in 1784 by Massachusetts for townships in Maine and by New York for its turbulent western region, and in Jefferson's own square township proposals for western Virginia in 1777 and 1779.[22] When he chaired the committee that first drafted the land survey system, Jefferson also drew on the southern land management system that used government land offices for title claims, registrations, and payments. Both northern and southern interests were also served by alternating very large tracts—undivided 36-square-mile townships—with townships divided into square-mile sections. All the seaboard colonies contributed toward the uniquely American agricultural landscape: the scattered independent farm tract housing a single family, instead of the Old World agrarian community.

When Thomas Jefferson let his fertile imagination run free, he often drove his fellow workers to distraction. As chairman of Congress's Grand Committee to devise a plan for the new public domain, in 1784 alone he submitted three different tract-size plans to the committee—1,000 acres, 850 acres, and 640 acres. The first, with Jefferson's compulsive bent for improvement upon tradition, would have revolutionized surveying by replacing Gunter's Chain measure (used since 1620) of 66 feet with a nicely rational decimal-standard 100 feet, just as Jefferson would persuade the new nation to settle on 100 cents to the dollar. An acre was 10 square chains, but the subdivisions would be called "hundreds." But Jefferson could not budge his committee from Gunter's Chain, of which Stilgoe says, "no mathematical ratio is more important in the American Enlightenment landscape."[23] Jefferson also fiddled with the mile. He sometimes used the geographical mile of 6,086 feet, giving 850 acres per square mile, but eventually he agreed to the statute mile of 5,280 feet, generating 640 acres. Jefferson's experiments with different systems of measurement make it clear that the survey was not cast in stone from the first but began its history as a matter for debate and negotiation.[24]

Jefferson's interest in easy sale and quick title to the public lands was not self-serving. In 1776 he argued that the public lands should not be sold at all but should be given away to deserving yeoman farmers. Otherwise they would "settle the lands in spite of everybody" as squatters. Jefferson indirectly condemned George Washington and Robert Morris when they held out good land for higher prices or squatter improvements. He anticipated the long-term conflict between public good and private profit: "Whenever there is in any country uncultivated lands and unemployed poor, it is clear that the laws of property have been so far extended as to violate natural right."[25] In the debates concerning disposal of the public domain, Jefferson never backed off from the principle that "the small land holders are the most precious part of a state." To his contemporaries, his righteousness made him almost unbearable.

In May 1784 Jefferson provided his committee with details about practical surveying instructions. A base line or surveyor's line would be crossed by meridian lines at mathematically regular intervals. In addition, "the surveyors shall pay due and constant attention to the variation of the magnetic meridian, and shall run and note all lines by the true meridian, certifying with every plat what was the variation."[26] Jefferson also insisted on careful surveys with a standard chain, to be "plainly marked by chaps or marks on the trees . . . exactly described on a plat." Ever the practical farmer, he hedged his mathematical approach by insisting that useful terrain descriptions be marked on the plat, with "all water-courses, mountains, and other remarkable and permanent things" marked in distances from base and meridian lines.

Congress adjourned for the summer of 1784 without acting on the proposal. Jefferson reluctantly left the committee's unfinished business to others when he was appointed ambassador to France. But he became a more determined advocate of a government- controlled land system to serve the freehold farmer after visiting Versailles's formal gardens, which absorbed an area equivalent to one-quarter of all of Paris. The park was the playground of the aristocracy, regardless of the farming needs of the common man. Jefferson was convinced that unless Congress acted quickly and rightly, America's prime farmland could easily be lost to speculators with no public conscience.[27] Jefferson thought perhaps the land should not be sold at all to the small farmer, but freely granted. Only large-scale holdings by nonresidents should pay the nation's bills.

By early 1785 deepening financial incapacity forced the Confederation Congress to act quickly. Only rapid and large-scale sales of western lands would keep the national government solvent. In April a new committee, with one representative from each state, did little more than tinker meretriciously with Jefferson's plan before sending it to Congress for debate and vote. The geometric pattern remained, with townships set at 6 (statute) miles square. Only David Howell of Rhode Island is recorded as complaining that moneyed speculators won a bloodless victory over Jefferson's yeoman; the resulting ordinance was "the most complicated and embarrassing subject before Congress. . . . Infinite pains are taken by a certain set of men vulgarly called land robbers, or land sharks to have it in their power to engross the best lands."[28] Outright sale of land already surveyed would bring in funds more rapidly than the southern warrant method, which necessarily waited for land to be selected and marked. Sales could also be at public auction, with a standard price of a dollar an acre, barely accessible to ordinary citizens, tantalizing to the wealthy speculator, and far beyond the reach of the subsistence farmer. Those who held veterans' scrip or other depreciated paper might gain land, however, for pennies an acre.

Considering the special interests swarming over a weak Congress, rampant speculation in western lands by the legislators, and the trouble the new land system would have with existing titles and claims, the passage of the Land Survey Ordinance on 20 May 1785 is surprising. The western lands were not an untouched tabula rasa, and the Congress contained few innocent idealists. No one, not even Jefferson, doubted that the square farm units were artificial and arbitrary, impossible to link to the actual geographical variety of the West. But all the alternatives seemed worse.

The ordinance had one objective: the "Western Territory . . . ceded by individual states to the United States," and "purchased of the Indian inhabitants," was to be "disposed."[29] Congress created three new positions: one official geographer to administer the survey and sale and thirteen field surveyors assisted by thirteen chain carriers. "And each surveyor shall be allowed and paid at the rate of two dollars for every mile, in length, he shall run, including the wages of chain carriers, markers, and every other expense attending the same." They were to proceed to divide the Western Territory "into townships of 6 miles square, by lines running due north and south, and others crossing these at right angles."

According to Pennsylvania's 1681 proprietary charter, the western boundary of the colony/state was five degrees west of the Delaware River. This is Pennsylvania's current western border where, at its junction with the Ohio River, the north-south and east-west township and section lines began. To ensure initial accuracy, "the geographer shall personally attend to the running of the first east and west line; and shall take the latitude of the extremes of the first north and south line, and of the mouths of the principal rivers." Townships and sections were to be numbered "from south to north" sequentially, beginning in the southeastern corner.

After Seven Ranges were surveyed, platted, and the results returned to the Board of Treasury, the secretary of war had first claim "for the use of the late continental army" to satisfy Revolutionary War veterans' claims. Minimum price for all other tracts was an expensive "one dollar the acre," but significantly "to be paid in specie, or loan-office certificates, reduced to specie value, by the scale of depreciation, or certificates of liquidated debts of the United States." The first township was to be sold whole, the second by lots or sections, "and thus in alternate order through the whole of the first range. Lots numbered 8, 11, 26, and 29 were reserved for the national government, without explanation. Lot 16 was held out for the maintenance of a public school in each township. Both reservations were ineffective and were later eliminated. Also set aside were "one-third part of all gold, silver, lead, and copper mines" to be held or sold by Congress, but this condition was soon dropped.

The surveys, plat maps, auctions, and sales that followed demonstrated that the ordinance was not going to function as Congress hoped. Fixed prices were undermined from the beginning, and discounted and depreciated certificates became the standard means of acquiring land at pennies an acre. Reserved land, first held only for veteran priority and the public sections, set controversial precedents for later railroad and other speculator withdrawals. Nor were limits set on the number of tracts available to individuals or companies or any requirements made for settlement or improvement.

The ordinance seemed tailor-made for cash-rich speculators, as Congress probably intended. As long as Jefferson was absent in Paris, the small farmer had no effective advocate; thousands of frontier squatters or preempters already on the public lands were ignored. But even Jefferson was not likely to be sympathetic toward the rough and ready Scotch-Irish, a lawless breed of "bold and indigent strangers" who moved into unsettled tracts in "an audacious manner." Yet Jefferson might have agreed with their credo: "it was against the laws of God and nature that so much land should be idle while so many Christians wanted it to labor on to raise their bread."[30] Versions of this argument would bolster squatters' claims throughout American history.

O H I O
LAND GRANTS & SURVEYS WITH EARLY FORTS & SETTLEMENTS

Fig. 6. Graphical summary of the land purchases, survey tracts, and land grants in Ohio. Major precedents for public land sales and private speculation were established as settlers moved into Ohio. To avoid conflict over titles, to limit baronial private fiefdoms, and to allow orderly federal control, the ordinances of 1785 and 1796 initiated the geometric survey at the point where the Ohio River crossed from Pennsylvania into Ohio (Seven Ranges). From *Historical Geography of the United States*, by Ralph H. Brown. Copyright 1948 by Harcourt Brace Jovanovich, Inc; renewed 1976 by G. Burton Brown, Nancy Revsbech, and Laura L. Schrader. Reprinted by permission of the publisher.

Despite its faults from the beginning, had the Land Survey Ordinance of 1785 not been passed, Americans might well have spent the years since then buying land solely from a series of powerful and autonomous private land companies with virtual feudal powers over personal fiefdoms. Already the Ohio Company had succeeded in acquiring more than a million acres, at a discounted 8¢ an acre, just below the Seven Ranges. A number of congressmen were openly involved in the 5 million acres sought by the Scioto Land Company, which got government approval in 1787 but failed to raise enough capital. A consortium including Aaron Burr sought 2 million acres on the Mississippi. The Connecticut Company received 3.8 million acres in the Western Reserve. But with the 1785 law the United States instead became the dominant seller of America's western lands. If privatization had taken place, the government might have been compelled to intervene at an early point to regulate prices and conditions and to guarantee orderly western expansion.

For want of enough good surveyors a frontier was nearly lost. The Confederation Congress could groan and birth a law, but it fell into its usual inept ways in the simple discharge of the ordinance of 1785. Skilled surveyors were hard to find; they were most often self-taught "measurers." Many quasi-amateurs were put to work because they had found and platted their own perimeters and those of a few neighbors. Although few could use instruments, virtually all surveyors and chain carriers could follow the secondary instructions of the ordinance by noting springs, watercourses, land quality, and other terrain features. Most Americans had fundamental agricultural experience, which helped compensate for their limitations as surveyors.

The Ohio terrain of the Seven Ranges is chopped up into myriad stream hollows and hills. Survey equipment had been recently improved, but a good surveyor, working with a knowledgeable assistant, had a long and laborious task before him, depending as he did upon multiple sightings and complex mathematical calculations for each position. Congress had put the survey on an impossibly accelerated timetable, but it proceeded so slowly that the land sale income Congress needed so desperately might dribble in only after the government's collapse. Lack of money from the public domain did hasten the failure of the Confederation government and rushed the constitutional debates.

By February 1787, after about twenty months of work, the field surveyors, much to the dismay of Congress, had surveyed only four of the Seven Ranges and located them on plat maps. When the geographer of the United States, Thomas Hutchins, reported his leisurely advance, the Board of the Treasury angrily concluded that "considering the surveyors have already been employed two years, it is not probable that in the course of another, they will have completely surveyed the first seven ranges."[31] The board urged that the ordinance be quickly bypassed to put the four surveyed ranges on the market immediately. The land was to be sold at a minimum price of a dollar an acre until all sites were purchased, with one-third down and the rest payable in three months. The price was not cheap, nor were the terms easy. But Congress hoped the deeply discounted land paper that seemed to flood the nation would encourage buying. In the autumn of 1787 the first national public land sales and transfers to private ownership were completed: 72,934 acres for $117,108.22, all to small purchasers. Despite the intent of the ordinance and the hopes of Congress, no entire townships were sold. At the prevailing prices, wealthy private land companies, though many had vast amounts of ready cash, did not patriotically step in to bail out the fledgling government.

The Confederation Congress learned hard lessons that would not be forgotten by legislators throughout American history. The income generated by land laws geared to serve small farmers was hopelessly low. Congressional dedication to Jeffersonian yeoman-farmer ideals was never strong and probably was spurious. Now with proof in their empty pockets, the legislators, who had never stopped listening to the speculator lobby, rushed ignominiously into the embrace of Hamiltonian entrepreneurs. Since no upper limits had been set on land sales, the solution to financial stress was to sell very large tracts, far larger than entire townships, gobbling up private capital for government coffers. Any concern that the nation was squandering its capital resources to pay daily bills seemed minor in light of the vast stretches of real estate north of the Ohio River. Not for the last time, Congress openly ignored the intent of the ordinance of 1785. In a breathtaking move, it sold 1 million acres of the Western Territory to the Ohio Company. The company in turn used depreciated land certificates it had been quietly accumulating and paid out less than 10¢ an acre in real cash. Widely known backroom maneuvering included the intense pressure that the Reverend Manasseh Cutler, a major beneficiary in the Ohio Company, put on William Duer, secretary of the Board of the Treasury. The government, not for the last time in its land dealings, sold out to special interests. Within a week Congress enhanced the value of the company's new holdings when it passed the Northwest Ordinance to create new and equal states in the Ohio and western regions.

The Ohio Company's special interests surfaced again in 1787, when representatives from several states gathered wearily in Philadelphia to prepare for the impending collapse of the Confederation government. Its single asset was the western lands. Land was the silent participant in the negotiations for a new government, and the Ohio Company, with its aggressive claims, the not-so-silent partner. Most delegates came to Philadelphia in May and June 1787 intent on scrapping the Confederation in favor of a better-organized and more powerful central authority. Some came to make certain the barely united states would fall into several reasonably sized Balkan-like entities. Quickly the parties divided between states with enormous surpluses of unoccupied land or claims upon unoccupied land (Massachusetts, Pennsylvania, Virginia, North Carolina, South Carolina, and Georgia), and fully occupied states (New Hampshire, Connecticut, New York, New Jersey, Delaware, and Maryland). These unoccupied lands were bargaining chips with which the Constitution was negotiated. James Madison was wrong in his analysis that the division was over population; the average "large" state had 307,000 residents and a "small" one had 278,000—only a 10 percent difference.[32] Divisions between federalism and states' rights would depend on whether the public domain came under control of the new central government or whether the states or private speculators acquired a voice in final disposition. Hundred of millions of acres of unoccupied land were at stake.

On 29 May 1787, Governor Edmund Randolph of Virginia made a ritual denunciation of the Articles of Confederation and opened debate with his Virginia or Large States Plan. It reserved most government powers, primarily land policy, to the states. The landless states quickly perceived Randolph's proposal as a public domain land grab by states with claims, which could then profitably sell them and prosper in ways inaccessible to the landless states. Within two weeks William Paterson, attorney general of New Jersey, replied with the New Jersey or Small States Plan, not unexpectedly granting most powers to the central government, with the important proviso that acts of Congress were superior to all state laws. With considerable bravado, the landless states sought to give Congress the power to slough off portions of existing states that could be then admitted as separate states. This would have been little more than stealing the lands of underpopulated states. These delegates also proposed, half-seriously, to abolish the states altogether and place all power with the national government.[33]

Roger Sherman, spokesman for tiny Connecticut, had already captured the huge Ohio Western Reserve tract for his state in 1784. Now he worked behind the scenes with the South Carolina vote to guarantee a strong central government, in which land powers would be embedded in the Senate. But America's farmland future was decided on 23 July when the Confederation Congress, still in lame-duck session, sold a million acres of Ohio land to the Ohio Company for two-thirds of a million dollars. The Ohio Company, now infiltrated by Connecticut financeers, paid the bill in depreciated paper worth less than $100,000.[34] The new Ohio Company territory was one-third the size of Connecticut. Sherman suddenly lost interest in his private talks with South Carolina, and jurisdiction over the public lands was turned over to the Supreme Court without a fight. Connecticut, or its more prosperous citizens (the same thing, at the Convention), had more land than it could digest and dropped its aggressive stance about where control of the land resided. From this point on land-hungry delegates and the speculator lobby worked to make certain the new government would continue the lucrative policy of trading land for distressed or discounted government paper, at one-fourth to one-eighth of face value. Speculators also knew well that a strong national government would raise the real value of government paper. Before 1787, public land worth $10,000 could be negotiated for $2,000. If the Constitution was adopted, the same deal might cost $6,000 or even the full $10,000, a prospect that horrified speculators and drove them to intensive lobbying.[35] Under these pressures, the Constitution would stay silent about land.

In the fall of 1787 Congress authorized other large sales to be "not less than one million of acres in one body." The Very Reverend Mr. Cutler forged an agreement that sold a large tract to his Scioto Company. Another million acres went to the equally wealthy and clever John Cleves Symmes. After special interests and friends were satisfied by these immense transactions, Congress shut the door. In one of its last major acts, in early 1789, the Confederation Congress, which had virtually voided the ordinance of 1785 by its extraordinarily self-serving sales, now ordered the Board of the Treasury to survey and sell the rest of the Seven Ranges under the original conditions. This was a second attempt to revive small-scale land sales. But sales ground to a halt as the new nation waited anxiously for the outcome of the Constitutional Convention and approval of the new Constitution by the original thirteen states. Not until seven years later would the new federal Congress attempt to resolve the muddled interests, priorities, and policies that controlled the public domain.

CHAPTER 2

Land and Liberty, Individual Rights, and the Constitution

Most people who came to the colonies were in search of land on which to plant and prosper. The possession of land . . . everywhere . . . was recognized as the one indisputable stake in society. If the ease with which it could be acquired, especially by well-placed officials and their favorites, released torrents of greed that made a mockery of equality, it also released the energies of tens of thousands of men who were willing to sweat for the good life.

Clinton Rossiter, *Seedtime of the Republic*

The Pistole Fee Affair

Americans have from the earliest days reacted strongly to invasions of private property. In the 1750s Governor Robert Dinwiddie of Virginia walked unsuspectingly into a hornet's nest when he decided to put a stop to the casual way Virginians for many years had speculated in land. George Washington's renowned avarice was tame compared with that of his fellow Virginians, some of whom had made their constant buying, selling, and trading into a perpetual money machine. Dinwiddie ordered that land would henceforth be granted only after rigorous review and payment of a fee of one gold pistole, a universal coin worth about $3.60 in colonial Virginia. The House of Burgesses, crawling with speculators, was dumbfounded. After decades of unregulated development, Virginians believed in the total autonomy of their private property. They indignantly fought off government intervention and public "taking" of private assets. From Dinwiddie's perspective, he stepped in to regulate an uncontrolled rush for highly profitable land. The House of Burgesses claimed protection under the British constitution not to be deprived of property without their consent. They quoted the Royal Declarations "that no man's life, member, freehold or goods, be taken away or harmed, but by established and known laws."[1]

In the major pamphlet circulated during the debate, Richard Bland joined liberty and property into a seamless argument. Both were "precious vessels whose soundness is destroyed by the least flaw and whose use is lost by the smallest hole."[2] While admitting that land acquisition was highly profitable, Bland and the burgesses believed they were also protecting the liberty of private property, which has since prevailed continuously as the single most powerful feature of American society. Liberty meant above all the right of the individual to buy, own, improve, and sell property without interference. The right of private individuals to hold land and profit from it became the driving force behind debates about private property, personal rights, and political liberty.

The Pistole Fee Affair demonstrated that landownership was at the heart of the debate over American liberties. Freedom to acquire, improve, sell, trade, and speculate in land was the one subject that was not negotiable. It was more than a matter of principle. It was the opportunity to make one financial killing after another, virtually without risk. Few other attempts at intervention and regulation could have aroused Virginians so much.[3]

Landownership: Not an Original Colonial Right

Landownership was not an original right when the Virginia Company settled Jamestown in 1607. The company owned the land, and its employees were paid for their labor in food and supplies out of a common storehouse. But their lack of motivation contributed to Virginia's infamous "starving time" and nearly wiped out the settlement. The company abandoned its corporate ownership and gave each employee a three-acre "garden" as an incentive. Such a landholding was far superior to anything available back in England. One visitor to Jamestown reported that employees now did in one day what had taken a week under the old conditions: "Since the private allotment of land," three men harvested as much corn as thirty.[4] The system was so rewarding that the company began regular distribution of land. In turn the colony prospered, and in 1700 the company offered each new settler a "headright"—fifty acres. Headrights attracted hardworking farmers in all the colonies outside New England.

The Body of Liberties of Massachusetts Bay in 1641 insisted unqualifiedly on the absolute autonomy of fee-simple ownership:

"All our lands and heritages shall be free from all fines and licenses upon alienations, and from all hariotts, wardships, liveries, primer-seisins, year day and wast, escheates, and forfeitures.[5] From the first, land titles were generally unencumbered, under acquisition of land in "free and common socage," or a free and clear title. Again, the novelty and profitability of a free and clear title cannot be over-stated. Unrestricted land title created a wide new class in early America.

The ability to buy land was perhaps the greatest attraction of all to the prospective immigrant, particularly in light of the impossi-bility of doing so in the Old World, even with cash in hand. Any settler who was determined enough, and land hungry enough, could acquire a tract whose size would make an Old World land baron envious. In a typical observation John Wentworth, governor of New Hampshire, said in 1768 that even the highest wages in the empire, prime working conditions, and full choice employment could not keep people off the farm: "Scarcely a shoemaker, a joiner, or silver-smith but quits his trade, as soon as he can get able to buy a little tract of land and build a cottage in the wilderness."[6] New York's gover-nor, Henry Moore, observed nine years later that "servants imported from Europe . . . as soon as the time stipulated in their indentures is expired . . . immediately quit their masters, and get a small tract of land . . . poverty . . . is patiently borne and submitted to with the greatest cheerfulness, the satisfaction of being landholders smooths every difficulty."[7] Moore noted that even skilled artisans among such indentured servants almost universally chose a piece of land and lived on it despite opportunities for "comfortable subsistence" in their trade. All income and savings seemed destined to go to pur-chase land at the earliest opportunity. Colonial America became "a good poor man's country," with unprecedented horizontal and ver-tical mobility.

Invasion of Private Property: Sufficient Cause for Revolution

Colonial Americans were quick to take advantage of the new land rights.[8] Freemen possessed absolute control over all matters involv-ing their tracts. The earnest landowner could draw on powerful Saxon, German, or English "ancient rights." Jefferson called them *allodial rights,* orginally the powers attached to "an estate held in absolute dominion without obligation to a superior—i.e., the early Germany and Saxon freehold farmstead." He believed that the future success of the nation depended upon "personal property, in absolute dominion, disencumbered with any superior."[9] This commitment to freehold as the core of personal independence was so deeply embedded in Western ideas of natural rights that little new theory (after the common law, Harrington, and Locke) was needed to justify it in eighteenth-century America. Whether colonials became radicals or stayed conservative, they agreed on certain fundamental beliefs: republicanism, a strong legislature, individual rights, the separation of powers, and property qualifications. It is difficult to think of the political climate of early American history without ownership of land as the primary ingredient to guarantee the individual's autonomy.

Land Rights in the New Nation

Colonial commitment to protecting private property from encroachment did much to bring on the Revolution. The Declaration of Independence directly attacked George III for his "long train of abuses and usurpations" and singled out colonists' decade-long complaint about property-taking "taxation without representation." Had not John Locke said, after all, that a government that attempts to interfere with an individual's natural right to the entire value of his property deserves to be overthrown? In 1764 James Otis concluded, "What one civil right is worth a rush, after a man's property is subject to be taken from him at pleasure, without his consent?"[10] Otis created an important distinction for the nervous rebels: American land rights derive not from the colonial charters or from English law, but from natural, inalienable rights. Landownership, and all property rights, existed independent of any Crown grants, commercial charters, or the mother country's benevolence. Samuel Adams agreed: " It is acknowledged to be an unalterable law of nature, that a man should have the free use and sole disposal of the fruit of his honest industry, *subject to no control.* "[11] The long history of American landholders' complaints about the infringement of their rights by taxation and regulation stretches from the Revolution to the present. The American rebel in the eighteenth century could be the bedfellow of the modern conservative property owner: both would complain that the government was violating their rights as freeholders to control the disposition of their property. (See Chapter 11.)

The revolutionary debates were conservative in nature, intended to protect the existing property rights and landholding independence of the colonials. But the problem of how to put into practice Everyman's right to acquire property was left untouched to vex the new nation. John Adams and others argued only vaguely for a free society based on a wide distribution of "landed estates" to "the multitude."[12] Although Adams wrote, "if the multitude is possessed of real estate, the multitude will take care of the liberty, virtue, and interest of the multitude in all acts of government," the new United States, for all its innovations, was not based on egalitarian land reform.[13] No plan was broached among revolutionaries to force widespread land franchisement, despite fears that most Americans, like Europeans, might end up landless. New state constitutions in Virginia, Massachusetts, New Hampshire, New York, Pennsylvania, and Vermont did promote universal "natural right" landholding. They included "right to acquire" clauses to ensure the "happiness and safety" of free and independent citizens. But no promise was made to the masses.

Unencumbered private access to land, and the profits it generated, prevented rigorous colonial land-use planning. When the new United States came into being, it was compelled to find its own solution to the landownership problem or abandon the West entirely to private control. If a modern people's revolution means confiscating landed estates for redistribution to socialist communes or possibly small farmers, then American independence was not gained through a people's revolution. Land reform, though a constant refrain, was carefully sidestepped at the Philadelphia Constitutional Convention. Despite veteran and squatter unrest, James Madison did not believe that the western empty lands ought to be treated as a safety valve to satisfy the demand of the common man for his share of the benefits of the new government. Free redistributed land must not be used to prop up the central government. The high value set on private property was already too deeply embedded in American life. As Madison and other state delegates worried the constitutional process along, they ingeniously devised a strong central government to guarantee both private property and the democratic tendency.

Their extraordinary step was to apply private landholding to the multitudes. In the 1770s and 1780s property holding as a universal right was used as a litmus test of democratic principles. The logic behind it was profoundly conservative: only property owners

deserved the right to vote and hence gain access to political power. The convention delegates sailed into untested waters over the
unusual new American reciprocal interaction between democratic
principles and property rights. More accurately, how could the convention keep the democratic tendency under control and guarantee
propertied citizens their privileges? Madison's genius was to argue
that the rights of the individual in a democratic society were protected more by a strong centralized constitutional government than
by landownership.

Anti-federalists in 1787 quickly retorted that the new powerful
central government would speedily become a greater threat to property rights and individual liberties than mob rule by the democratic
masses. This complaint that the greatest danger to landownership
came from government intervention would be repeatedly picked
up into modern times by advocates of private property rights. On
the other hand, the challenge of the masses against the propertied
classes would play a lesser role in America than in other national
revolutions. The unexpectedly large numbers of American freeholders found their private property was not attacked for the sake of land
reform, but rather was admired and aspired to. America's revolutionary era may be unique in its emphasis upon protecting private property and other personal rights. This is reflected in the speedy passage
of the Bill of Rights and its incorporation into the Constitution.

In an unexpected twist of events, the federalist and anti-federalist
wrangles meant that the Constitutional Convention almost entirely
ignored the question of freehold landownership and private property,
even though these had been central to colonial and revolutionary history. When the constitutional debates began in May 1787, although
farmers were strongly represented among the delegates, the issue of
freehold did not arise. The delegates did not even debate a general
statement they made about the duty of government to preserve private property.[14] It is likely the constitutional debates may have been
saved because they did not engage the issue of private landholding.
In turn, however, private landholding was set adrift from specific
government policy and the democratic process. But it was widely
understood that it would not be touched. If the right to hold land was
watered down, the core of the new American society would be lost.
The complete autonomy of each citizen's private property was one
cornerstone principle about which there could be no debate and no
compromise.

Yet Gouverneur Morris kept at the conservative stance: land-

ownership and political power must be yoked together. Paradoxically, twentieth-century conservatives work hard to keep land and government apart. For Morris the long-standing logic of the eighteenth
century still held: landholding gave a person independence, which
in turn conferred freedom of thought and action, which in turn was
essential to responsible participation in public affairs. Ordinary landless "mechanicks" were considered irresponsible and easily bent to
the vagaries of popular moods. Every colony required property ownership as the qualification for voting and holding office.[15] The condition of freehold for the franchise was not seen as repressive and as
restricting the vote to a wealthy few, since "any man worth his salt
could get fifty acres or earn three pounds," particularly in the New
World. Even after most freehold qualifications for voting rights were
dropped, landownership still demonstrated a "stake in society," a
point taken from William Blackstone's *Commentaries on English
Law*.[16]

Most of the so-called founding fathers, including John Adams,
Samuel Adams, Benjamin Franklin, John Dickinson, James Otis,
Thomas Jefferson, and Alexander Hamilton, had condemned England as a feudal society where a privileged aristocracy lived off the
disfranchised. The new American society, in sharp contrast, was
founded on virtuous labor on freely owned land. Jefferson boldly
insisted that American colonials held their land not because of feudal
grants or English goodwill, nor even from Lockean natural right, but
because they had wrested it from the wilderness by hard labor: "As
much land as a man tills, plants, improves, cultivates, and can use the
product of, so much is his property. He by his labor does, as it were,
exclude it from the common. . . . God and his reason commanded
him to subdue the earth, i.e., improve it for the benefit of life, and
therein lay out something upon it that was his own, his labor . . .
thereby annexed to it something that was his property."[17]

The Constitution: A Landless Document

But, curiously, the word *land* is rarely and indifferently mentioned
in the Constitution.[18] Nowhere is land given the detailed attention
anyone would expect who followed the western land cessions and
the land ordinances of the 1780s. This neglect may be intentional,
but the omission means that the Constitution does not treat the

United States as a physical reality or geographical entity. In this regard it is a document dealing with abstractions. Neither is the more specific concept of *public domain* mentioned, although the public lands were the new nation's most extensive natural resource, which the struggling Confederation government tried to exploit for income, status, and sovereignty. In contrast to this constitutional silence, the earlier 1781 article 9 of the Articles of Confederation referred specifically to "the private right of soil," to state land grants to private parties, and to litigation over land between individuals and states.[19]

The closest acknowledgment in the Constitution that the United States has a geographical location is in article 4, section 3, second paragraph: "The Congress shall have power to *dispose of* and make all needful rules and regulations respecting the territory and other property belonging to the United States" (italics added). Emphasis here is placed on *disposal* not to the states, nor back to the native peoples, nor in terms of disputes with foreign nations, but to private individuals.[20] Most important, the Constitution did not claim the public domain as a permanent and irrevocable possession. The national government had many historical precedents for holding the land perpetually. But the Constitution's rare statement on territory was also an extraordinarily radical statement in light of global feudalism. Instead, *land disposal* was to be national policy. Land disposal was also to take place with all deliberate speed. This brief statement about congressional powers established national public lands policy. It began the process of rapid decentralization of landownership, with benefits and limitations that would shape the American character. It continued the government's plan for the intentional privatization of the public lands, which would make American society distinctively individualistic. Not least, laissez-faire free enterprise received a shot in the arm as land opportunities became entrepreneurial opportunities for both low-cost development and highly-profitable speculation. The Constitution thus provided an early indirect subsidy for nationwide capital enterprise.

This generous disposal of the public domain and protection of private investment in land can be traced back to the 1785 Land Survey Ordinance: "Be it ordained by the United States in Congress assembled, that the territory ceded by individual states to the United States, which has been purchased of the Indian inhabitants, shall be *disposed of.*"[21]

In addition, the Northwest Ordinance of 1787, significantly passed just before the Confederation Congress collapsed and in the midst of the Constitutional Convention debates, gave Congress superior rights to "the primary disposal of the soil." The 1787 ordinance pointed back to 1785 by guaranteeing "any regulations Congress may find necessary for securing the title in such soil to the bona fide purchasers." The 1787 ordinance also fought for the autonomy of federal lands: "no tax shall be imposed [by the states] on lands the property of the United States." To reassure the speculator lobby, the law also insisted that "in no case shall non-resident proprietors be taxed higher than residents."[22]

The Land Survey Ordinance of 1785 was implicitly incorporated into the Constitution through article 6, which continued all "debts" and "engagements" under the Confederation.[23] Also included were the territorial details spelled out in the 1787 ordinance. These two acts, in a step that was surprising in a largely feudal era, put sovereign territory on the market. They claimed the principle that public land could, and should, be legally bought and sold: "and real estates may be conveyed by lease and release, or bargain and sale, signed, sealed, and delivered." This did away with any remaining vestiges of primogeniture, entail, or inheritance controls over free sale and put teeth into the repudiation of any "title of nobility" in article 1 of the Constitution. To avoid the rise of another landed aristocracy in new clothes, the ordinance of 1787 decreed that the political power of new states turned not on territorial size or land wealth, but upon the number of "free male inhabitants, of full age."[24]

Treatment of western regions had been on the early agenda of the Philadelphia meetings. But the delegates sidestepped the pressing issues of speculation, exploitation, and preemption and the respective roles of federal, state, local, private, and Indian interests. The ordinances of 1785 and 1787 would at least hold off major distortions or unacceptable takeovers of western lands. There was no hurry. Apparently most Americans agreed with Thomas Jefferson when he concluded that it would take a hundred generations (instead of the actual five) to explore, settle, and populate the West.

The Constitution and its amendments are peppered with surrogate or substitute terms for land. Crucial words—property, nobility, taxation, debts, credit, due process, compensation, internal improvements, general welfare, new states—all carry land-use freight that continues to fill legislative, judicial, and agency books.

The Fifth Amendment in the 1791 Bill of Rights states in part: "No person shall . . . be deprived of life, liberty, or property, without due process of law; nor shall private property be taken for public use, without just compensation." In 1868 this was specifically applied to the states in the Fourteenth Amendment, which also protected "the privileges or immunities of citizens of the United States." Once the government disposed of territory to private interests, it could not recover it by confiscation. The Constitution admitted the higher rule of private property.

The Philosophical Debate over Private Property

Much of American history revolves around two words, *private* and *property*, treated separately and together. The two terms become extraordinarily powerful concepts when used to define land-ownership and land use. *Private* means *not* public, not held in common, separate from government. In the context of American history, *private* has been associated with each person as an autonomous entity, characterized by laissez-faire independence, free from intervention by government, and owing no competing public "duty." As for *property*, Americans were grounded in John Locke's definition: "Property . . . is the right a man has . . . for subsistence and comfort of his life . . . for the benefit and sole advantage of the proprietor, so that he may even destroy the thing . . . by his use of it, where need requires . . . government being for the preservation of every man's right and property."[25]

Much of early American history can be explained as the attempt to acquire and guarantee land as private property and the struggle to keep it independent of public intervention. The move toward continuing *privatization* of the physical territory of the United States is an extraordinary surrender of national worth and even national identity into the hands of private persons for their free profitable disposal. One alternative—perpetual federal ownership of the public domain as a national commons—was never seriously considered. The neglect of land treated as a national treasure, and the commonplace acceptance of private landownership, is not at all surprising.

This obsession with land as private property did not originate with the American fervor for independence.[26] Compared with revolutionary ideologies in the nineteenth and twentieth centuries, American independence did not seek radical land reform to shift ownership from the wealthy land baron to the common dirt farmer. American views were appropriated ready-made from English common law and the natural rights philosophies of James Harrington and John Locke in particular. It was as if, to paraphrase Henry Steele Commager, England imagined and America realized the fundamental belief that individual freedom, private property, and personal ownership of land are closely linked.[27] James Harrington concluded that the unexpected passions of the English Civil Wars broke out when no one power, neither Stuart monarchs, Cromwell and his New Model Army, nor the propertied classes of Parliament, dominated ownership of land. Land as physical property dominated human affairs. Land was the invariable source of wealth. In his 1656 *Commonwealth of Oceana,* Harrington's "Agrarian" possessed a combination of land, ownership, and sovereignty that was quickly appropriated by Americans, even as they smugly sat out England's struggles and built up their holdings free of England's intervention.[28]

Harrington stood in the tradition of Renaissance heroic individualism. Individual autonomy was humanity's first, natural, and most spontaneous trait. He defined freedom as personal independent ownership of land, without constraints. Landless men were servile and dependent, inevitably corruptible and invariably corrupted. A nation of self-sufficient agrarian freeholders would approximate the perfect society.

In 1689, when John Locke put together pregnant ideas in *Two Treatises on Government,* he did not dream it would become a handbook for American rebels. To Locke private property meant far more than today's personal possessions—even more than the autonomy made possible by ownership of land. Locke's property included all the qualities, powers, rights, and capacities related to human individuality. "Every man has a property in his own person." It was akin to the totality scientists today apply to the chemical, physical, and electrical "properties" of basic elements such as barium or potassium. Thus Locke would not distinguish life, liberty, and the pursuit of happiness from "enjoyment of property." Eighty-seven years later, as Thomas Jefferson reworked his first draft of the Declaration of Independence, he shifted comfortably from "life, liberty, and property" to "life, liberty, and the pursuit of happiness."

Locke said, and Jefferson agreed, that in their primeval state of nature all people had a natural right to property, just as metaphysical "accidents" are tied to "substance." The right to property was first of all a right to *subsistence*.[29] All people rightfully had access to land and its fruits so they might not starve. Land must be available to provide bread and water for basic needs. Americans quickly appropriated the Lockean logic of land right and linked it to Harrington's simple farmer:[30] the natural right to individual freedom depended upon owning land. Men without land were dependent, servile, and possessed by others; their condition was terrible, and they were without their rightful properties. Jefferson wrote: "Dependence begets subservience and venality, suffocates the germ of virtue, and prepares fit tools for the designs of ambition."[31] Landholders became free as they became independent of others for food and other benefits of land. The primary function of government was to guarantee private ownership of land.

For John Locke, the discovery of America meant the liberation of humanity. Vast unclaimed and unowned estates lay in a "state of nature," ready to be claimed by private individuals for their own pleasure. What would have delighted Locke was that more than 70 percent of adult white males qualified as freeholders in the new United States. He expected that a very few would hold enough land to participate in government, and that the landless lower classes would be excluded entirely.[32] But property, and its wide range of benefits, became in the new United States a "natural right" accessible to most inhabitants, not a barrier thrown up to protect the privileged few from the mob. In an extraordinary and unexpected turnaround, private landed property became the ally of democracy. John Adams concluded that the formation of a government of the people "had more relation to property than to liberty."[33] The American Revolution and the new United States made everyone a potential landlord instead of creating a universal peasantry. Adams described the proposed new government as "no other than a government in which the property of the people predominated and governed." The availability of land for all comers—for subsistence, for profit, and as an inalienable right—set the United States apart.

But conflict arose because private individual possession of land was treated both as an inalienable right and as the pathway to wealth. All Americans deserved land, even the poorest farmer. At the same time, land was to be valued at the highest possible market prices. This American preoccupation with individual landownership as Everyman's birthright, and the attention concentrated on land as a negotiable economic commodity, would profoundly affect the course of American history.

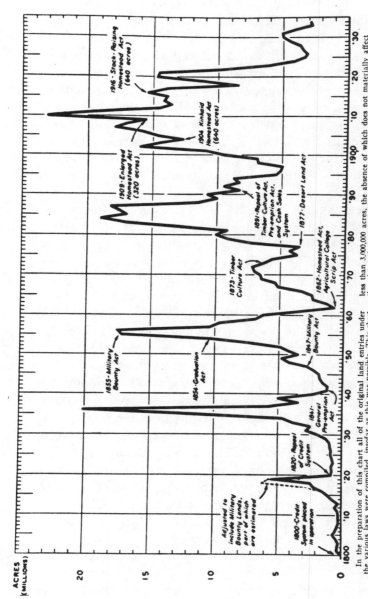

ACRES (MILLIONS)

20

15

10

5

0

1800 | '10 | '20 | '30 | '40 | '50 | '60 | '70 | '80 | '90 | 1900 | '10 | '20 | '30

1800-Credit System placed in operation

Adjusted to include Military Bounty Lands, part of which are estimated

1820-Repeal of Credit System

1841-General Pre-emption Act

1855-Military Bounty Act

1854-Graduation Act

1847-Military Bounty Act

1873-Timber Culture Act

1862-Homestead Act; Agricultural College Scrip Act

1891-Repeal of Timber Culture Act, Pre-emption Act, and Cash Sales System

1877-Desert Land Act

1909-Enlarged Homestead Act (320 acres)

1904-Kinkaid Homestead Act (640 acres)

1916-Stock-Raising Homestead Act (640 acres)

In the preparation of this chart all of the original land entries under the various laws were compiled, insofar as this was possible. This chart includes the following types of cash entries: Private cash entries, public auction sales, preemption entries, Indian land sales, timber and stone entries under the Act of 1877, mineral-land entries, (small), coal-land entries (small), abandoned military reservations, and miscellaneous sales. It also includes entries made with military warrants and various kinds of scrip. Original entries under the Homestead, Timber Culture, and Desert Land Acts are included.

It was not possible to secure data concerning all the land entered with scrip and military warrants, the amount not included in the chart being less than 3,000,000 acres, the absence of which does not materially affect the picture here presented.

It should be pointed out that this chart is for original entries. A chart of final entries or one showing the amount of entries going to patent would be substantially different as a large amount of homestead, timber culture, and desert-land entries never were proved up.

The chart does not include lands granted to railroads or States, nor certain small grants to individuals. Nor does it include Indian land sales prior to 1879 nor the sale of Indian allotments at any time. (*From Bureau of Agricultural Economics*)

CHAPTER 3

The Great American Land Boom
(and Bust)

Possibly never in the world's history has a new government, representing so few people, had so free a hand in deciding what kind of an agricultural economy it wanted to develop on so large an area of rich and reasonably accessible lands.

Murray Benedict,
Farm Policies in the United States, 1790–1950

We presume that the gentlemen speculators formed their plans on the commonly received principle, that the public is a goose, and that while its enchanting plumage offered so many temptations to pluck a few feathers, no other danger was to be apprehended than that of being *hissed at!*

1819 editorial in the
Ft. Clairborne Courier (Alabama Territory)

Having once been saddled with an ineffective national government, in the spring of 1789 Americans approved the new federal government by only a narrow margin. Would the new United States soon collapse into thirteen independent and warring small nations, each bent on grabbing as much territory as possible? Some states gravely regretted their western land cessions of 1781. Speculative interests like the Ohio Company worked feverishly to protect their investments. Small independent family farmers also looked to the bountiful Ohio country to make their fortunes.

Not until August 1790 did Congress order the Department of the Treasury to revive the survey of the Seven Ranges and restart public sales. The survey edged westward as slowly as before. Congress also waffled about new land legislation for the next six years, allowing massive land grabs by speculators and large-scale intrusions by squatters.

Struggle over the "Uses" of the Public Domain

Speculators and investors must have been pleased when Congress dumped the vexing western lands problem into the hands of Alexander Hamilton, secretary of the treasury. He quickly set out specific policies in his 1790 *Report of a Uniform System for the Disposition of the Lands, the Property of the United States.* Hamilton paid scant attention to earlier land-sale policies: the Jeffersonian yeoman farmer had little disposable cash. Instead, the public lands were to be made as lucrative as possible for large investors. Hamilton did not feel committed to either the letter or the spirit of the Land Survey Ordinance of 1785; it stood in his way. He sought to void prior survey in favor of indiscriminate location. Regardless of the survey system, the government must be free to sell large tracts that cash-rich buyers might find attractive: "any quantities may, nevertheless, be sold by special contract, comprehended either within natural boundaries or lines, or both."[1] The smallest tract, the full 640-acre section, priced at $1,280, remained far beyond the means of the yeoman farmer. But for very large holdings, perhaps 10 miles square or more, he urged low prices attractive to investors, a steal at 30¢ an acre. Tracts of more than 100 square miles could be bought on credit. The newly constituted House of Representatives, teeming with speculators, amiably passed Hamilton's bill to establish a General Land Office for convenient sale and title, and it even reduced the price of large tracts to "twenty-five cents 'hard money' per acre." But the Senate balked at the potential giveaway, and the bill perished. The pressing problem of the public lands remained in limbo for six more years.

Jefferson looked to the disposal of public domain as a singular opportunity to redirect the course of civilization if a truly democratic society could be built on the freehold farmer. From his experience as ambassador to France, Jefferson had become highly conscious of the danger of unrest and revolution if the common man felt he had no future. Jefferson urged easy access to the land in small units. The nation's public land laws, perennially caught on the horns of the Hamiltonian-Jeffersonian dilemma, seemed always on the verge of causing a class war.

Both Hamilton and Jefferson, in very different ways, promoted new uses of the West. Hamilton advocated unregulated free enterprise, which would also serve to support a strong central government. Jefferson's commitment to the virtuous yeoman farmer turned the

West into a vehicle to guarantee the farmer's dominion in the new nation. Either move marked a radical departure from the controlled feudal patterns of the past. Nor can the land hunger of Americans be overestimated. Crèvecoeur had once asked the classic question, What is an American? and answered: everyone who strove to be a landowner, an independent entrepreneur making his own fateful decisions and fortune, completely freed from all controls, public or private. Murray Benedict wryly concluded that this "pioneer philosophy still pervades much of our thinking on agricultural problems —at its best providing the foundations of a sturdy, productive citizenry; at its worst defending doggedly the right of the individual to wreck the soils entrusted to him, and to rearrange land patterns and tenure in ways that create social problems of first magnitude."[2] Rapid landownership by private interests precluded a national agricultural-lands policy. Or more accurately, the fastest possible profitable transfer of public lands into private hands *was* national agricultural policy. Ninety percent of the people worked directly on the farm. Everyman's dream centered on free and clear title to productive farmland.

The next half-century saw history's fastest transformation of wilderness into farmland and a wholesale gobbling of land by private interests. A new land rush followed Anthony Wayne's Fallen Timbers "final solution" to the Indian problem in 1794. The Treaty of Greenville not only brought peace, but created an identifiable line, which could be fixed on maps, between white and Indian lands. Settlers enthusiastically rushed into the new empty Ohio country without waiting for legal niceties, like survey and public sale, from an eastern government. The population of the new state, Ohio, mushroomed from 50,000 to 600,000 between 1803 and 1820. The public sale of Ohio's public domain was undercut by far cheaper tracts from large private estates already in the state. In turn settlers expected that the government must sell at a discount. The private investor John Cleves Symmes, whose title to a million Ohio acres went back seven years to 1787, reported that freshly arrived settlers "almost laugh me full in the face when I ask them one dollar per acre for first-rate land, and tell me they will soon have as good for thirty cents" from the government. Tens of thousands of farmers also infiltrated the untended public lands, built their homes and barns, cultivated the land, and dared anyone to push them off. Most settlers were honest, law-abiding citizens who admitted that indiscriminate taking of land was illegal. But was it not their patriotic duty to clear the wilderness and build farms and towns? Aggressive preemption ignored the standardized survey and controlled sale. Squatting was the time-honored means for go-getting pioneers to acquire quality farmland.

Rumors spread that the struggling federal government could regain some semblance of control over the chaotic public domain only by hasty capitulation to the demands of squatters and private specu-lators. Symmes complained that "all Kentucky and the back parts of Virginia and Pennsylvania are running mad with expectations of the land office opening in this country—hundreds are running into the wilderness west of the Great Miami [River], locating and mak-ing elections of land."[3] The unfortunate governor of the Northwest Territory, Arthur St. Clair, still shadowed by his 1791 Indian defeat, wrote in his 1796 report: "What the intentions of the government, are with regard to the sale of the lands in the country I am entirely ignorant, but it is my duty to inform you, sir, that in my opinion, if they are not disposed of soon, such numbers of people will take possession of them, as may not easily be removed."[4]

Reinventing the Wheel: The Land Law of 1796

Belatedly, reluctantly, Congress once again turned to the western public lands. Advocates of the independent settler took the initiative and appeared to gain the upper hand in congressional debates. Albert Gallatin, the Swiss immigrant representing western Pennsylvania, claimed to champion the small farmer. He projected a statesmanlike vision: "If the cause of the happiness of this country was examined . . . it would be found to arise as much from the great plenty of land in proportion to the inhabitants, which they as citizens enjoyed, as from the wisdom of their political institutions."[5] In direct rebuttal to Hamilton's earlier patronizing of wealthy speculators, William Findley, another representative from western Pennsylvania, told Congress that "they ought not only to keep a wholesale but a retail store."[6] But Congress then ignored the advocates, added some light rephrasing and updating to the ordinance of 1785, and reenacted it as the Land Act of 1796.

The law of 1796 covered "the sale of the lands of the United States, in the territory northwest of the river Ohio, and above the mouth of the Kentucky River." The conditions for sale dismayed advocates of cheap land for independent settlers. Just as in 1785, half the townships were to be sold whole. The other half were to be sold in sections of 640 acres each. The price was $2 an acre. This might seem a bargain for the incredibly fertile farmland available across the Northwest Territory, but it put land costs far out of reach for most prospective settlers. Credit was so limited as to be virtually meaningless, based on a 5 percent immediate down payment, with payment of 50 percent within thirty days and the balance within one year. In an era of a barter economy, when poor farmers rarely saw $100 cash in a year and the moderately successful might scrape up $100 in savings over several years, only a few farm families had $64 on hand for the down payment, and they would be most unlikely to come up with an additional $574 within thirty days, much less the balance of $640 at the end of a year. Congress showed its true colors by granting a substantial 10 percent discount to cash-rich buyers who paid in a lump sum.

America's western public land policy, in this second attempt, still served the same investor class and largely excluded the pioneer settler. No wonder small farmers simply picked up and settled on unclaimed (and often unsurveyed) but fertile land. In the unlikely event that they were reading John Locke at the hearth by a sooty fire, they would have agreed with the philosopher that land was worthless until improved "by the labor of his body and the work of his hands." Locke argued that land became the farmer's private property when "he hath mixed his labor with, and joyned to it something that is his own."[7] Jefferson had already argued in a 1785 letter to James Madison that human beings have a "fundamental right to labor the earth," enjoy its produce and dwell on it, and in the process of such improvement to claim it as their property. "The small landholders are the most precious part of the state."[8]

The first advertised sale took place quickly; legislation passed on 18 May became effective on 24 October 1796.[9] But once again, bids for public lands were few. Only a paltry 108,000 acres were converted into private property, one-third (35,000 acres) in a single purchase by two investors, Alexander Macomb and John Edgar, who soon forfeited their land back to the government.[10] In 1796 the Treasury Department earned an embarrassing $4,836, which peaked at $83,540 in 1797 and collapsed to $11,963 in 1798 and only $843 in 1799. Gallatin reported that by May 1800 a total of 121,540 acres had been sold at well under a dollar an acre.[11] The federal debt went down less than 1 percent, since government debt securities, sharply depreciated to 12¢ to 15¢ on the dollar, were widely applied at face value to land purchase. At this rate the national debt in 1796 alone would not be paid off for a hundred years.

With this disappointing beginning, President Washington found few takers for the thankless new position of surveyor general. He finally nominated Rufus Putnam, territorial judge in Ohio, but also chief agent for the notorious Ohio Company. Washington knew full well that making Putnam surveyor general was like letting the fox into the chicken coop, but the president hoped Putnam's familiarity with the speculative market would give the government a shrewd and knowledgeable negotiator to make the best of the public domain. By the fall of 1797 Putnam had his surveyors in the field; plats were being mapped and available tracts registered with Treasury. Putnam worked out the survey with scrupulous detail, even checking field notes himself (and remembering them for future investment), despite Indian troubles, a bad 1797–98 winter, procedural confusion, and survey mistakes. The field surveyors Putnam hired were mostly small-time speculators themselves; good surveyors were already in the Ohio country making their fortunes. The government could do little to prevent surveyors from taking advantage of their insider information. Lack of confidence in the integrity and impartiality of government land officials and surveyors would mar settler-government relations for most of the nineteenth century. In favor of Putnam's work, within four years he spread the survey westward from the Seven Ranges faster than ever before. By 1797 his crews reached and surveyed the Greenville Treaty line.[12]

Tinkering: The Land Law of 1800

In 1800 the Ohio country had reached its second stage toward statehood and sent William Henry Harrison as its nonvoting delegate to Congress. Even though Harrison was Symmes's son-in-law, he championed the desires of his constituents, mostly subsistence squatters seeking some means of legitimizing their tenuous claims. Harrison worked hard for lower prices, smaller tracts, economical credit terms, local land offices, and in particular some favorable resolution of the preemption problem. He was joined by Tennessee congressman William C. C. Claiborne, who in the best Jeffersonian tradition preached the protection of the independent yeoman for future American greatness in the western dominions. Claiborne insisted that preference for farmers must include the exclusive right to move freely onto the public lands, improve land for their own benefit, receive protection from sharklike speculator claim jumpers, and be awarded first right to half sections of 320 acres at minimum legal prices. Congress shouted down Claiborne in a lopsided vote. It showed its contempt for settler-squatters by passing a special act that rescued the major speculator, John Cleves Symmes. He had sold Ohio land to settlers for profit without troubling to pay his purchase price or acquire title. The outraged buyers were heard by Congress, but instead it let Symmes off the hook by granting the settlers minimum prices ($2 per acre) with two years' credit and preemption on their tracts. Symmes pocketed his money, and the settlers had to buy their land twice.[13]

In the Land Act of 10 May 1800, Congress did move to bring the government closer to the people. It created four land districts with offices at Cincinnati, Chillicothe, Marietta, and Steubenville. But many prospective settlers were disillusioned when Congress held the price line at $2 an acre minimum. Minimum acreage went down to 320 acres, or a half section. This created the precedent for later tract-size reductions, eventually down to 40 acres. In 1800 a farmer could put down $160 to buy his 320 acres, but this was still a formidable sum. After two years $160 more was due, plus $57.60 interest. One year later another $160, and $19.20 interest, came due. The final payment was $160, and $9.60 interest, by the fourth year, for a total of $726.40, compared with $1,280 within one year as required by the act of 1796, four years before. For the frontier settler who needed five years to break even and who might need years to overcome a mortgage of a few hundred dollars, the new terms were still beyond reach.

Simultaneously the government sold millions of acres to the Holland Land Company, John Cleves Symmes, and the Ohio Company for as little as 12¢ an acre. Alexander Hamilton's prophecy that the nation's land development belonged to the big investor was verified in the early 1800s. One senator for the newly minted state of Ohio, John Smith, bought 30,000 acres. An Ohio judge and the founder of Steubenville, Belazeel Wells, entered 24,000 acres. Every twelfth purchase before 1806 was a speculation buy of more than two sections (1,280 acres), at a time when a typical prosperous Ohio farm probably stood at less than a hundred acres. Sales soared.[14] Despite his own squatter problems on his million acres, John Cleves Symmes sold prime tracts at half the government price, with generous credit terms and discount incentives for large purchases. It was far easier for the westering farm family to go to private land offices than to public sale centers. In their aggressive advertising, private investors also offered roads, town sites, and smaller lots with convenient loans and credit, and they even bartered for grain and animals or for an eastern farm, which the government could not do. Agricultural history on the Ohio frontier may well read more like a private capitalist venture than a public development.

New squatters poured into Ohio, even though they knew that it would take more years to bring their new farms to profitability than the law allowed for payment. But perhaps possession *was* nine-tenths of the law. While small farmers found better deals elsewhere than government claims, speculators rushed to buy the public domain. Almost 397,000 acres were transferred in 1801 alone, which more than doubled the totals of the previous five years together. Now credit bookkeeping also entered the picture. By 1804, when 1,310,000 acres went into private hands, immediate receipts reached $1,116,000. But, ominously, more than $3,800,000 would be due the government within four years.[15] By 1806 over 2.4 million acres were sold for $4.9 million, with a debt of $2.5 million due by 1810. Ohio was selling for $3.78 an acre.

A Study in Speculation: The New Madrid Claims

The land boom transformed cautious, cash-poor settlers into speculators hungering to take advantage of every new loophole in government policy. Some of the most blatant opportunism came with the "New Madrid Claims," after the famous earthquakes that hit the boot heel of southeastern Missouri on 16 December 1811 and on 23 January and 7 February 1812. Seismologists have estimated that the shocks from the New Madrid fault measured 8.4 to 8.7 on the Richter scale. Brick walls swayed, spilled kitchen fires were stomped or splashed out, the dust settled out of collapsed chimneys and roofs, and horses ran screaming through the streets as the shaking stopped and the eerie postearthquake stillness shut itself in everyone's ears.

Stunned town and country people picked themselves up and staggered outside to view the damage. Some people remembered a "subterranean thunder" rumbling deep in the earth since summer. The ground sank with the January quake. The ruined town was soon underwater, and it was completely submerged with the 7 February shock.[16]

Today New Madrid County would quickly have been declared a disaster area eligible for federal emergency aid. Back in 1812 Congress gave emergency relief by granting earthquake victims tracts of land "on any of the public lands of the said [Missouri] territory."[17] But in its humanitarian haste, Congress's grants created a legal sieve subject to easy manipulation. Like some twentieth-century Congresses, the legislators had simply thrown money at a problem. Even the simplest frontiersman had become an experienced land dealer who relentlessly exploited every loophole to turn a profit and, with luck, gain a windfall. Soon "New Madrid Claims" became notorious for their power to generate quick cash or acquire prime Missouri farmland. They entered regional folklore about frontier smarts and government stupidity. Congress had not made its grants inalienable; they could be traded or sold. Secondary markets soon covered buying, selling, and even separating "rights" to be sold for cash or credit. By an enormous lapse of legislative judgment, New Madrid grants could be applied to land anywhere in the Missouri Territory. Nor did Congress put a time limit on final location. The grants and rights to grants became floating authorizations over millions of acres. A few New Madrid people actually turned their grants into local land. But in most cases enterprising local frontiersmen bid up prices to speculators, who in turn used the floats to locate on valuable new town lots across the territory. Samuel Hammond, receiver at the St. Louis land office, had to protest in February 1815 about floating rights. He ominously warned Josiah Meigs, General Land Office commissioner, that speculators were using the grants to capture improved land held by squatters who had been unable to gain clear title because the survey had not reached them. Very often long-term squatters had become respectable settled farmers and were embittered by the land grabs. Any stranger wandering around a preemption farm was hustled off. It was not difficult for local people to trace their troubles back to a scheming Congress and its local land office representatives.

Land Mania after 1815

After the nation's trial by combat of 1812–15, postwar America was fragile but ebullient. Settlers wrote back home of "Ohio feever" and the "Missouri and Illinois feever" that would never, they said enthusiastically, let them see Massachusetts or New York again. The Kaskaskia *Western Intelligencer* observed in its 28 February 1818 issue that "almost every person has in a greater or less degree, become a dealer" in public land.[18] When they were not dealers, squatters "simply settled down to grow a crop at the expense of the government." Ohio set a record with 831,000 acres turned into private ownership in 1815 alone. The English traveler Morris Birkbeck wrote in astonishment that where he had expected empty wilderness, "We are seldom out of sight, as we travel on this grand track, towards the Ohio, of family groups, behind and before us. . . . [bearing] a little store of hard-earned cash for the land office of the district; where they may obtain a title for as many acres as they possess half-dollars, being one-fourth of the purchase money."[19] The St. Louis *Missouri Gazette* reported in its 26 October 1816 issue that "every ferry on the river is daily occupied in passing families, carriages, wagons, negroes, carts, etc. etc.—respectable people, apparently able to purchase large tracts of land."[20] One patient Pittsburgher counted 260 wagons moving down the Allegheny valley in nine days. The public domain of Ohio was largely consumed by 1820, and settlers moved on to Indiana, Illinois, and Missouri. The combination of an efficient survey, Indian removal, tens of thousands of illegal trespassing settlers, a few thousand bona-fide farm owners, and a speculative economy would bring new public-land states into the Union almost annually: Indiana in 1816, Mississippi in 1817, Illinois in 1818, Alabama in 1819, and Missouri in 1821. Less clear is whether both speculator and farmer benefited despite or because of the land-law confusions.

The Farmer's Downfall: Short on Cash, Long on Debt

But the speculation boom that made everyone believe their future riches could be hitched to the high-flying "land office business" collapsed in the rightly called Panic of 1819.[21] Western money, credit, capital, and cash flow depended upon hundreds of unregulated private local banks that issued their own bank notes, not always negotiable. This "junk money" was easy to acquire when a farmer had land as collatoral. Both farmer and speculator tied up their futures to cheap money and easy credit. But the flurry of paper money doubled between 1813 and 1819, induced inflation, and brought on federal controls. In the summer of 1818 the Second Bank of the United States, in a dramatic reversal of its benign neglect of the private banks, demanded immediate repayment of large sums they had borrowed. Banks failed across the West. The crisis became desperate when the Second Bank of the United States took local bank currency in payment for its loans only "at a discount proportioned to the distance from the place at which it is payable." The western land boom abruptly ended. Virtually no one could afford the standard price of $2 an acre in hard currency. Most speculators and farmers discovered, to their dismay, that much of the local currency paid them for land had become worthless. The disaster turned into catastrophe for western farmers, not for the only time in American history, with a simultaneous collapse in commodity prices. Wheat fell from $1.45 a bushel in 1818 to 91¢ in 1819 and 72¢ in 1820, similar in scale to price collapses exactly a century later. After a decade of cheap money and easy credit policies, frontier landowners owed the government $23,000,000. And "Land Office Money"—federal bank notes—became so valuable that it received a premium of 15 percent over face value. Local bank notes fell into deeply discounted worthlessness and profoundly depressed the price of land as cash became short. "The settlers never dreamed that . . . the common currency of the country would be so depreciated that $100 would only pay $85 debt at the land office," said an Alabama newspaper in 1820.[22] In the process, the real value of government land rose to new levels, once more too expensive for the ordinary farmer.

Tightening the Screws: The Land Act of 1820

Congress backed up Second Bank action with the Land Act of 1820. Beginning 1 July 1820, all public land went for cash only; the credit system was summarily abolished. Perhaps to muffle protest, the base price was reduced to $1.25 an acre and the minimum purchase to 80 acres.[23] The new act immediately brought an end to land sales, already stifled by scarce money. Pioneer settlers once again were excluded from an expensive market. Cash had virtually disappeared since 1818. Even affluent speculators had to change their tactics, since they depended upon the credit system, meager as it was, to carry them through until their own land sales raised the money to cover their debts. The act of 1820 could have bypassed these overwhelming problems if it had allowed preemption, by permitting pioneers to take tracts of public land and giving them time to settle in with improvements until they raised capital to buy them. But Congress could think only in terms of a no-credit policy, now inappropriate in the desperate times of 1819. The land debt of over $22 million in late 1819 was reduced by September 1822 to $10.5 million, and by mid-1825 to $6.3 million. But continuing tight money and uncollectable debt led to further legislative repairs by Congress in 1821, 1822, 1823, 1824, 1826, 1828, and 1832, for a total of eleven relief measures. Eventually all settlers and speculators who had lost money in forfeited land were certified for replacement tracts. But the certificates, often discounted, created a market of their own, and the land system, already unraveling, came entirely apart.

Orderly and progressive disposal of public land into private hands, begun in 1785, had seemingly disappeared. Congress would not look to a liberal pro-farmer credit system for the rest of the century. By 1825 few contemporaries could fathom the complexities of the nation's public land laws. Landowners who still owed money to the government received the impression, with all the relief acts and exceptions, that a general forgiveness soon would save them. Many stopped payments, and the debt became an apparently fixed national burden. Yet survey historian Malcolm Rohrbough has concluded that the revisions of the 1820s, despite their confusions, "managed to keep much of the land that had been sold in the boom years between 1815 and 1820 in the hands of the purchasers, and to this extent it served the national purpose."[24]

CHAPTER 4

Looking for Alternatives:
The Squatter's World

On 6 January 1984, dozens of modern squatters acquired title to their California desert land. For more than fifty years the original squatters and their heirs had lived in homes on public land in the silver-mining town of Red Mountain. The mine had closed in 1929, but the people stayed on. Not until the early 1960s, in the words of a Bureau of Land Management official, had the federal agency "noticed that we had an entire town living on federal lands, technically in trespass."[1] Told at a hastily called public meeting in Red Mountain that they would have to buy or vacate, most residents petitioned to buy their house lots.

But then problems arose that would not have surprised two centuries of squatters on empty public lands. The judge appointed in 1965 to handle the transfer died in 1975 without filing the necessary papers. Federal bureaucrats told the squatters they could do nothing unless they filed new land transfer applications, but the officials did not realize that the legislation involved, the Townsite Act, would shortly expire. By the time the squatters had done their new paperwork, it was void. Appeals led California congressman William Ketchum to introduce a special relief bill, but he died before it could be acted on. By now, a local official said, "I guess the people in Red Mountain thought the gods were against them." In 1981 the squatters formed the Red Mountain Townsite Association, an old-fashioned claims club. It appeared that they would get their titles in May 1983, but silver prices rose, and the company holding the silver-mining rights revived its old claim. The Bureau of Land Management (BLM) official reported, "We went ahead and told the people the land could not be sold. They were a bit upset to say the least." The frustrated townspeople now raised an uproar with congressmen, federal officials, and the media, and the BLM shortly announced that they would get their land. Thirty-one acres were to be sold in lot-sized parcels for $200 an acre. One resident said, after fifty-five years of squatting and twenty-seven years of title contest, "Finally, I guess all the letters and persevering all paid off."

In 1815, as Daniel Ashby carved out a farm in the hills of Missouri, his gnarled hand wrote, "I drove out three hundred and seventy-five head of stock hogs, and squatted in the west part of the settlement of Howard County. There I lived as happy as Lord Selkirk on his island. I was monarch of all I surveyed. My rights—there were none to dispute."[2] But Ashby had settled on the public domain. When the federal government's surveying team appeared and the new land office opened, widely advertised public auctions were scheduled and speculators rushed to buy with cash in hand. Ashby's utopia began to come apart.

The Survey Ignored

Contrary to popular democratic mythology, private frontier land-lords, and the government officials who managed the public domain, did not generously welcome cashless farm families who worked their way west to seek their fortunes. These farmers, in turn, were more interested in government intervention to give them free access to public land than in keeping their vaunted free-enterprise independence. The happy frontier was full of bickering adversaries.

When George Washington visited his own western holdings in the summer of 1784, he complained of squatters "in defiance of the [1783] proclamation of Congress. They roam over the country on the Indian side of the Ohio, mark out lands, survey, and even settle them."[3] The Land Survey Ordinance of 1785 had made trespassing on public lands unlawful. Even posting troops into the Ohio country to remove settlers and protect surveyors brought little change. Pioneers, convinced they had a moral right to the land by way of "improvement," fought to keep soldiers, Indians, and other interventionists away. In 1786 Colonel Joseph Harmar wrote that despite the forcible removal of illegal settlers "off as far as seventy miles from this post . . . the number lower down the river is immense, and unless Congress enters into immediate measures, it will be impossible to prevent lands being settled."[4]

Land authorities and eager frontier settlers had been on a collision course since colonial times. The British had set a memorable precedent with the inflammatory Proclamation Line of 1763, which closed the region west of the ridge of the Alleghenies to settlement, even when frontier farmers already dotted the Ohio Valley landscape. After independence, government proclamations and the laws of 1785, 1796, and 1800 legally sealed off western territory until the Indians were removed, the survey made, and auction opened. But aggressive frontier farmers, tantalized by the world's richest soils coupled with a benevolent climate in the Ohio country, were not going to be denied. It was one thing to make the survey system the law of the land. It was another matter to enforce it.

An important but unexamined distinction is that the geometric survey established by the ordinance of 1785 was *not* the first historical settlement pattern on western public lands. Rather, the survey was a configuration very often overlaid on existing frontier landholdings. Irregular squatters' fields and homesites peppered the Northwest Territory, where they took over the best soil and terrain, watercourses and woodlots. The territory was also overlaid by private investor tracts the size of small kingdoms, together with large military reserves, as well as Indian and foreign claims. The geometric survey did not often invade an American "empty quarter." To settlers hunkered down in the wilderness, the survey was another source of serious trouble. The only aspect of the new system that suited them was potential clear title to their property. American public land history is very often the record of legislation, policies, regulations, and customs that conveyed land *outside* the survey.

Squatters or "preempters" did not expect sympathy from the private landowners they invaded, but they quickly learned they had few friends in government to protect them. Rather, antisquatter laws passed in 1804 and 1807 included a $1,000 fine and a year's imprisonment, a heavy penalty if enforced. Between 1785 and 1791 American troops were sent to evict and burn out squatters, but this was quickly dropped as embarrassingly similar to Indian removal. Presidential proclamations from Jefferson, Madison, and later Jackson condemned trespassing as theft of the national treasure, but these proclamations fell lightly in the West. Instead, preempters flooded Washington with petitions for exemptions. They also argued that the government created its own woes because of the snail-like pace of the survey. They complained that Congress was spineless when pressed by lobbying speculators. Most trespassers honestly believed that the public lands were a national commons available for free settlement and profitable development by the first taker. Squatters claimed it was their patriotic duty to stake out and clear a wilderness tract, improve and domesticate it into prime farmland through hard labor, and receive a prior right of ownership for their efforts. This patriotic activity deserved praise, they insisted, from all right-thinking Americans. The squatters said they were an unusually freedom-loving and diligent breed of citizen. One petition to Congress set out the rights and limitations of individual land use: "Every man was entitled by nature to a portion of the soil. . . . [No man] ought to possess more than two hundred acres."[5]

Before the 1815 land boom, violent encounters between squatters and legal landowners were unlikely in the vast midwestern expanses. But as farms and claims began to overlap, Thomas Sloo, agent for the Ohio land office at Shawneetown, reported to Land Commissioner Josiah Meigs: "Several persons have called on me as the public agent to give them peaceable possession of their lands. Persons who are residing on them now and were previous to the sale refuse to give them up . . . the rightful owner is kept out of possession . . . [and] thinks his case a hard one to be compelled after paying the government for a tract of land, to be reduced to the necessity of commencing a suit at law to obtain his just right."[6] Possible land wars led President James Madison to intervene with an executive proclamation on 12 December 1815. Madison's words outraged frontier settlers: "many uninformed or evil-disposed persons" currently living on unsold government land were to "forthwith to remove therefrom" on threat of "such military force as may become necessary."[7] Madison's proclamation was read by western farmers to mean that the eastern government had hypocritically turned against them. In an impassioned letter to Secretary of State James Monroe, Ohio congressman John McLean argued on 19 January 1816 that "not one in fifty of these persons were conscious of infracting the laws of their country." McLean told Monroe: "They have fought, and some of them have bled, in defense of their homes. Does policy require that the arm of the government should be lifted against them?"[8]

Within weeks, by 25 March 1816, Congress granted new exemptions to Ohio trespassers. Cash-poor farmers quickly picked up to migrate into the western public domain because they felt confident in "the [future] lenity of the government in keeping them in possession" of tracts they would soon occupy and improve.

One English traveler watched the dreaded survey teams move into squatter country. Soon land offices set up dates for auctions. He dramatically wrote home:

> The hour approaches: the poor squatter runs about the town; he has been laboring all the year that he may buy the land on which his house is situated; perhaps for want of a dollar or two, it will be taken from him by greedy speculators. A jobber accosts him, pities him, and offers to withdraw his pretensions for the sum of three dollars; the poor simpleton gives them to him, not doubting the jobber. . . . This is what is called hush money.[9]

Congressman Balie Peyton of Tennessee carried the same bathos to Washington:

> That poor man who had blazed the trees and planted the potatoes had chosen that spot as the home of his children. He had toiled in hope. He had given it value. . . . When the public sales were proclaimed, if that poor man attended it, he might bid to the last cent he had in the world, and mortgage the bed he slept on. . . . He might have his wife and children around him to see him bid; and when he had bid his very last cent, one of these speculators would stand by his side and bid two dollars more, and thus he would see his little home . . . pass into the hands of a rich, moneyed company.[10]

Government survey teams were rushing to catch up with trespassers. On 11 March 1815 Thomas Sloo wrote to Josiah Meigs that "there are nearly a thousand improved places in this district that are not located. . . . if the government does not adopt some energetic measures to nip this conduct in the bud—it will retard the sale of all those places."[11]

The government stood by the orderly 1785 method, slightly adjusted in 1796 and 1800, and continued to send out survey teams, record their data on plat maps, and sell at public auction the geometric tracts off the plats. The deputy surveyor was the field agent. Working diligently in the wilderness, he could line out 4 or 5 miles a day and survey about 30 miles in a seven-day week. Based on the government piecework scale of $3 or $4 a mile, he could generate a gross income of more than $100 a week. This was a grand wage, but each surveyor had out-of-pocket costs for chainmen, woodsmen to open the line of sight by removing brush and timber, and sometimes a hunter to provide meat. Yet no one learned more about the terrain, woods, watercourses, and soil quality than the surveyor. He saw his efforts as a good investment.[12] His temptation to hide the best tracts by not reporting their features in the field books must have been enormous, and it was often yielded to. An ambitious surveyor could also gain effective control over large regions by bidding for large contracts that he could not possibly map himself but that could be subcontracted at profitable rates. The surveyor's trade became a road to riches. Two who retired comfortably after survey-ing tens of thousands of lines were Ohio's Edward Tiffin and the self-proclaimed world's greatest surveyor, William Rector of Indiana and Illinois.

The government also closed in on intruders when the Department of the Treasury created the General Land Office in 1811.[13] Its road to bureaucratic success lay in orderly, uncomplicated surveys, field reports marked clearly on plat maps, the publicized open auction of new empty lands, and after auction, the private sales at minimum government prices or higher. Although it had no police power to remove squatters, land office policy was unsympathetic and unco-operative toward them. Squatter and land officer confronted each other from different economic and political worlds. Some contem-poraries feared a class war involving government agents, individual preempting farmers, private-enterprise speculators, and manipula-tive congressmen.

The most powerful and feared tool of the General Land Office was the public auction. Outsiders, land speculators, loan sharks ("those harpies"), and their agents—identifiable by their fancy manners, "ruffled shirt . . . and a bit of jewelry"—showed up in large numbers at major auctions to buy townships and sections and halves and quarters out from under the outraged squatters. The stakes were high. The Wisconsin *Green Bay Intelligencer* in July 1835 publicized that land paid off at 20 to 30 percent every year. In March 1836 it told readers that Manitowoc prices went sky-high in a week, from $10 to $250 an acre.[14] Some auctions in Indiana drew a hundred or more outsiders, who bought up tracts running to 15,000 acres. By 1837 agents converged on Indiana from New England, New York, and the middle and southern states to lay hold of 236,000 acres.[15] In Illinois Daniel Webster grabbed up several thousand acres of La Salle County prairie, and the John Griggs consortium of Philadelphia took 124,000 acres near Springfield. Almost a third of Wisconsin's public lands, 553,000 acres, fell into speculators' hands by 1840, averaging 6,430 acres among only eighty-six owners.

But the western squatter was a hardy breed, surviving onslaughts of Indians, weather, speculators, bad markets, surveying teams and land auctions, and threats of removal. The government continued to treat the western domain as closed and empty land, then gave it a rigid survey woefully unrealistic for farming and set impossibly expensive terms for individual ownership. As a result, squatter-farmers rather than owner-farmers spread over most of the frontier. Repeated relief acts encouraged such settlers to believe they would not be removed but would be treated as pioneering heroes. Some squatters simply dared the authorities to act against them. This was particularly true in desperate years of low agricultural prices following the Panics of 1819 and 1837. Repeated legislation in 1785, 1796, 1800, 1804, and 1807 had already revealed the ineffectiveness of removal orders and heavy penalties. Strong action to forcibly remove intruders also went against public opinion.

Both squatters and legitimate owners claimed the absolute rights of private property guaranteed by the Fifth Amendment. A quagmire of due process and just compensation led Congress not to meddle. Nor was it likely that legislation would move contrary—as it would in the twentieth century—to the historic American principle of complete autonomy by owners to buy, sell, trade, improve, or otherwise manipulate private property. The squatters, like all Americans, could turn to "the right of the people peaceably to assemble," guaranteed by the First Amendment, "to petition the government for a redress of grievances." Aspects of the First and Fifth Amendments stood in conflict between private rights and public interest. Squatters formed powerful claims clubs that effectively undermined federal land policies. The clubs were forerunners of the nation's most potent interest group of the next century, the farm lobby.

A Classic Case: Claims Clubs and the 1830 Burlington Auction

Rumors filtered east that eastern Iowa contained the best farmer's land yet encountered, with well-watered chernozemic soil six feet deep—primeval stuff. Rumors that Iowa's gently rolling countryside was even better than Illinois farmland brought a rush onto the land long before the government could send survey teams, make plats at the land office, and hold public auctions. Tens of thousands of squatters took the best sites, plowed the rich fields, built their homes and barns and outbuildings, and prospered. But ultimately the survey did reach them. Auction dates were set. Speculators appeared in their ruffled shirts. But the farmers had learned how to fight back. In 1838 when the Burlington, Iowa, auction was called, local newspapers reported that a pushing crowd of 20,000 local farmers converged on the day of the sale. They had already formed themselves into claims clubs to use collective influence (and muscle) to intimidate outside buyers and purchase their own farmland as cheaply as possible without competition. One eyewitness noted that "the hotels were full of speculators of all kinds from the money loaner, who would accommodate the settler at fifty per cent . . . and a worse class of money sharks . . . who wanted to rob the settlers of their lands and improvements . . . holding that the settler was a squatter and trespasser, and should be driven from his lands."[16]

Tension was high when the Burlington auction opened. United States Army general Ver Planck Van Antwerp opened with a public reading of the act of Congress of 31 March 1830, which listed the penalties for attempting to prevent open competitive bidding. There were also severe penalties for secret deals to buy land for immediate prearranged resale. Alongside General Ver Planck Van Antwerp stood John C. Breckenridge, receiver and registrar of the Burlington land office. The reading brought "a silent smile on the settlers' faces [which] spoke their contempt." In the days after the auction was first announced, new faces at the local land office found a stony silence when they asked about local conditions and opportunities. A good strong lie to throw the speculator and his agent off the track became a virtue. At least eighteen local claims clubs, one for each township, existed for the sole purpose of protecting farmers' interests at the open auctions. When the auctioneer opened the bidding, the designated bidder for the clubs had already jumped to his side. All tracts where squatters had claims went quickly for the minimum price of $1.25 an acre. In contrast, eleven unclaimed tracts went for speculation as high as $2.86 an acre.[17] The clubs did not intervene on unwanted land, but there was no doubt who was in control. The stakes were high: between 1838 and 1840, 1.14 million acres of the nation's best farmland were sold at the Burlington and Dubuque land offices. If an absentee owner did acquire some acreage, local citizens made certain it was taxed to the limit, timber and other removables were quickly "hooked," and cattle were put to graze. Absentee land was treated as a local commons. Squatters' claims clubs anticipated the self-protection associations of frontier mining

towns, Great Plains cattlemen's associations, and western town vig-
ilantes. The squatters' "law of necessity" in the 1830s would become
"the law of the West" in the 1880s.

America's Great Speculative Land Boom

The early 1830s saw the greatest land boom thus far in American history, which gradually came under the control of the General Land Office as the survey moved westward to overrun squatter invasions.[18] The opening of public land and its transfer into
private hands took on gigantic proportions. The government had
been adding an unprecedented 2 or 3 million acres a year to the market. In 1834–35 alone, a phenomenal 28 million acres were shifted
from closed to open land. Two years later the Van Buren administration dumped 56,686,000 acres on the market. And the regions offered
were perhaps the richest virgin soils in the world, across Illinois and
Iowa, Alabama, Mississippi, Arkansas, and Missouri. Rumors came
from Missouri that citizens planned to cast "every man into the poor
house" who was not "worth more than $10,000."[19] Michigan land
did not come on the market until 1828, but by 1834 25.6 million acres
had been surveyed. By 1834 almost 144 million acres of the public
domain were carved up into townships and sections and 35.5 million
acres of it had been sold.[20] The land mania also fueled inflation; from
1830 to 1836 land prices rose 150 percent across the nation.

Monopolistic speculation included the government-favored
American Land Company, bankrolled by Andrew Jackson's pet
banks, which owned 322,000 acres of farmland. Its Mississippi agent
openly admitted he used his fat bankroll to eliminate competition
by the local farmers. "If it is wrong to over-bid a settler for a piece of
public land, the fault is with those who, by legislation, have ordered"
sales to the highest bidder. Company policy was openly Darwinian
tooth and claw: "The strong will prevail over the weak, and the first
settlers, who are generally poor, must go to the wall."[21] In acts of
open collusion, the Treasury would shut the local land office as soon
as the company enclosed a large territory. Newly arrived settlers,
down to their last dollar, repeatedly discovered that the American
Land Company was the only land agent for miles around.

Public outcry against the sovereignty of the American Land Company rose as its connections with the Jackson administration, con-

gressmen, and prominent bankers and investors became known. By the summer of 1839 the influential *Albany Evening Journal* complained that the American Land Company now "over-shadowed the Republic." It charged:

> Such a combination of wealth and power had never before existed among us. The highest officers in the general and state governments were stockholders in this gigantic monopoly. . . . Its agents were sent abroad through the new states and territories to monopolize all the valuable lands. . . . The surplus revenue then in the pet banks, was at the service of these speculators. Millions of dollars were invested in Michigan, Illinois, Wisconsin, Mississippi, etc. The stockholders in this overgrown monopoly were selected from the men in power. Vast political and pecuniary influences were combined. Standing at the head of the Albany stockholders were Messers Crowell and Burt, editors and proprietors of the state paper. Then came John Van Buren, the son of the President of the United States. Silas Wright, Jr., a senator in Congress, through whose influence the deposits were placed in the reach of speculators, was a stockholder in the monopolizing "American Land Company."[22]

Other newspapers, including the fledgling *New York Times*, questioned the propriety of the connections and also noted that the highly profitable venture was taking prime farmland out of the hands of the deserving small farmers who had made the nation great.

Similar surefire investing led the Philadelphia publisher John Griggs to acquire 115,000 acres in prosperous central Illinois. In later years the Brown-Ives-Goddard venture capital group out of Providence, Rhode Island, teamed up with William Scully to develop a 148,000-acre "landlord estate" on prime land in Nebraska.[23] By the 1870s Ira Davenport, operating from his office in Bath, New York, had acquired 65,000 acres of Nebraska. Complaints rose about "speculator's deserts"—land that absentee owners held off local markets for years awaiting higher prices. The acres languished undeveloped, producing no taxes for local roads and schools, inhibiting trade and commerce, and often stripped of trees and other movable resources.

Cooling off the Boom

To everyone's astonishment, President Andrew Jackson intervened into the land "phrenzy." The president was notorious for his own shrewd, hard-driving, and profitable speculation. But the Specie Circular presidential order of 11 July 1836 limited public land purchases to specie, or hard cash only, in gold and silver coin. Land sales stopped, with no real revival until the mid-1840s. The resulting financial collapse utterly devastated western farmers, who, like their descendants in the 1970s, were using cheap money, easy credit, and inflation to improve their land in anticipation of escalating prices. Instead they were once again caught in a desperate squeeze between falling land prices and falling commodity prices.[24] For the second time since 1819 western farmers were convinced they bore an undeserved burden of the nation's troubles. The long history of high farmer vulnerability to market conditions is still not over today.

Squatting: A Permanent Alternative to the Survey System

Not everyone praised the underdog squatter-farmers. The Englishman James Flint described them as "men who take possession without purchasing, are afraid of being turned out, or of having their pastures abridged by newcomers." They were no better than speculators and "wish[ed] to hold the adjoining lands in reserve for themselves" until they could round up enough cash. Flint warned that "the prudent will always be cautious of explaining their views, particularly as to the spot chosen for purchase, and without loss of time they should return to the land-office and make entry."[25]

But claims clubs subverted the law of the land across some of the nation's best agricultural areas in Indiana, Illinois, Wisconsin, and Iowa. In northern Illinois, "If a speculator should bid on a settler's farm, he was knocked down and dragged out of the office, and if the striker was prosecuted and fined, the settlers paid the expense." Speculators discovered that settlers were ready to shoot them at close range, "burn powder in their faces," even at the risk of being recognized. Some Wisconsin moralizing was typical: "Our neighbors have been dealt with in an unfeeling manner, driven from their homes, their property destroyed, their persons attacked, and their lives jeopardized by bad laws and greedy speculators."[26] In open self-congratulation, a Wisconsin club also insisted on privileged status earned by patriotic sacrifice. "We have left our friends, deprived ourselves of the many blessings and privileges of society, have borne the expenses, and encountered the hardships of a perilous journey, advancing into a space beyond the bonds of civilization." In 1836 the Squatters' Union of Lake County along Lake Michigan wrote its own constitution and acted as a private vigilante government to control land sales, claims records, and title transfers and even to arbitrate internal conflicts. It was not alone when it ran its own surveys and boundaries from township lines.

Claims clubs or squatters' associations served many of the same functions as homeowners' associations in the twentieth century. This occasionally included early versions of protective covenants, exclusion of the "wrong" people (speculators), and early versions of zoning (unsettled land had no rights; value-added "improved" farms enjoyed exclusions and protections). The claims clubs even offered "discounted" land at the original $1.25 minimum per acre.

Government officials, like treasury secretary Albert Gallatin and General Land Office commissioner Josiah Meigs, were convinced that the crowds of illegal settlers, like grasshoppers descending on the plains, were beyond control. Squatters' success threatened the last chance for orderly distribution of the public lands under the survey system.[27] The debate over preemption was a struggle over the government's control of its own domain. All Americans agreed that the public lands were destined to go into private hands. But it was not so clear who would be eligible or had the power to buy. The "open" auction favored the cash-ready speculator. Preemption might shift the balance toward the settler; whether it preserved the skeleton of survey and sale was another matter. Or would preemption abandon the public domain to chaos?

The Preemption Act of 1830

In 1828 the House Committee on Public Lands, which had always been a bulwark against illegal intrusion, now reversed itself to endorse a general preemption act: "It is right and proper that the first settlers, who have made roads and bridges over the public lands at their expense and with great labor and toil, should be allowed a privilege greater than other purchasers."[28] The bill failed. In 1830 Missouri senator David Barton argued effectively that "the old law" of 1807 was antidemocratic because it "created general inequality" and held off the American natural right "to elevate the numerous non-freeholders of our country to the proud rank of freeholders."[29]

Congress passed and Jackson signed the Preemption Act of 1830. Settlers who fulfilled "the fact of cultivation . . . and possession" in 1829 were given sole first rights to buy up to 160 acres. Squatters used the 1830 law to buy 243,000 acres in 1830 and 558,000 acres in 1831. Land registrar Gideon Fitz complained, "They come like the locusts of Egypt, and darken the office, with clouds of smoke and dust, and an uproar occasioned by whiskey and avarice."[30] In 1829 only 2,600 acres had been granted to squatters.

Now government policy gave preference to settlers who "would occupy the land for agricultural purposes alone."[31] Two worlds were on a collision course—both legal, and both widely supported. Fitz concluded that the 1830 act allowed anyone to take "a general sweep . . . of the most valuable lands of the United States . . . at as low a price as that which the poorest person in the nation, would have to pay for the poorest pine barren."[32] Rampant speculation proved the great American national truth: Americans will always lie when tempted by a land deal.

Preemption acreage, which had fallen to less than 32,000 acres in 1833, shot up to twenty times that much in 1834—637,600 acres.[33] What had started out as minor relief for a few weak and vulnerable squatters in the 1820s became America's most lucrative bargain-hunting ground in the 1830s. But most squatters could no more come up with $200 for their 160-acre quarter section then than in the 1820s. "A class of citizens . . . simply meandered over the face of the western country," almost an early version of depression-era migrant workers.

The Survey Subverted: The Preemption Act of 1841

The lauded Preemption Act of 1841, touted as a historic solution to a nasty problem, merely legalized a western reality. Squatters still had a formidable opponent in Henry Clay. He tore into the "lawless rabble." "The whole preemption system is a violation of all law, and an encouragment to persons to go on the public lands and take the choicest portion of them." The real choice before the public was between law and lawlessness. A New York newspaper described the government's preemption laws as "granting bounties to squatters engaged in cheating the government out of the best tracts of public lands."[34] Debate in Congress was now "between the log cabins and the palaces." Senator Clement C. Clay of Alabama argued that the venerable auction system had always suited the speculator.

> Was not the question distinctly presented, whether the government was to sell the public domain in small quantities to men of small capital, who would immediately occupy, improve, and render it productive, or whether it was better policy to sell at auction to bands of speculators and capitalists in large quantities, to lie idle and unprofitable till they could extort the desired profit from those whose necessities compel them to have it?[35]

When passed in a garbled and truncated version, the act of 1841 recognized that settlers on the *surveyed* public lands were no longer committing legal trespass or intrusion. Settlers could move in advance of land office jurisdictions and secure 160 acres at the minimum price of $1.25. But few people noted that exceptions were written for the new alternate sections in grants for "public improvements" for railroads, canals, and roads.

In 1976 Roy M. Robbins, the modern historian of the American land, called the 1841 act "the most important agrarian measure ever passed by Congress. . . . a victory of pioneer America. . . . the capstone in the democratization of the public land system." In 1843 Horace Greeley had called it "a curse to the West and to the whole country."[36]

CHAPTER 5

The Survey and Its Competitors

In truth, disposal of the public lands was never dedicated to building up a vast agricultural domain in the American heartland, despite lofty protestations in the halls of Congress. The only constant policy was surrender of an entire national landscape into utterly independent private hands. The marketplace has been the only consistent measure of land value.

The hasty transfer of land from public into private hands, often at tens of millions of acres a year, is unique in history. Independent family farmers were often the victims of this comprehensive transfer, but they also regularly benefited from such privatization. Historically, American farmers have consistently made more money profiteering in land than in farming. They have depended upon the unearned capital appreciation of land for their immediate financial needs and long-term staying power, and to guarantee a patrimony to pass on to future generations. The pattern is not surprising. Buffeted by low prices and high costs in carrying out daily farming activities, American farmers turned to rising land values for their primary investment. Despite their complaints, independent farmers were very often smaller versions of the big-time speculator. These conditions prevailed throughout the nineteenth century and persist in the twentieth. The idealistic creation of a vast national agricultural heartland is another matter.

The Contrasting Worlds of Prairie and Plains

By the mid-nineteenth century, the venerable survey and auction stood as only one of several competing means by which public land passed into private hands. The always dubious hold of the survey and auction system had clearly been broken. The intentions behind government land policies had always been murky, and seventy years of extensive adjustments and exceptions brought little clarity or direction. By midcentury, as settlers moved onto the public domain, they could hardly escape entering several different "worlds."

FREE LAND "WAITING TO BE USED"
Wherever the survey had not yet carved up terrain into rectangular tracts as small as 40 acres, migrating settlers looked upon the land as an off-the-map unrestricted wilderness. An unsurveyed Illinois prairie might as well have been a moonscape untouched by humans. Settlers, with an eye to successful farming, moved onto irregularly shaped patches of land based on fields the horse and plow could follow, streambeds and drainage patterns, and access to woodlots, rivers, and roads. The best land did not come in squares and rectangles. Good farmers looked for soil quality, level terrain, a source of water, trees for fuel, fences, and buildings, and an acceptable growing season. They took more to the easy lands of central Illinois and eastern Iowa than to hilly southeastern Missouri or the arid, cold, windy Dakotas. If independent farmers had been the only buyers and settlers on the public domain, they would have left large "empty zones" of second- or third-rate land. Some regions, such as southern Indiana, might have remained unsold for decades.

Had the public domain remained unsurveyed, without the auction sale process, it would have become a multimillion-acre patchwork quilt of farmland, irregular and scattered, amid a national wilderness, like occasional clearings in a vast forest. This was the actual public domain settlement pattern as settlers leapfrogged ahead of the survey. Until the 1840s this original land-use configuration was also an illegal trespass onto the public lands.

THE SURVEY LANDSCAPE
Once the survey restyled the landscape, geometric rationality overwhelmed traditional agricultural standards for good land. The survey had the virtue of producing an orderly, exact, and continuous fix on the land—not a single obscure acre was missed. Tracts were easy to locate on the abstraction of the plat map, but the survey offered little else. Virtually every tract contained bad land along with good. An otherwise prime 160-acre quarter section, lined up from some distant axis, might miss water and woods by fifteen feet. Or a quarter section on a steep slope would be vulnerable to severe erosion of topsoil. A quarter section is also hard to work if it has a swamp dead

center. Once the survey intruded, farmers had to work hard to match land quality with cadastral survey. The consistently prime quality of land across much of Illinois and Iowa had the advantage that it often matched the survey geometry. The land along the Red River of the North suited the survey well. But these were exceptions. Wherever the survey went, its great virtue was its reliability in locating individual tracts and the trustworthiness of accurate title to land.

"IF YOU WAIT LONG ENOUGH, THE LAW WILL CHANGE"

Another world covered time as well as space. Squatters knew that eventually their "bit of heaven," carved by hard work out of wilderness following the terrain, would be rearranged by the gridiron survey. But they also learned that if they stood their ground they could control the auctions encompassing their land, and that Congress would eventually cave in to their petitions. At the very least, most settlers worked hoping for repeated delays in the surveys, public auctions, and final title. They learned that government policy was a moving point on a moving line as politicians constantly tinkered with the land system. Within a lifetime prices could shift from $2 to $1.25 to $2.50 an acre or even to free land, aside from private market fluctuations. By the tortuous process of "graduation" (see below), "old" public land, left vacant after auction and private sale, would be treated not as leftover wilderness, but as low-quality farmland for sale at deeply discounted prices. Minimum acreage scaled from 320 acres down to 40 acres. Maximum acreage depended upon one's bankroll and credit rating; even after farmland limits were set at 160 to 320 acres, an otherwise honest and patriotic buyer often winked at the law and got not simply a farm-sized tract, but a region larger than many European principalities. A watchful preemptor might have done well waiting out the twelve years between 1830 and 1842. Far out in the western wilderness, a durable squatter probably wondered which would arrive first: the survey and auction, opportunities for preemption, or the right to free land. The less scrupulous buyer found generous loopholes giving discounted prices for far more land than the law allowed. Residence requirements changed often, from none at all to five-year settlement guaranteed by oaths, witnesses, and depositions. Farmers also lived on seasonal time scales, as well as the notorious three-year "make or break" pioneering cycle and the equally famous "ten years to profitability" agricultural cycle.

THE COMPLEXITY OF THE PUBLIC LANDS

The status of land became so intricate that it could overwhelm the understanding of farmer or speculator. One might be looking at unopened public land, or open but unsurveyed public land, or surveyed land not yet open for sale, or surveyed land open for sale. Land once open for sale might be withdrawn and held for competing "internal improvement" (canal, road, railroad) interests. Land supposedly open for sale might be tainted by squatter or "float" or scrip claims. Soon this would be complicated even further by decreasing graduation prices as available land got "older" and by claims for free land. In most cases, when Congress introduced new public domain policies, it did not bother to remove older contradictory rulings. Farmer-settlers, who earnestly wanted to get down to working their land productively, often found themselves embroiled in constant tangles to claim, pay off, acquire title, and keep their farms. In the long run, the farmer needed security while the speculator thrived on fluctuating regulations, on markets created by loopholes, and on loose management of the western lands.

LAND AS A PRIVATE ECONOMIC UNIT

Still another "world" can be tied to the land office system, with its geometric survey and public auction. The land office followed one policy: to transfer, for a price, the domain out of public and into private hands. Thus it stood as the nation's long-term direct promoter of *privatization*. Alternative policies were rarely if ever considered until well into the twentieth century, when most of the nation's farmland was already privately held. Laissez-faire individualist capitalism, perhaps the most compelling and most durable of all American institutions, has persistently looked upon the public domain as the origin of personal wealth and corporate profitability. The keys were the inviolability of private property and the autonomy of the free market, summed up as freedom from government controls. Above all, the survey and auction policy produced a convenient, speedy, and reliable way of translating public real estate into private cash value. The land seeker looked at the plat maps not for their agricultural capacity but for their dollar value controlled by a speculative market. By the 1870s, as western arid lands were opened, the government intervened to keep a sometimes runaway and sometimes collapsing market from destroying land values. Even here government intervention, as it always had, worked to place valuable land in private hands.

LAND AS HOME FOR A WAY OF LIFE

Less clear is America's emotional involvement with the world of individual farmers, romantically imagined as toiling happily on their self-sufficient, independently owned plots. Until early in the twentieth century, the vast majority of Americans had the experience, skills, and outlook of farmers. America's "Everyman" supposedly looked to landownership not primarily for its rapid profit turnover, not as a site for a suburban house, but for the prosperity it promised in a stretch of soil to cultivate. An early nineteenth-century backwoods South Carolina farmer summed up an American dream: "My farm gave me and my family a good living on the produce of it; and left me, one year with another, one hundred fifty silver dollars, for I never spent more than ten dollars a year, which was for salt, nails, and the like. Nothing to wear, eat or drink, was purchased, as my farm provided all. With this saving, I put money to interest, bought cattle, fatted and sold them, and made great profit."[1] Without going as far as the bucolic claims of Crèvecoeur or Jefferson, most Americans were convinced that if they had their health, reasonable ability, and commonplace agricultural skills, together with a quarter section, they could be fairly certain of a comfortable existence. Viewed from the perspective of humans' seven-thousand-year experience with agriculture, the nineteenth-century American farmer became one of the world's most successful agriculturalists—almost a mythic figure. But it is a real myth that government land policies served the farmer well. The stilted language of an 1828 House committee admitted the value of the farmer to the nation. It was "just and proper that he who renders a benefit to the public, who by his enterprise and industry has created for himself and his family a home in the wilderness, should be entitled to his reward. He has afforded facilities to the sale of the public lands, and brought into competition lands which otherwise would have commanded no price and for there would have been no bidders, unless for his improvements."[2] But only much later, beginning with the 1930s, was the American farmer legitimized by government protectionist policies.

Graduation: Bargain-Hunting at a Fire Sale

By 1854 John Wilson, commissioner of the General Land Office, began to doubt the practicality of the land system. After decades of the fastest geographical expansion of any society in history, large tracts of unsold and unwanted public land languished amid the parcels already sold, traded, or gifted into private hands.[3] Where Jefferson had imagined a hundred generations to reach the Pacific, half the distance had been covered in patchwork fashion within a generation and a half. Every year the government continued to throw 10 million new acres on the market, though public sales required only 1 to 3 million acres. Wilson noted that approximately 8 million acres remained unsold each year. These overenthusiastic releases contradicted the original survey policy of controlled, compact, and contiguous settlement. Very often the unsold public land—sometimes a rocky quarter section, sometimes a swampy lowland, sometimes thousands of acres of badlands—would be treated as a "common land" by neighboring settlers, used as pasture for cattle and horses, and stripped of any timber, with roads routed over it rather than over private land. The worst sort of wandering squatters might take over and create a woodlot notorious for harboring unsavory gypsies or hoboes. Was the leftover land no-man's-land or every-man's-land? If a county or township had too many ownerless and neglected tracts, the tax burden weighed on the remaining farmers.

The large tracts of rough and poor land unsold in southern Indiana and southwestern Missouri had inhibited growth. In contrast, most of Ohio, Illinois, and Iowa sold quickly as compact, continuous settlement. As late as 1854 Indiana had 458,700 acres available, some of it thirty-five years on the market. Missouri in 1854 had not attracted buyers for almost 14 million acres, half on the market since 1820.[4] Under tremendous pressure from his constituents, Missouri senator Thomas Hart Benton became an advocate for a marvelously simple solution: reduce the price in gradual stages based on how long the tract had been available. As early as 1824 Benton showed the near contempt in which the survey and auction laws were held when he reminded the Senate that the government was foolishly selling its best land for $1.25 when its privately owned equivalent went for $15 to $20 an acre, while refuse land, good only for foraging pigs or cutting firewood, might not be worth 50¢ an acre.[5]

By 1828 Benton tried to establish a precedent by having several district land offices classify their lands according to agricultural cash value. The land offices reported that large tracts were inferior or worthless, so overpriced at $1.25 as to be unmarketable. Ohio offices valued unsold land from $1.03 an acre to 50¢. In Indiana valuations ranged from $1.25 to 44¢ and in Missouri from 62$\frac{1}{2}$¢ to 12$\frac{1}{2}$¢. Pressure grew to let prices float at market levels, as they had done between 1836 and 1850 with almost 4 million acres of the Chickasaw cession selling at less than 80¢ an acre. Opponents complained that gradua-tion merely anticipated plans for free land for homesteaders. Horace Greeley, probably the most influential nonpolitician of the day, com-plained in his *New York Weekly Tribune* that the national treasure would be squandered by "graduation, loose preemption, or direct cession." Condescendingly, Greeley proposed that any hardworking American, virtuously tilling the soil, avoiding frivolous expenses, and receiving fair price for produce, needed only a year to save $100 for an 80-acre farmsite. Greeley would soon change his mind and become a national champion for free-land homesteading.

The title of the act of 1854 promised "to Graduate and Reduce the Price of the Public Lands long on the market to actual Settlers and Cultivators."[6] But the law was miserly, not generous. Acreage not sold for ten to fifteen years would be reduced to $1; for fifteen to twenty years to 75¢, for twenty to twenty-five years down to 50¢, twenty-five–thirty years to 25¢, and if unsold for thirty years or more, down to one bit, or $12^{1}/_{2}$¢.

Nevertheless the 1854 act released pent-up land zeal to bring on one of the greatest land rushes in American history. The St. Louis office, serving one of America's larger survey backwaters, reported that on 2 November 1854 people crowded into lines, slept on stairs to be first in the morning, and in their press broke down the office's doors.[7] After the 1854 act, sales at new low prices soared from 2 million acres a year to 40 million. Ohio gave away only 70,000 acres at bit prices, but Missouri sold 6.5 million acres at $12^{1}/_{2}$¢, more than three times the acreage sold at higher prices. Bit land in Alabama covered more than 8 million acres. Nationally, between 1854 and 1862 more than 77.5 million graduation acres were sold, including more than 25 million as bit lands.[8] Less than 25 million acres of the public lands went for the regular minimum price of $1.25. By 1862 almost all land designated for graduation had been sold in Ohio, Indiana, Illinois, and Iowa.

Critics condemned Congress for dumping valuable government land. Before the bill was passed an Alabama senator asked, "What clause in the Constitution authorized Congress to give away lands?" He was reminded that article 4, section 3, gave Congress power to "dispose of" United States territory. But in anticipa-tion of twentieth-century politics southern senators worried, "if

Congress gives away land to the landless, it might give money to the moneyless."[9] The 1854 act claimed to serve "actual settlers and cultivators," but its thin regulations served speculators. Some Missouri bit land turned a $15 an acre profit. Horace Greeley wrote that "any shrewd monopolist can drive a coach and six through" the Graduation Act. General Land Office commissioner John Wilson reported that within weeks the act was "productive of much fraud and perjury, and proved seriously injurious to the actual settlers on the public domain."[10] Wilson appealed to Congress for legislation with teeth. For his efforts he was removed from office in 1855; many legislators openly colluded with speculators and land officers.

Crusading for Land Reform

Nineteenth-century American land reform, pursued by farm groups, liberal newspapers, professional reformers, western politicians, and radical labor advocates, was surprisingly weak and misdirected. Their common, often-repeated slogan was safe enough: "All men have a natural right to the soil, else they will be deprived of life, liberty, and the pursuit of happiness."[11] Early land-reform activists such as George Henry Evans and Thomas Skidmore drew wrong-headed comparisons with Europe's landed aristocracy, feudal society, and downtrodden peasantry, predicting an inevitable class war and a socialist revolution. There seemed to be little understanding of the widespread dedication on all levels of American society to private enterprise and the entrepreneurial spirit as the primary means for upward mobility. Land reform in the United States would never take on the radical and revolutionary character adopted in Europe, Asia, Africa, or Latin America. Yet Evans's program—free homesteads, homestead exemption, and land-use limitation—would, like many radical and socialist reforms, eventually be incorporated into American life.

In 1841 a Maine newspaper argued that the land issue always involved larger principles. It was "a struggle between aristocracy and democracy. . . . the rights of the poor man . . . to settle upon and improve a portion of the public domain."[12] Critics condemned free land as a direct attack on the right of property. Homestead advocates were vilified for trying to "vote yourself a farm." By the 1840s land reform had been captured by idealists of the new National Land

Reform Association. Their self-appointed spokesman was Horace Greeley.[13] Quoting the Bible but sounding like John Locke, Greeley condemned the policies that sold the national treasure for cash, as if it were "mere merchandise, like molasses or mackerel." Land was a divine gift to be apportioned as Everyman's natural right.[14] Personally repelled by all speculation, Greeley condemned independent farmers' lack of moral fiber when they profited from several additional quarter sections. Free land was Greeley's equivalent to motherhood, the flag, and apple pie. Free land would in one step solve the nation's ills, including foreign immigration, urban blight, unemployment, and factory slavery. The National Reformers lobbied intensively to take away presidential powers to open new lands for sale, to repeal the cash sale law of 1820, and to restore withdrawn lands reserved for private business entries. When the Homestead Act neared passage, they worked to include these safeguards, but in their self-righteous moralizing they naively ignored and lost to special-interest groups and the inherent temporizing attitude of Congress.

Homesteading: Crippled Attempt to Help the Farmer

By 1862 passage of the legendary Homestead Act for the independent farmer was more pitiable than honorable. Yet today the Homestead National Historic Monument just west of Beatrice, Nebraska, is revered as sacred ground. By Lincoln's signature 160 acres drawn from the public domain was donated to anyone who would settle on the land and work it for five years. But even the dubious advantages of the 1854 Graduation Act were more generous: 80 acres could be immediately titled for only $100, without the residence and improvement required for the often-impossible five years.[15] In reality the Homestead Act was a severely crippled step that contradicted existing land policies. Homesteading did not rescue Jefferson's hallowed yeoman farmer. Nowhere was homesteading the only way to acquire land; it competed everywhere with preemption for the same tracts. Public auctions continued on other lands, as did private sales. Nor was the cash value of homesteads protected, since the government regularly put new lands on the market.

In the first seven years only one-quarter of the nation's new farms were homestead applications. In the 1860s the most homestead filings in any single year, 26,000, were made in Minnesota. By comparison Illinois, containing expensive land with none available for homesteading, had a single-year high of almost 60,000 new non-homestead farms.[16] Kansas added over 13,000 homesteads in the 1860s, but also 28,000 other farms. Only Nebraska added more homestead entries—16,000—than other farms—9,500.[17] In the 1870s, 300,000 homesteads were outdistanced by 1.3 million other new farms.

Some states offered little land for homesteading. Most of the Old Northwest was unavailable. But the act helped populate the tier of states and public land crossing the nation's famous midpoint, the 100th meridian: midway across Kansas, Nebraska, and the Dakota Territory. Yet only 780,000 acres were open in Kansas, a state—like Iowa and Minnesota—where public lands had been captured by railroad withdrawals. More than 5 million acres could be homesteaded in Nebraska. The Dakota Territory was completely open, since nothing had been offered before 1862.[18] The Dakotas had been considered too remote and mostly too cold and arid for farming. But free land made settlers reconsider and, unfortunately, carried thousands of farmers into harm's way beyond acceptable rainfall. The only Dakota homesteaders who avoided disaster invaded the belt of land along the eastern edge of the area near the Red River of the North. Here they were far more likely to have the minimum twenty to twenty-five inches of rain needed each year for farming. By 1880 Dakota homesteading surpassed that in all states and other territories when it reached 8,600 homesteads covering 1.3 million acres. But, ominously, five years later only 3,500 titles, fewer than half, were made final on 548,000 acres. Even in good farm country not all homesteaders stayed long enough to claim their land. Almost half of Michigan's homesteaders gave up their valuable land and improvements between 1880 and 1885. About 63 percent held out in Wisconsin, 60 percent in Iowa, and only 46 percent in the harder Missouri country.

The public domain designated for homesteading seems stupendous, almost 84 million acres. But already the government had donated three times that acreage to the railroads alone. Also excluded were 140 million acres donated to states and 175 million acres of Indian lands. Homesteading was restricted to land already surveyed. Considering the public lands Congress could have included under the Homestead Act, its actual donation was paltry, covering leftover surveyed lands after the interests of auction sales, preemption, grants to states and railroads, private entries, and withdrawals had been taken care of.

Speculators' business went on as usual: 159,000 acres of valuable agricultural lands along the Minnesota River were acquired by fifty speculators in tracts ranging from 750 to almost 17,000 acres. The local land office registrar and receiver, making the most of their insider information, acquired 3,500 exceptionally fine acres. Lawful acreage limits were ignored, as were regulations on settlement and improvement. Yet in 1890 the commissioner of the General Land Office dared say, in a tone of bravado or disingenuousness, that "the great objective of the government is to dispose of the public lands to actual settlers only—to bona fide tillers of the soil."[19] In reality hundreds of thousands of acres still fell into the hands of a few men, among them the Englishman William Scully and the Rhode Island investors John Carter Brown and Robert H. Ives.

Farmers: Neither Innocent nor Helpless

Idealistic land reformers like Greeley, had they taken a closer look at their beloved honest, struggling farmers—like lifting a rock to find bugs swarming underneath—might have taken a real dislike to their constituency. Enterprising settlers enjoyed the new loopholes. They could now acquire 160 acres as homesteaders, another 160 acres as preempters, a third quarter section as regular buyers at public auction, and perhaps even a fourth through a "relinquishment." And because the act was carelessly written, a squatter could file a free homestead application instead of a preemption claim.[20]

Most farmers believed multiple acquisitions were not only "smart" but a moral duty to their families, to make the future less harsh. A similar secondary market, equally questionable but widely worked, was the sale or mortgage of homestead or preemption claims that had not yet been "proved up" or paid for. A settler would file a claim on a 160-acre homestead, but long before inhabiting the land and working it long enough to have clear title, would use it as collateral to borrow money. But the loan was not applied to homestead improvements; it was used to make a down payment on another quarter section. By selling the document giving him the right to final title, the settler could tap still another market to generate yet more capital. The midwestern novelist Hamlin Garland, in *A Son of the Middle Border,* said he had rushed to buy land in the 1880s in Dakota's James River region not to farm but to have property with an instant rise in value: a preemption cost him $200, which he immediately mortgaged for $200 cash, giving him a piece of land for no cost that was worth at least $200.[21]

Seth Humphrey was the local agent for Boston investors in 1889 on the Dakota frontier. He made usurious loans to distressed settlers who needed cash to avoid losing their farms by default. The times were particularly harsh after a series of severe winters followed by dry summers, combined with grasshopper plagues and pandemic low prices. As he crisscrossed the high dry plains, Humphrey described the migrants, some desperate and others speculative, perpetually on the move in search of the American dream:

> On came the settlers by train and by prairie schooner from Minnesota, Wisconsin, and states farther east: bona fide farmers thrown together with ne'er-do-wells, forever shifting westward; renters tired of renting; others merely tired of the places they were leaving; and a heavy sprinkling bent only on "proving up" their titles to quarter sections of land with the minimum of improvement required by law and selling out at a profit.

Humphrey wrote of "pseudo-settlers . . . who, though more or less sincere, never would be successful farmers—restless clerks, tired professors, schoolm'ams." The fluid society included

> chronic settlers—men who followed the taking up of government land as a habit. How did they manage to file on land in each of their several migrations, since the law allowed only one right to an individual? This disturbed them not at all. Bill Jones of the Wisconsin boom thought of himself as Hank Brown in Minnesota, then shifted to John Smith for his filing in Dakota.[22]

Humphrey complained that the western farmer found it easy to borrow up to $1000 on land and then skip town, abandoning his tract to the soulless eastern bank.

Most western settlers piously claimed the right to "flexibility," which meant laissez-faire opportunism on the brink of sheer anarchy. Paul Gates writes, "Settlers had 'hooked' timber from public lands, ganged up against Federal marshals trying to levy upon stolen timber, packed juries to free the accused, and managed to turn the law against officers trying to protect government property."[23] Cash-poor farmers, without thought of payment, rushed to engross two or three quarter sections. Everyone knew that so much acreage could never be plowed, planted, cultivated, harvested, or fenced by one family. John Ise's famous account of sod-house life quotes an 1877

Kansas homesteader bending the law:

> We took out homesteads directly. We might have "filed" on the land, and that filing preemption would have been good for 30 months, at the end of which time [or before] we could have bought the land or put a homestead on it. As it is, we must live on it five years. The first two years we live "off and on"—that is we must sleep on it once in a while and make some improvements on it within 6 months, or it will be forfeited. It is to be our home, but we can hire out by the day or month as we like.[24]

Paul Gates has generously concluded, "When [the local farmer] swore that he was not making the extra entry for others he was committing perjury but his crime, if crime it was, was commonly done and was not as harmful as if he were making his entries for a cattleman, a timber baron, or a large capitalist estate builder . . . abuse of the legislation was less serious than the success in making it possible for the man with little capital to get started on the road to farm ownership."[25] Unlike the National Reformers, westerners did not treat the Homestead Act piously; they saw it as a golden opportunity to make a series of quick killings.

CHAPTER 6

Trading Land for Technology

Some opportunities for the federal government to build up the nation were simply too providential to pass up. Over a period of fifty years, roughly from 1820 through 1870, the United States became a compact, efficient, and well-linked nation through the simple expedient of trading large land corridors through the public domain for a network of completed roads, canals, and railroads. This fashioned yet another land pattern overlying the farmland grid. In many cases such routes were located and set aside before the survey reached the new region. Once again the survey landscape was not the first land-use arrangement on the public domain; empty and open unsurveyed regions were crisscrossed with predetermined corridors that would often contradict the survey.

As early as 1806 the Jefferson administration looked forward to the benefits of the new National Road, authorized to run an extraordinary 250 miles from the port of Baltimore to the Ohio River hamlet of Wheeling, deep in the western wilderness. Construction began in 1811, and the road, completed in 1818, gave new overland access to the agrarian Midwest. By 1833 the National Road would press westward 130 miles to Columbus but with an unexpected development. Between Baltimore and Wheeling the road had crossed no townships, sections, or quarter sections of survey land. But in the survey lands west and north of the Ohio River a surprising omission was discovered in the land ordinances. The law did not allow for rights-of-way for transportation; one family's quarter section simply abutted its neighbors' continuously across the countryside. This simple omission would change the course of American land use, agriculture, and private enterprise.

Ohio Precedents for Right-of-Way Land Grants

The 1803 Ohio Enabling Act made it clear that the federal government rather than the states controlled transport and communications routes.[1] An 1808 treaty with Indian tribes in Ohio gave the United States a strip of land 120 feet wide running from the rapids of the Miami River at Lake Erie to the western edge of the Connecticut Reserve. In a step significant for subsequent American history, the treaty set aside "all the land within one mile of the said road, on each side thereof, for the purpose of establishing settlements along the same." This land was then withdrawn from the survey gridiron to stand as an independent land corridor. Sale of the mile-wide zone on each side was to pay for road construction and maintenance. This provision was most felicitous for the federal budget, since road costs would be self-contained without further government expense. The grant totaled a generous 60,000 acres. The 1808 treaty included an additional 120-foot strip from the upper Sandusky River to the Greenville treaty line, for a road only and no settlement zone. Congress intervened in another historic step by withdrawing from public sale alternate survey sections along the right-of-way. It then donated the withdrawal to Ohio on condition that the private Columbus and Sandusky Turnpike Company sell the land for road-building funds. This giveaway was rationalized on the grounds that the alternate survey sections not ceded would grow in value and compensate the government for its concessions.[2] The Columbus and Sandusky Turnpike Company received 31,600 acres to build its road. All in all, Ohioans and Congress were well satisfied with the 336 miles of roads gained by releasing 93,500 public acres into private company hands.

Few politicians could ignore the "canal fever" of the 1820s and 1830s. Farmers along the Erie Canal sharpened their speculator's skills in the sudden change from bare-bones subsistence to profitable commercial farming. Canal fever led Ohioans to build almost 400 miles of canals using $5,145,000 of state funds and private investments, but most developers turned to government financing, based on lucrative alternate-section land along rights-of-way.[3] By 1848 Congress mandated a 458-mile Wabash Canal, the nation's longest, running from Toledo to Evansville, funded by a land grant of 1,750,000 acres. Ohio officials ultimately squandered 1,230,000 acres of federal land for less than $1,800,000. In contrast, Illinois officials by 1871 had turned 324,000 acres into $5,860,000, admittedly based on the valuable 1827 Illinois and Michigan Canal route from Lake Michigan's Chicago River to the Illinois River flowing into the Mississippi. This grant included "a quantity of land equal to one-half of five sections in width, on each side."[4]

Abuses of right-of-way land grants were sometimes spectacular. In Wisconsin in the late 1830s only one mile of a canal was built from Lake Michigan at Milwaukee to the Rock River flowing into the Mississippi, although the grant took almost 125,000 acres of Wisconsin farmland from the nation's coffers.[5] A proposed water link between Green Bay and the Mississippi, using the Fox and Wisconsin rivers, shifted 820,000 acres into private hands. Dams and locks proved defective, capital was drained by eastern financiers, and even the most credulous knew that the Wisconsin River was passable to steamboat traffic only during the brief high-water season. No water link was ever made.

Railroads Transform the Nation

The American love affair with the steam locomotive made it impossible to oppose the rush to trade land for a railroad network. James H. Lanham wrote eloquently in an 1840 issue of *Merchants' Magazine*: "All patriotic and right-minded men have concurred in the propriety of their construction . . . iron monsters . . . dragons of mightier power, with iron muscles that never tire, breathing smoke and flame through their blackened lungs, feeding upon wood and water, outrunning the race horse."[6] John Stuart Mill had an early insight into the railroad on the American land: it was an honest machine of unparalleled might that, with its useful carrying power controlled on permanent tracks, was the perfect means to master a vast wilderness. Mill rightly predicted that American farmers, surrounded by a wild and uncultivated expanse, living bravely off their hard physical labor, would delight in the dramatic victory the steam locomotive symbolized over the creeping pace of ordinary human intervention into the wilderness. Alexis de Tocqueville wrote that America's spacious regions, through man's steam engine, would "yield freely of their treasures to his researches and toils. . . . He has almost annihilated space and time. He yokes to his car fire and water, those unappeasable foes, and flying from place to place with the speed of thought carries with him, in one mass, commodities for supplying a province."[7] The French traveler Michel Chevalier said that the typical American "has a perfect passion for railroads; he loves them . . . as a lover loves his mistress."[8]

No wonder, then, that in the brief span of twenty-one years

between 1850 and 1871 the federal government joined in the national love affair by donating western lands on a scale that allowed some private railroad corporations to own more territory than entire eastern states. Twenty percent of Kansas, over 10 million acres, fell to the railroads, as did 15 percent of Nebraska, more than 7.75 million acres.[9] The new steam locomotive, completely unanticipated, overnight became the greatest magnet for private enterprise and government subsidy. It was a grand collaboration.

Once the unyielding rule of rural time and space had been that a loaded wagon behind a team of horses could make a round trip of no more than fourteen miles between farm and town. (Hence the nineteenth-century American rural landscape was peppered with towns fourteen miles apart, so that no farmer was more than seven miles from a place to trade.) The railroads created totally unexpected universal *access* across the broad nation. The United States in a short generation collapsed into itself like a dense star. It changed from an unmanageably enormous geography, where there would exist perpetually empty and unknown remote regions, to an interconnected landscape where no one, no matter how distantly settled, was ever quite out of reach. In 1868 Walt Whitman summed up the national passion:

> I see over my own continent the Pacific railroad
>   surmounting every barrier,
> I see continual trains of cars winding along the
>   Platte carrying freight and passengers,
> I hear the locomotives rushing and roaring, and the
>   shrill steam-whistle,
> I hear the echoes reverberate through the grandest
>   scenery in the world.[10]

Victory of Enterprise over Land

But in the astonished rush across the shrinking landscape, no one spoke out for democratic public ownership of the railroads. Instead, American private enterprise would take a quantum leap to the grand scale it has today. Railroad companies were treated as untouchable utilities—a public good in private hands. Private ownership, with the sole objective of unregulated profit, was never at serious issue until the collapse of the railroad system a century later in the 1960s, ironically brought on by federally subsidized trucking and highway enterprise.

Congress slipped easily into trading land for railroads.[11] The first session of the Thirty-first Congress in 1850 received twenty-three bills for land grants to guarantee railroads in every public-land state. Senators Stephen A. Douglas and John Wentworth tried to minimize the immense grant of a 100-foot right-of-way running from Chicago to Mobile on the Gulf of Mexico, including half the land in even-numbered sections for 6 miles on each side of the line. Douglas told Congress this was no new risk venture but an extension of the worthy federal practice going back to 1827 in Ohio. He also used his formidable persuasive powers to argue that the alternate sections along the proposed line would double in value to $2.50 and the government would lose nothing.[12] Douglas carefully ignored evidence from Wisconsin that settlers refused to buy $2.50 land wherever $1.25 land was available. Then the confusion began. Where land was already in private hands along the line, alternatives *(lieu land)* would be selected by the railroad 6 to 15 miles on each side. Douglas's rhetoric, together with heavy pressure from eastern financial interests, got the bill passed, and then signed by the new president, Millard Fillmore.[13] The Chicago and Mobile bill created a privately owned public utility that ultimately became the highly profitable Illinois Central Railroad. Railroad speculators scrambled for federal grants. By 1856, 700 miles were in place, based on the sale of over 1.2 million acres of once-public land for $14,210,000, averaging $11.80 an acre. In 1850 there were only 1,276 miles of track in the upper Mississippi valley; five years later there were 4,567 and by 1860 over 11,000, mostly financed by the public domain.[14]

President Franklin Pierce was joined by a few congressmen in attacking the land giveaway as unconstitutional. Already George W. Jones of Tennessee and Andrew Butler of South Carolina held that land grants for railroads were beyond the power of Congress to convey. But in 1852 and 1853, 1,322 miles were added to the 1,333 miles already granted, based on 4,400,000 acres added to the existing 3,750,000 acres.[15] President Pierce belatedly asked whether the public interest was served by leaving all railroad construction in private hands. That Congress had the *authority* to grant land did not mean it had a *duty* to do so. Pierce ordered the commissioner of the General Land Office to return to public offering 30 million acres that had been withdrawn in anticipation of railroad grants. Nevertheless, the combination of special interests, expansive public opinion, and the self-interest of speculators in Congress was not to be denied. By 1855 private railroad companies besieged Congress for 20 million acres in trade for 5,000 miles of track. In seemingly uncontrolled releases of the public domain, 78 million acres were given up by 1857. This included most of the remaining public lands in Iowa's agricultural paradise and other rich farmland states.[16] The pressure of public indignation and the Panic of 1857 restored 18 million acres for purchase by settlers. But the Panic, and the collapse of capital, only temporarily halted construction to wait for better times.

Transcontinental Railroad Corridors

Asa Whitney made the first proposal to build from the Mississippi and Missouri rivers to the Pacific Ocean. In 1844 he suggested building from Milwaukee through Wyoming's South Pass to Puget Sound.[17] The plan depended upon a continuous strip of land 60 miles wide carved out of the public domain along the entire route, at a cost to Whitney of no more than 16¢ an acre. The famous Pacific Railroad Surveys speedily examined alternative western routes independently of the General Land Office survey.[18] In contrast, the land office survey struggled slowly westward according to the guidelines set back in 1785 and 1796.

With southern obstructionism removed during the Civil War, Congress moved quickly toward land grants for the transcontinental line. The generous Pacific Railroad Act of 1862 chartered the private Union Pacific Railroad to receive a 400-foot right-of-way through withdrawn public lands. Additional grants gave twenty odd-numbered sections for each mile of line constructed from Omaha on the Missouri River to the western border of Nevada. The same subsidies were granted the Central Pacific Railroad to build to the California border. The secretary of the interior was to withdraw all corridor lands immediately—first 15 miles on each side according to the 1862 act, and in 1864 this was extended to 25 miles on each side—cutting a 50-mile swath from Nebraska to California. All new homesteads and preemptions were excluded from this corridor, although existing claims would be honored, to a maximum of 160 acres each for homestead and preemption. The 1862 and 1864 acts created 2,720 miles of right-of-way while surrendering some 34,560,000 acres of public land. This generosity toward the central route did not match the forthcoming gift to the new Northern Pacific Railroad Company: a 400-foot right-of-way, twenty sections of land for each mile in states and forty sections for each mile in territories, with 10 additional lieu land miles on each side. The resulting swath of land was 80 miles wide in the states and 120 miles wide in the territories—an area, as Paul Gates noted, larger than the state of Missouri.[19] This grant passed through 2,128 miles from Duluth to Portland and Tacoma, totaling 45 million acres. It covered 23 percent of North Dakota and 15 percent of Montana. In sum, the five transcontinental railroads received between 100 million and 110 million acres of free land, which became their private property to dispose of at their pleasure. In addition state grants increased railroad profit potential. Texas owned its own public lands and granted away 21 percent, over 35 million acres, of its entire land area.[20] Congress donated a grand net total of more than 127 million acres to subsidize private railroad construction. When state grants are included, the total rises to 213 million acres.[21]

As early as 1865 the General Land Office set the tone of federal generosity when it granted the Burlington and Missouri Railroad a free hand over the nation's entire public domain: the company could select land from geographically distant regions unrelated to the railroad's line. Each site, whatever its location and value, was then withdrawn from the public marketplace. Two years later, Nebraska governor Paddock angrily denounced "the evil effects of this baleful system of land grants . . . this rapid absorption of the public domain . . . by railroad monopolists and land speculators."[22] By the mid-1860s railroads were relocating their lines in open disregard of their grants. They claimed lieu lands (when their grant was already in private hands) almost at will across the public domain. The government had also long given up the argument that it could compensate for lost land by selling its reserved sections along the right-of-way for double the minimum price.[23] By the 1870s and 1880s, the railroad grants were buried under layers of protection.

The railroads became the greatest private landowners in the nation. Only public institutions—the states and the federal government—were larger. When reform passions reached national proportions and became violent in midwestern farming regions, Congress

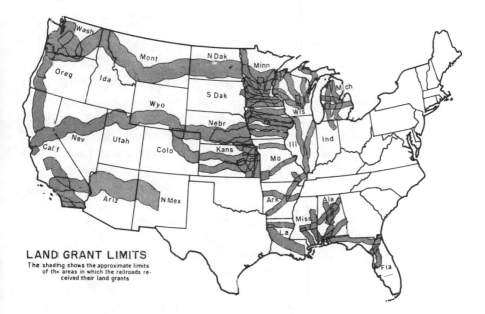

LAND GRANT LIMITS
The shading shows the approximate limits
of the areas in which the railroads received their land grants

Fig. 8. Federal land grants to railroad companies to guarantee their profitable expansion often dominated western expansion. The shading shows the approximate limits of the areas in which the railroads received their land grants. Such private interests often overwhelmed the federal survey and sale to independent farmers. See especially Iowa, Minnesota, Kansas, and Nebraska. From *History of Public Land Law Development*, by Paul W. Gates (Washington, D.C.: Public Land Law Review Commission, 1968).

belatedly responded. Petitions from state legislatures—Pennsylvania, Ohio, Indiana, Wisconsin, Missouri, and California—told Congress that the gifts of land to the railroads, and withdrawals of enormous zones from public sale, were a "violation of the spirit and interest of the national Homestead Law and manifestly in bad faith toward the landless." To soothe outraged settlers, the 1869 grant to the California and Oregon Railroad, a forerunner of the Southern Pacific, incorporated the famous "homestead" clause: "The lands granted . . . shall be sold to actual settlers only, in quantities not greater than one quarter section to one purchaser, and for a price not exceeding two dollars and fifty cents per acre." As Paul Gates observed, "There is no known evidence of government officers in the 19th century trying to enforce them."[24] The 1870 Holman resolution concluded that "the policy of granting subsidies in public lands to railroads and other corporations ought to be discontinued . . . [public lands are for the] exclusive purpose of securing homesteads to actual settlers."[25]

Following one last large grant to the Texas Pacific, the railroads received no more land subsidies after 1871. But it was not until 1890 that railroads were compelled to return (forfeit) unsold tracts to the government. Enforcement was so poor that some major holdings, like the huge Northern Pacific fiefdom, were never recovered. The nation was compensated by rapid westward settlement based on an unequaled transportation network.

Commissioner Sparks Takes on the Railroads

President Cleveland's new land commissioner, William J. A. Sparks, complained that reform measures passed by Congress in 1879 were "an unmixed evil." They "promoted unnecessary and improvident expenditures, premature and worthless surveys, the corruption of public officers, and the unlawful appropriation of vast bodies of the most valuable unsettled public lands."[26] Sparks came to the General Land Office with a reputation as a combative reformer and a tendency toward "unparliamentary language." He had been receiver at the Edwardsville land office between 1853 and 1855 and had served four undistinguished years in Congress. But in his first annual General Land Office report Sparks came out swinging against virtually all special interests.[27] He raged at "absurd claims" that had been transformed into "impregnable rights." Forty percent of all homestead entries were "fraudulent;" innumerable western cattle entries were "fictitious and fraudulent." Timber culture entries were "conspicuously fraudulent" and involved collusion by government officials. Widespread timber cuttings were "universal, flagrant and limitless." Undeveloped railroad withdrawals "arbitrarily and cruelly" deprived honest settlers of land opportunities. Sparks concluded that deception in land dealings was the rule, tolerated and even covered up by land office officials. Although a loyal Democrat, Sparks followed the lead of his president by showing no favorites in his denunciation of corruption. High officials, including earlier commissioners, felt his wrath: they had used their office "to the advantage of speculation and monopoly, private and corporate, rather than the public interest."

Sparks saved his angriest assault for the railroad grants. When the public domain became the private property of the railroads, he argued, the grants were treated like sacred groves. They received all conceivable exemptions and privileges. In cases of conflicting and often dubious claims, the railroads invariably got the benefit of the doubt. In addition, land was withdrawn from public access and held indefinitely for the railroads without authority. Railroad companies were consistently allocated more land than authorized. Sparks complained that well-paid railroad attorneys could blow up small grants into vast holdings with government acquiescence. In favoring the railroads the General Land Office had run roughshod over the honest needs of ordinary settlers. Most litigation was so time consuming, adverse, and expensive for settlers that "at every point in every stage . . . it became easier for claimants to buy the land from the railroads" than to pursue their just cause. Sparks was not all wind: by 1887 he had recovered more than 21 million acres of Northern Pacific lands and restored them to public entry. Sparks eliminated long-standing "special" considerations given powerful speculators. He fought illegal fencing of large tracts—one Nebraska cattle company had enclosed 84,000 acres of public land. In 1887 he persuaded a reluctant War Department to bring in cavalry to remove illegal fences in Wyoming.

Land Reform

In 1879 the prestigious new National Academy of Sciences voted to intervene in government land management and force land reform. As a respected independent organization, its voice would be heard in Congress and among government agencies. The members of the academy said they were responding to the enormous waste and irretrievable losses inherent in the existing land system, the apparent incapacity of Congress to bring meaningful change, and public clamor for reform. A year earlier John Wesley Powell, as government scientist and explorer, in his *Report on the Lands of the Arid Region of the United States,* had exposed the scope of federal mismanagement when he urged major changes in land survey and sale to suit new conditions in the arid West. The National Academy of Sciences appointed its own investigative committee to look into the clutter of 3,500 laws, more than 10,000 regulations, myriad policy statements, and uncounted court cases, which had created millions of independently owned tracts of land blanketing the United States west of the Ohio-Pennsylvania line.[28] The committee's most specific advice was to establish a long overdue classification of public lands, based on economic use and strategic value: irrigable, arable, timber, pasturage, swamp, coal, mineral, and so forth. Once again, it sounded the old refrain: Congress must explore the best means to make public lands available to actual settlers.

Congress astonished reformers when in 1879 it created without debate the nation's first Public Land Commission. Equally surprising, the commission was not stacked with self-serving politicians but included some of the best informed and most dedicated professionals of the day, including James A. Williamson, the reform-minded commissioner of the General Land Office; Clarence King, influential head of the Geological Survey; Alexander T. Britton, a Washington attorney with experience in the land office and a close associate of Carl Schurz, secretary of the interior; the redoubtable and controversial John Wesley Powell; and the muckraking Idaho land official Thomas Donaldson, who would emerge as the hardworking policymaker for the commission.[29]

The most compelling land issue facing the nation stood where settlers had recently moved, on lands along the 100th meridian. Here, for the first time in settlement history, rainfall was far too limited for successful "eastern" farming. But the commission did not cope with the problem by examining the workability of existing legislation, particularly the Homestead Act, for the independent settler of limited means. In addition, alarming problems swirled around relinquishments, the abuse of Morrill scrip, delayed titles owing to litigation, and other misuses that did not enter their deliberations.

Although the commission avoided politically controversial recommendations, it did look toward the future. It proposed to divide the public domain into agricultural and nonagricultural lands. Nonagricultural land was divided into mineral and timber classes and then graded into three quality and quantity levels. The commission did not examine agricultural land types in any detail but merely separated farmland into eastern-style humid traditionally "arable" land, and western "arid but irrigable" farmland. Much western land would be categorized as pasturage for grazing. Unfortunately, the commission offered no criteria for division. It also proposed that pasturelands, as yet undifferentiated, should be sold in unlimited amounts at decreasing prices over several years, beginning at $1.25 an acre in 1886 and dropping to 75¢ in 1890, to 50¢ by 1896, 25¢ in 1902, and down to one bit in 1905. With a small bow to Powell's 1878 report, the commission proposed pasturelands purchase of 2,560-acre homesteads on surveyed, unsurveyed, and unappropriated public lands.[30] The commission's final 1884 report concluded that perhaps only 5 million acres of useful farmland remained available for sale to the public. It called for the repeal of the Preemption, Timber Culture, Desert Land, Timber and Stone, Swamp Land Indemnity, and cash sale acts because of the widely acknowledged fraud connected with them.[31]

The commission concluded that the frontier of open land was virtually at an end because agricultural land workable by the small independent farmer was gone. Hence the laws that controlled western expansion into the empty public domain, particularly the 160-acre Preemption Act and Homestead Act, should be repealed and replaced by more practical ranching and resource-development acts. New standards were to be applied to the remaining public domain. The commission's viewpoint is at first glance hard to reconcile with the intensive homesteading taking place in Kansas, Nebraska, and the Dakota Territory, which had not yet reached its peak in 1884. But farm failures would soon soar. The 160-acre tract seemed less and less relevant west of the 100th meridian, as Powell predicted. But without direct intervention by the commission or Congress, homesteaders and preempters continued to press into the arid western wastelands, only to find themselves in high-risk situations.

In his reforming zeal, Commissioner Sparks took an unprecedented and probably suicidal step to set matters right: on 3 April

1885, after only a month in office, he suspended all further private entries on public lands in order to allow adequate time for the investigation of fraud, deception, and abuse.[32] Even the most optimistic western land boosters had begun complaining that railroad grants now covered vast corridors 20 to 80 miles wide ranging across the landscape. These private zones were being held off the market for a decade or more, awaiting higher prices, thus inhibiting frontier growth. Sparks also shut down sales because he was profoundly disturbed by the widespread contempt western settlers had for federal laws. Sparks took it personally when he concluded that his own agency's policies tempted simple American farmers to perjure themselves. The land acquisition process had become so distorted, he concluded, that government regulations encouraged settlers to subvert their fundamental integrity: "Men who would scorn to commit a dishonest act toward an individual, though he were a total stranger, eagerly listen to every scheme for evading the letter and spirit of the settlement laws, and in a majority of instances I believe avail themselves of them. Our land officers partake of this feeling in many instances, and if they do not corruptly connive at fraudulent entries, modify their instructions and exceed their discretionary powers in examinations of final proof."[33]

Sparks moved toward an across-the-board cleanup. His second annual report, in 1886, focused on incompetent and fraudulent surveys, which were costing the government large sums to resurvey and replat. The survey had long ago been compromised by political appointments reaching all the way up to the sixteen surveyors general. Fraudulent lines and corners set to capture a strategic well or crossroads became all too common. Over the decades the surveyors had never become professionalized. Contracts were let to unqualified private persons or companies. Some survey markers were merely blazes on trees, wooden stakes on raised mounds of earth, and other temporary signs that could easily disappear or be readily moved. The long-standing government fee—$6 per mile—had always been inadequate for more difficult terrain and was laughable for mountainous regions. Back in the eighteenth century most men of ambition or means had acquired simple surveying skills as part of their agricultural experience. George Washington was typical. But gradually surveying became a more sophisticated professional skill, an important aspect of civil engineering.[34] While the General Land Office survey did have its professionals and skillful amateurs, too often the all-important responsibility of turning out lines, determining corners, and formulating plats and maps was ineptly, carelessly, or fraudulently done.[35] To give the survey system its air of permanence, the law had from the first stipulated that once the survey was completed and the plat registered at the land office, it was permanent. This made it extremely difficult to undo either honest amateur mistakes or fraudulent lines and corners. While virtually every state found it necessary to revise the survey, California surveys were the worst, sometimes a quarter-mile to a mile off, with corners and lines that could not be located on the land itself, demanding expensive and time-consuming resurvey. The land office sometimes found itself reworking a survey three or four times before the lines and corners could be rationalized. The survey was losing its credibility; yet its primary virtue since 1785 had been its apparent reliability, which guaranteed settlers their land without controversy and litigation.

Sparks drew enthusiastic support from Grover Cleveland's secretary of the interior, Lucius Lamar, and from the president himself. Congressmen Lewis Payson of Illinois and William S. Holman of Indiana joined Sparks to form a formidable reform faction. But when the wrath of the railroads, large landowners, opportunistic speculators and foreign money interests descended upon Congress and the Cleveland administration, Sparks found himself abandoned. He had frozen western land entries and reopened inquiry into long-standing exemptions and privileges. As a result he had effectively nullified loopholes inserted into the Preemption, Timber Culture, and Desert Land acts to guarantee some of the most profitable enterprises in American history. Forced to resign in November 1887, to the end Sparks fulminated against the bad laws, ineffectual administration, and open fraud that led to "the gross piracy of public lands." Paul Gates called Sparks a "prickly, self-assured moralist, perhaps the ablest Commissioner the Land Office had in the 19th century."[36]

For five years after the resignation of William J. A. Sparks, Congressmen Lewis Payson of Illinois and William S. Holman of Indiana carried on the commissioner's reform efforts to free legitimate land entries from the cloud of fraudulent claims that muddied the public domain. But not until after a congressional housecleaning in the election of 1890 were the votes mustered to repeal the badly abused forty-nine-year-old Preemption Act and the corruption-prone Timber Culture Act. The General Revision Act of 1891 also cleaned up Homestead Act commutation, desert land entries, and presidential powers to create forest preserves and made innumerable small corrections.[37] Once again, in the seemingly futile attempt to limit large land grabs, the act sought to limit total land entries by one individual to 320 acres (homestead entry plus one other). Following the precedent set by Commissioner Sparks six years earlier, the act took the historic step of shutting down all further public offerings of land. After 106 years of survey and sale, the General Revision Act of 1891 was the first direct attempt by Congress to examine land reform in a disciplined way, to remove outdated or abused legislation, and to tighten working policies. The reforms of the 1891 act did in large part eliminate the "flexibility" cherished by western boosters and speculators.[38] Yet General Land Office commissioner Binger Hermann complained in 1897 and again in 1902 of bureaucratic ineptitude, continued open fraud, and even a "systematic conspiracy." A land office agent in Nebraska reported that while many homestead entries were made in the early 1900s, local farmers openly boasted that no "genuine, legal homestead entry" had been made in years.

Iowa and Kansas Vanity Atlases

Enterprising publishers' agents roamed the newly prosperous midgrass prairie country west of the Mississippi River. They promoted "official" atlases that, for a price, would feature local farms as prime examples of midwestern agricultural success. Farmers, in turn, hoped to attract land buyers at higher prices when the atlases were published. The following pages include typical "enhanced" steel engravings to promote farms in Iowa and Kansas, together with county plat maps, presumably to enable interested buyers to locate the farms. Maps and illustrations are from A. T. Andreas, *Illustrated Historical Atlas of the State of Iowa* (Chicago: Lakeside Press, 1875), and *Official State Atlas of Kansas* (Philadelphia: E. H. Evert's and Company, 1887).

Fig. 9. Morning scene on the large stock farm of John D. Rivers, Des Moines Township, Dallas Country, Iowa. Iowa farmer John D. Rivers offered up to 4,000 acres for sale "at rare bargains" and included his address in Polk County. On the far left horizon, Rivers had the artist suggest that the railroad town, Dallas Center, was nearby, although it was nine miles away. From Andreas, *Illustrated Historical Atlas of the State of Iowa.*

Fig. 10. Stock farm and residence of H. H. Taylor, Delaware, Polk County, Iowa. This illustration must have pleased Taylor, displaying as it did a prosperous farm and good roads. From Andreas, *Illustrated Historical Atlas of the State of Iowa*.

Fig. 11. Farm residence of Calvin Thornton, Polk County, Iowa. Des Moines is in the distance. Thornton's farm was in Section 6 of Grant Township. From Andreas, *Illustrated Historical Atlas of the State of Iowa.*

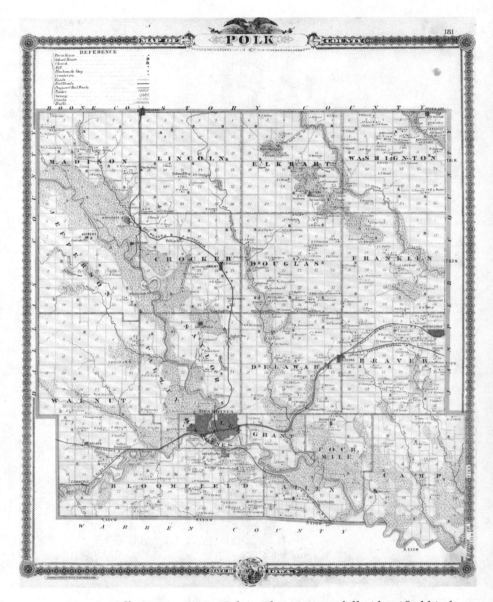

Fig. 12. Polk County, Iowa. Calvin Thornton carefully identified his farmland in north central Grant Township (Section 6), just east of Des Moines
above the curving rail line. Taylor's place is in north central Delaware Township (Section 8), which is directly above Grant Township. Thornton has
another (Section 9) tract identified as being nearby Taylor's. The atlas sales-
man may have hooked the two subscribers at the same time. From Andreas,
Illustrated Historical Atlas of the State of Iowa.

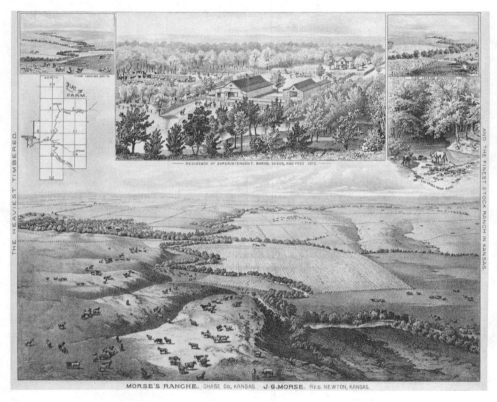

Fig. 13. J. G. Morse's Ranch, Chase County, Kansas. It was advertised as "The Heaviest Timbered, the Best Watered, and the Finest Stock Ranch in Kansas." Morse had the artist show a prosperous cattle farm with more trees and water than it was likely to have. He also included, on the upper left side, a plat of the farm, which was adjacent to the curiously named town of Worsevu. From *Official State Atlas of Kansas.*

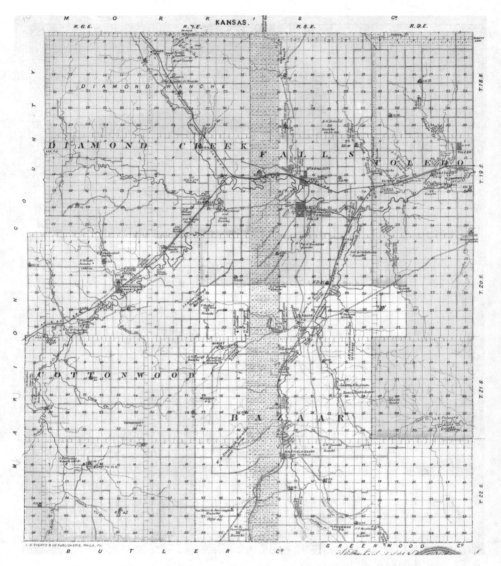

Fig. 14. Chase County, Kansas. Morse's Ranch could also be located on the Chase County and Cottonwood Township map, which indicated that Wonsivu (variant spelling) had a post office and that the Atcheson, Topeka, and Santa Fe Railroad was only eight miles to the north. From *Official State Atlas of Kansas.*

CHAPTER 7

In Harm's Way

The government bets 160 acres against the entry fee of $14 that the settler can't live on the land for five years without starving to death.

Idaho senator William E. Borah, 1912

Like Moses in the desert, John Wesley Powell brought command-ments to safeguard the American farmer in the hard, dry lands of the American West. Dryland settlers would prevail only with a land "system less arbitrary than that of the rectangular surveys now in vogue. . . . It is best to permit the people to divide their lands for themselves." The timeworn survey, hardly changed since 1785, would put settlers in harm's way on its platted tracts: "The lands . . . are not valuable for agricultural purposes in continuous bod-ies or squares, but only in irrigable tracts; . . . they should not be hampered with the present arbitrary system of dividing the lands into rectangular tracts." Powell's official 1878 *Report on the Lands of the Arid Region of the United States* was prophetic about the true nature of the West and its impact upon settlers. In sum, Powell argued, "practically all values inhere in the water."[1] The West had some limited potential "if the lands could be divided into parcels, governed solely by the conditions under which the water could be distributed over them." Powell was too pessimistic about the scale of irrigation, but not about the dangers to the small farmer, or the need for land reform or the inevitability of massive federal intervention.

Following unexpected droughts and financial panics, the opti-mistic 1870s became the pessimistic 1890s. All but the most ex-treme boosters admitted that the empty arid lands of the western United States did not naturally have enough water for farming and settlement. But tens of thousands of farmers had already been pushed west to put down roots. Nor did the situation improve in the future. For seventy years, between the first settlements of the 1870s and

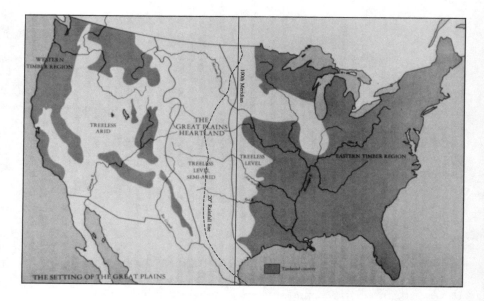

Fig. 15. Middle American heartland. Settlers encountered new conditions in the Midwest and plains, particularly the open prairie country and lack of adequate rainfall. The limits of the geometric survey quickly became evident. Map revised from Robert V. Hine, *The American West: An Interpretive History*, 2d ed. Copyright © 1984 by Robert V. Hine. Reprinted by permission of Little, Brown and Company.

the government-inspired recovery in the 1930s, plains farmers were thrown into near-starvation conditions, leading to the displacement of tens of thousands of families, the creation of a debtor class, and a major failure in America's vaunted frontier settlement. Eventually federal farm policies sacrificed land and water resources, and eventually cash, on a massive scale to produce abundant cheap food for consumers and to rescue small farmers. But in the interim conditions were acceptable on the plains for only two decades out of the seventy years between 1870 and 1940. The era from 1900 to 1920 is still considered the golden age of American agriculture; drought and desperation marked the other decades. In the process the arid West became the solvent that is now forcing the dissolution of the independent family farm as a potent force in American society.

The effort to preserve the myth of the West as a bountiful garden sometimes took a bizarre turn. In the late 1880s, as the picture of the drylands became clear and federal officials contemplated the disaster, someone remembered that heavy rains had descended upon the soldiers after the heavy artillery barrages of the Battle of Gettysburg. Similar downpours came, it was said, after the Battle of Waterloo and other artillery barrages during the Napoleonic Wars. In this light the Honorable Charles B. Farwell, senator from Illinois (the Sucker State), persuaded Congress to appropriate the substantial total of $10,000 for, as *Scientific American* put it, "a sufficient number of first-class bangings to condense moisture into rain."[2]

Shadowy operators in Washington, D.C., are not new. An obscure local lawyer, apparently smelling the money and publicity, got himself appointed special agent for the United States Department of Agriculture (USDA) to carry out the project. Robert G. Dyrenforth gave himself the rank of general and requested 200 Civil War siege guns from Senator Farwell's Rock Island, Illinois, arsenal, together with 40,000 blank cartridges, 50 tons of hay for wadding, 10,000 electric primers, over 600 men, and ground transportation, all of which would have cost the government $161,590. But USDA had only $20,000 for the project, so Dyrenforth compromised on $20,000 to send explosives up in balloons while at the same time setting off charges on the ground. The primary trials took place in August 1891 near Midland, Texas. Needless to say they failed dramatically, though some thunderclouds were reported thirty or forty miles to the north. The local farmers loved the entertainment. Reports of the fiasco showed up in papers across the country.[3] Dyrenforth was quickly nicknamed "Dryhenceforth." The USDA "cloud-compelling team" quietly stole away, and the government tried to forget the entire project. Later, during the Dust Bowl of the 1930s, President Franklin Roosevelt was called on to announce a national "Explosion Day" when each arid county would set off charges to bring rain. Unfortunately for the Republican party, Roosevelt did not follow through.

Apparently settlers did not easily comprehend, much less accept, real conditions on the arid western grasslands. Farmers working the new lands expected to match or exceed the bounty of Ohio, Illinois, or Iowa, where rainfall exceeded 30 inches a year. But athwart the 100th meridian, rainfall slackened to a risky 20 inches, and it would drop to a desertlike 12 inches along today's borders between Colorado and Kansas, Wyoming and Nebraska. Yet the pressures for westward movement and perennial frontier optimism induced repeated migrations and inevitably outmigrations on the Great Plains before settlers accepted the true nature of the arid lands.[4]

The arid western grasslands had been known as a dry region since the early nineteenth century. This was fixed in the national consciousness by Zebulon Pike's 1806–7 Arkansas basin expedition report.[5] By the 1820s the plains were widely known as the Great American Desert, an insurmountable barrier less easy to cross than the Atlantic Ocean.[6] In 1856 Joseph Henry, influential secretary of the Smithsonian Institution, lamented, "the whole space to the west . . . is a barren waste, over which the eye may roam to the extent of the visible horizon with scarcely an object to break the monotony . . . country of comparatively little value to the agriculturalist."[7] Settlers were edging into a wide and risky zone. In 1874 the commander of Fort Buford in Dakota Territory, Brevet Major General William B. Hazen, sent a scathing letter to the *New York Tribune* depicting the futility of the land. "This country will not produce the fruits and cereals of the East for want of moisture, and can in no way be artificially irrigated, and will not, in our day and generation, sell for one penny an acre, except through fraud or ignorance."[8]

Nevertheless, extremely strong expansionist pressures encouraged settlers to move westward. American "Manifest Destiny," like most patriotic gestures, swamped more reasonable opinions. As early as 1831 Joshua Pilcher wrote that anyone who saw the end of expansion "must know little of the American people, who supposes that they can be stopped by any thing in the shape of deserts."[9] In 1867 Senator G. S. Orth's junket into the western grasslands made him explain, "Our good 'Uncle Sam' has come here and he brings with him science and civilization. He intends to plant permanently a part of his great family; for he is now founding empires, and his mission will not be fulfilled on this continent until every foot of its soil will acknowledge his dominion and his power."[10]

The New Geography for American Agriculture

The earliest misgivings about the settlement of western lands began not at the high plains, but at the midwestern prairie. The endless vacant grasslands that stretch westward from today's Indiana-Illinois line shocked farmers because of the widely accepted European agrarian belief that land that did not grow trees could not support farming. Back in the 1780s, settlers called the first large prairie in Kentucky "the Big Barrens."[11] In 1803 James Monroe complained that Jefferson had squandered federal funds when he acquired the treeless Louisiana Territory.

But westering pressure led farmers to edge into the open tallgrass country of Illinois and Iowa. They discovered, to their delight, that lack of trees alone did not make bad farmland. In addition, they could avoid the tiresome girdling, cutting, and pulling stumps required in clearing land. Morris Birkbeck, an English settler in Edwards County, Illinois, wrote in 1821, "The people to the east of us are incapable of imagining a dry and rich wholesome country, where they may enter at once on the fine lands prepared for civilization, without the enormous expense of time and labor in *clearing*."[12] Birkbeck would have been outraged by Francis Parkman's hostility toward the open country in his 1849 *The Oregon Trail*.

In time the cornucopia of food that farmers created on the midwestern prairie gave verisimilitude to the logic behind the ordinances of 1785 and 1796: America's wilderness, no matter how poor it looked at first, was universally fruitful when settled by hardworking yeomen. A farmer could profitably settle on virtually any platted section in any township across the entire survey grid. The tallgrass prairie land of Illinois and Iowa suggested that every corner of every survey tract might be filled with well-watered deep soil, more fruitful than eastern farmland. In turn, rumors spread that the midwestern prairies were poor imitations of what was to come on the high western plains. C. W. Short and F. Gerhard in 1857 reported to potential settlers that the abundant grasses and flowers of the high plains promised agricultural marvels when the soil was touched by the plow. The western region was not, after all, the Great American Desert; it was the Great American Garden.[13]

In an unbelievable stroke of luck, or deception, this new frontier expansion coincided with a decade of unprecedentedly heavy rains from the mid-1870s to the mid-1880s, obviously an act of divine intervention in support of Manifest Destiny. Rains prevailed year after year across vast grasslands where such long-term wetness was not known in memory.[14] The effects of the heavy rains upon native grasses reinforced a groundswell of enthusiasm that the climate had truly changed in favor of the farmer. Wetter eastern grasslands, for which corn and wheat could be substituted, spread westward to replace the shortgrass prairie, barely acceptable for grazing. This seemed proof positive of the happy change. Tallgrasses

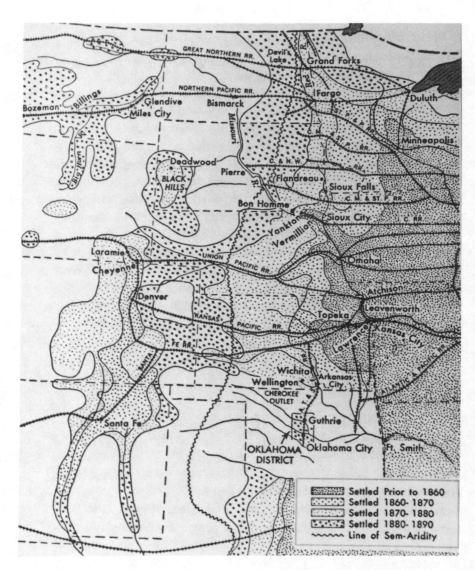

Fig. 16. Farmers' frontier, 1870–90. Successful settlement followed river valleys west of the line of semiaridity. After approximately 1880, settlers moved onto arid lands following a decade of unusually heavy rains and were often forced back when normal dry conditions returned. Reprinted with permission of Macmillan Publishing from *Westward Expansion*, by Ray Allen Billington and William L. Hedges. Copyright © 1974 by Macmillan Publishing Company.

(prairie cordgrass or slough grass, switch grass, wild rye, and particularly bluestem) were rapidly intruding westward upon medium grasses (western wheatgrass, june grass, side oats grama, three awns, needlegrasses and various dryland sedges), which in turn invaded historically arid shortgrass prairie (blue grama and buffalo grass).[15] Western grasslands became a veritable flower garden in the rain years of the later 1870s, enticing farmers where once they had encountered only a swardlike plant region. On this basis farmers, scientists, promoters, and government agents agreed that the old arid shortgrass prairie had been only a troublesome temporary interlude. America's true grassland was the flower garden of the tall and middle grasses, and now these spread westward as the advance guard for the westward-moving settler.

What agriculturalists did not realize was that they were seeing not a permanent change, but a long-term cycling of plant successions based on climate variations. They also wanted desperately to believe in a permanent shift of eastern grasses westward, since farming the tall and middle grasslands was already familiar and profitable. A massive immigration poured into the high plains, encouraged by government land policy, railroad interests, and land speculators, all based on the belief that successful midwestern farming would surely be repeated and then surpassed. The heavy rains continued until 1887, masking the true nature of the region.

When settlers moved west it seemed they changed the climate. Farmers were delighted to learn they could alter the forces of nature by plowing the land and planting trees. Already the midwestern prairie had been transformed into a garden; next the intractable desert would be conquered. As early as 1844 Josiah Gregg had concluded that "the extreme cultivation of the earth might contribute to the multiplication of showers."[16] Mormon settlers said that the level of the Great Salt Lake rose even as they irrigated and cultivated neighboring land. This belief was so pervasive, and so important to government expansionist policy, that when John Wesley Powell damned such views as unscientific and dangerous in his 1878 *Report on the Lands of the Arid Region of the United States*, officials inserted a corrective chapter, "Water Supply," by the respected scientist Grove Karl Gilbert.[17] Gilbert reported that "settlers . . . frequently told me that wherever and whenever a settlement was established, there followed in a few years an increase of the water supply." He quoted an 1869 study by a Professor Cyrus Thomas that had also been approved by the popular government explorer, surveyor, and scientist F. V. Hayden:

> Since the territory [Colorado] has begun to be settled, towns and cities built up, farms cultivated, mines opened, and roads made and travelled, there has been a gradual increase of moisture; . . . this increase is of a permanent nature, and not periodical, and that it has commenced within eight years past, and that it is in some way connected with the settlement of the country, and that as the population increases the moisture will increase.[18]

Gilbert attempted to validate the myth that a better climate followed human intervention in the arid West.[19] But in the next chapter, "Important Questions Relative to Irrigable Lands," Powell retorted,

> the operations of man on the surface of the earth are so trivial that the conditions which they produce are of minute effect, and in presence of the grand effects of nature escape discernment. Thus the alleged causes for the increase of rainfall fail; . . . if it be true that increase of the water supply is due to increase in precipitation . . . the fact is not cheering to the agriculturalist of the Arid Region. The permanent changes of nature are secular; any great sudden change is ephemeral, and usually such changes go in cycles, and the opposite or compensating conditions may reasonably be anticipated; . . . we shall have to expect a speedy return to extreme aridity, in which case a large portion of the agricultural industries of the country now growing up would be destroyed.[20]

Yet Powell agreed with Gilbert that human intervention, but through irrigation, was essential to western settlement and farming.

The human capacity to increase rainfall took hold as a supposed scientific fact. A Nebraska scientist, Samuel Aughey, wrote in 1880, "after the soil is broken, a rain as it falls is absorbed by the soil like a huge sponge."[21] Then the soil evaporates some moisture into the atmosphere each day, receiving it back at night as a heavy dew with more moisture than was evaporated. From this logic came the famous maxim "Rain follows the plow." Agriculture increased the absorbency of the soil by plowing, which in turn increased general humidity, ultimately bringing regular and reliable rains. It was also widely believed that the spread of the railroads encouraged rain, since the iron and steel rails modified the natural electrical cycles in an arid zone and induced more moisture in the air.[22]

F. V. Hayden lent scientific and government authority to the western grassland as America's new paradise. The best security to guarantee the new climate and prime farming conditions was planting trees in treeless zones.[23] Already in 1866 the General Land Office commissioner had said, "If one-third of the surface of the great plains were covered with forest there is every reason to believe the climate would be greatly improved, the value of the whole area as a grazing country wonderfully enhanced and the great portion of the soil would be susceptible of a high state of cultivation."[24] In 1873 Congress passed the Timber Culture Act, which offered land to settlers who would plant trees on their tracts. In the ebullient mood of the era, it seemed that climate could be changed by legislation. But trees did not grow well on the plains, and the act was repealed in the midst of the intense drought year of 1891.

The few remaining alarmists predicted not only an end to the rains, but also harm to the virgin soil. Their worries were swept away amid the boomer optimism. John Wesley Powell's 1878 government report opened with the forthright assertion, "the climate is so arid that agriculture is not successful." On the facing page he included an 1868 map of the United States shaded to show adequate eastern rainfall and low rainfall across the western half of the nation, aside from a thin dark Pacific Northwest shading.[25] Powell's argument was clear, direct, and precisely what potential settlers and land boosters did not want to hear. He complained that settlers were heedlessly rushing into harm's way as they crossed first into the "sub-humid region" that straddled the 98th meridian. Here it was possible to begin farming but impossible to succeed without a new and as yet unestablished water supply. This region, 10 percent of America's lower land area, had marginal rainfall ranging from 20 to 28 inches. To the west lay the enormous "arid region" making up 40 percent of the country. In some places irrigation could overcome the lack of rain. Unlike rainfall, Powell happily observed, irrigation was regular, reliable, and controllable in a region that otherwise posed too many uncertainties. But Powell raised eyebrows when he concluded that only 3 percent of the western arid lands were amenable to irrigation and settlement.[26] In addition, Powell argued that the day of the Jeffersonian yeoman farmer on the famous quarter section was long gone. The small-scale settler not only did not have enough land for survival, but could not cover the labor and capital requirements for irrigation projects. Future development would necessarily be cooperative and not individualistic, using public funds rather than private enterprise. The congressional bill attached to his report would have authorized irrigation districts overlaid on the remains of the survey system. Powell also worked hard to debunk the concept of dryland farming: irrigation was a better choice, since it would double productivity and promote settlement in otherwise hopeless regions. In its own way, Powell's report was a classic of western boosterism. But he argued the reverse of popular opinion: the arid lands were prone not to rainfall but to a persistent drought condition that made farming fruitless. In the meantime, the rains fell so heavily during the climate anomaly from 1876 to 1886 that settlers were being warned about mildew.

But by the 1890s arid times returned, with economic failures, mortgage foreclosures, and massive depopulation. As many as 200,000 settlers were displaced, second only to the 500,000 displaced in the 1930s. Landownership mattered little without water.[27] For the first time in American settlement history, the land and its improvements were abandoned. Wagonloads of farmers retreated eastward carrying a bitter slogan parodying the motto on government money more than divine providence: "In God we trusted, in Kansas we busted." The dryland plains came to represent human failure, not only in the 1890s but extending continuously into the 1930s. The blizzard of 1886–87 wiped out cattlemen. The extreme drought of 1887, which returned hot winds and dust storms, drove out the farmers. It was said that the main crop had become mortgage foreclosures. The widespread drought of 1894 was the worst, with only 8 inches of rain over much of the western grasslands.[28] The humid-region grasses retreated and the dryland shortgrasses moved eastward once again. The scale of the catastrophe was amplified by social and economic problems: the collapse of agricultural prices and the Panic of 1893, the most severe depression yet in American history. Drought and depression lasted to the end of the century. Western farmers lashed out with violence and unexpectedly radical politics.[29] They attacked those they believed had deceived them about western lands and then cheated them out of possible survival: eastern money interests, railroad developers, and federal policymakers, who appeared inept and deeply mistaken. The Populist party may have been America's most successful third-party movement.

Why Had Farmers Put Themselves in Harm's Way?

Settlers on arid western grasslands did not easily comprehend actual conditions. They worked from severely limited or mistaken views of agricultural needs. Their past experience in the East, no matter how rewarding, would mislead them. Not only would the rains mask the real situation, but farmers had limited information that did not take arid regions into account. They misled themselves about the minimum rainfall needed for good farming. Eventually major changes—beginning with dryland farming in the late nineteenth century and leading to massive government intervention and supports in the 1930s and to today's high technology, large capitalization, and mass market agribusiness—would allow profitable farming.

But the farmers were encouraged to settle on the arid grasslands because past experience made them overconfident, even cocky, about the capacity to master any landscape. This has been called the blind faith of a "boom psychology." They were too optimistic about the capacity of existing agricultural practices to cope with new situations. At issue were the pioneer farmers' perceptions of the real situation. What was normal? What was an anomaly? Pioneer farmers, when they moved into any new region, had a stake in a complex set of variables:

1. the soil and climate of the region
2. the capacity of agricultural technology to serve them
3. political, social, and economic backups
4. market conditions
5. human institutions
6. government land policies
7. available information

Success or failure depended on whether enough of these forces supported them and at what levels. Would a single aspect alone, such as soil conditions or water supplies or climate, deprive them of livelihood?

In addition, the settlers faced a higher-risk situation than established farmers or city dwellers back east. They were vulnerable to a multitude of threats, each one enough to drive them under: weather-sensitive crops, unpredictable weather, insect infestation, and vulnerability to outside economic factors such as prices. And as frontiersmen, they possessed a lower level of food, matériel, and cash reserves, less capacity to make conservative decisions when pressed by immediate needs, and a lower level of useful information.

On the other hand, frontier farmers on the American scene believed they had effective resources to survive risky conditions. These included an abundance of low-cost or free fertile land, benevolent government land policies that consistently granted friendly relief from burdensome laws or debts, a participatory political process, generous price and credit structures, rapid development of technological innovations, supportive family and community relations, and a "psychomilieu" that was freedom loving, independent, and entrepreneurial.

The arid-lands farmers believed they could cope with the risks involved in settling any new region and thought that the resources they carried along would allow them to exploit opportunities for a prosperous life. But as railroad boosters, Manifest Destiny, and providential rains drew them onto the plains, they failed to distinguish between signal and noise. That is, they did not separate useful information—the long history of a permanently arid region—from misleading and useless information—temporary heavy rains. To useless and misleading information can be added the settlers' own experience, national boosterism, and faith in single-family, self-sufficient subsistence farming. Nor was the "ripple effect" clear: Does a climate reversal affect ability to secure credit and mortgage money? It surely would affect their ability to pay debts. Commercial elements, such as railroads, could fade away during bad times or at best raise shipping rates to cover losses. Sometimes these *multipliers* would move the farm family toward internal conflict and possible breakup. All these elements suggest that society might not support farmers but actually hamper them under high-risk conditions such as climate change. Society not only can disperse risk conditions, it can also *amplify* them. When state agencies in the Dakotas and Nebraska provided welfare relief and the United States Army was ordered to make surplus supplies available to destitute farmers, the farmers' troubles were dispersed into society. But when farmers experienced low prices, commercial exploitation, and government indifference, their troubles fed back to them at increasingly burdensome levels.

New Laws for Arid Lands

In the arid West, as public-domain historian Roy Robbins wrote, "Here was pioneering at its worst—the difficulties involved in selecting land, building a home, finding fuel, drilling for water, fighting fierce winds, prairie fires, and grasshoppers were all but insurmountable. . . . the frontiersmen began the grinding process of harnessing nature . . . in its rawest form."[30] Government policy sought to keep the farmers on the unpromising land despite these extraordinary hardships and profound suffering. Farmers themselves believed it was un-American to desert their homesteads. It went against the creed of independence and self-sufficiency. Congress would spend decades tinkering with homestead laws to match western conditions and settlers' survival needs. By 1873 the Timber Culture Act had already encouraged settlers to move a more humid climate westward by planting trees. The Desert Land Act in 1877 promised an entire section of 640 acres for $800 if steps were taken to irrigate it within three years. The act applied to western states and territories ranging from the Dakotas in the north to New Mexico in the south, and west to the Pacific coast. But both the Timber Culture Act and the Desert Land Act were vaguely written to serve speculators more than farmers. President Rutherford Hayes thought so little of them that in his annual message in December 1877 he proposed extraordinarily different policies to suit western needs: "These lands [west of the 100th meridian] are practically unsaleable under existing laws, and the suggestion is worthy of consideration that a system of leasehold tenure would make them a source of profit to the United States, while at the same time legalizing the business of cattle raising which is at present carried upon them."[31]

After attempts at rainmaking had finally been set aside as a waste of time and money, irrigation was taken up as the solution.[32] In 1888 Congress tried to withdraw desert land from sale to keep settlers from mistakenly wandering out on it. But no program, not even the survey, had ever physically divided the bad land from the good. When congressmen debated about desert land, irrigable desert land, timber land, homesteading land, and countless other variations, the distinctions remained meaningless without a classification system. The land had not been sorted out by soil type, rainfall, potential use, terrain, or geographical location.[33] Failing at classification, Congress in 1890 reduced settlers' financial risk on irrigable desert land from 640 to 320 acres. Only 80 acres had to be irrigated, according to a provision in the 1891 General Land Revision Act.

The Desert Land Act failed, but it was not repealed until 1976. The Carey Act of 1894 provided relief for private irrigation companies in six arid states. But Lawrence B. Lee notes that almost sixty-five years later, in 1958, the Carey Act had been applied to only slightly more than a million acres whereas it had been intended for immediate application to 6 million acres.[34] The difficulty was not in government largess, but in the scale of irrigation needs. The experience taught that successful irrigation projects were probably beyond the technical, capital, and management resources of most individuals, private enterprise, or state agencies. It was also widely assumed that the federal government, holding most of the West as public domain, had the primary obligation, the legal right, the scientific management, and the financial capacity to establish irrigation opportunities. Nevertheless, the Carey Act has never been taken off the books.[35]

If settlement on more workable terms was the government's goal, then the Kinkaid Homestead Act of 1904 looked promising. It offered title to 640 acres of unsettled drylands in western Nebraska to anyone who would take up a farm for five years and institute $800 worth of improvements, equivalent to the minimum price.[36] A minor land rush quickly consumed the designated land, and pressure grew to expand the offering across other western states and territories. The Enlarged Homestead Act of 1909 used the same conditions, but reduced tracts to 320 acres.[37] Considering western Nebraska conditions and similarly difficult farmland elsewhere, it is not clear whether the Kinkaid Act and Enlarged Homestead Act were motivated by generosity or whether Congress dared settlers to try to survive. Local cattleman-historian John Clay sympathized with new Kinkaid Act settlers: "Those Sandhills are totally unfitted for agriculture." The act was "another instance of stupidity in land matters."[38] In 1912, when the interior secretary reported to Congress that the 1862 Homestead Act was irrelevant when it was not dangerous, Idaho senator William E. Borah charged that "the government bets 160 acres against the entry fee of $14 that the settler can't live on the land for five years without starving to death." In a calmer tone, the House Committee on Public Lands revived Jeffersonian rhetoric to remind Congress of its duty to the long-suffering independent farmer: "To reclaim and subdue our remaining public lands requires an expenditure of labor and money far beyond what is generally supposed; it requires determination, courage and energy of a high order, and continuity of purpose which are characteristics and virtues alone of good citizens."[39] In a rush of conscience, Congress reduced settlement restrictions from five years to three and added sievelike qualifications.

In the new century farmers continued to move onto marginal and submarginal lands, often in hope of recouping their losses by planting more acreage. The "great plowup" of 50 million acres in 1919–20 only made conditions worse. Some farmers laid great store by the promise of irrigated land when the 1902 Reclamation Act was passed by Congress. Others who acknowledged the real conditions of the Great Plains turned to the new "dry- farming" techniques to hold moisture in the soil. Additional motivation came with new strains of hard wheat from Russia and Turkey and the hope of new efficiency from machinery such as tractors. Nevertheless failures continued, and the region remained a frontier area. A turn for the better came from about 1900 until 1920, with higher prices and a spell of ample rain.

Lack of Water Revises American Frontier History

Land just west of the 98th meridian could be level and accessible, the soil the richest chernozem, yet without water it was a wasteland. Even today farming consumes 90 percent of the water available to the Great Plains. Agriculture is limited by its minimum needs; corn cannot grow on wheat's water consumption. The history of the public domain in the West is the history not of land but of the water that it needs and that sometimes is attached to the land. The result should be a new and very different history. Wealth for the speculator, survival for the independent farmer, food for the nation, and success for government policy depended directly upon local water supplies. These were rarely from rainfall, since arid America measures out at well under 20 inches a year (30 inches a year is needed for traditional eastern farming).

In this new landscape, the paths of survival did not follow east-west or north-south section lines but depended upon watercourses that snaked across townships and state lines. Plat lines often did little for settlers but mark out the terrible fact that they had no access to water. The Republican River basin crossed state and county lines, covering 25 percent of the states of Kansas and Nebraska.[40] Plat boundary lines became irrelevant. Rational maps began to follow river and stream valleys, to identify water holes and seepages, and to locate floodplains and sources of seasonal surface water. The major legal agreements controlling western farm growth in the twentieth century ignore the old gridiron landscape to enclose river valleys and watersheds. The historic 1922 Colorado River water compact may soon be paralleled by a Missouri basin compact. Oklahoma's 1980 Comprehensive Water Plan includes four interstate stream compacts covering the basins of the Red River, Arkansas River, and Canadian River.[41] With new pumping technologies and cheap energy, aquifer maps now are the most important agricultural maps in the West. Most often, western water comes from underground sources, the largest being the remarkable and vast Ogallala aquifer, which underlies 174,000 square miles of the central Great Plains from Nebraska to Texas.[42] But the Ogallala remained largely undiscovered and untapped until the 1930s.

Early on, new questions emerged for farmers, speculators, and congressmen to answer. In all the debates one unyielding rule prevailed: land alone had no value; the water attached to the land was the single most important source of its value. But who owned the water, and how was it attached to the survey units? Water, unlike land, flowed from one piece of property to another.[43] Could needy farmers divert the local river's water from its usual streambed into their irrigation ditches and holding ponds? Did water remain public domain after the quarter sections it flowed through were sold? Was water to be distributed according to landownership or agricultural need? Was water valued according to the marketplace or social need? Who sets water values? If ordinarily there was not enough water to distribute freely to all landowners, how was scarce water to be shared? These and other survival questions created new layers of laws and policies upon western farmers, adding to the patchwork of recent land adjustments.[44]

Water Rights

Property rights harking back to English common law long before John Locke were thrown out as useless for western water needs.

Riparian rights had for hundreds of years, back to the thirteenth century, dedicated water use solely to the owners of property bordering the stream or pond. This water was jealously guarded as private property, shared equally with the other riparian (based on a Latin word meaning the bank of a stream) owners. No one could divert the stream; it must be allowed to flow in its natural course.

But riparian rights were developed where rainfall was abundant. No thought had to be given to arid regions. Much land described by Powell and others as "irrigable desert land" did not physically touch a stream or pond but stood at a distance. Water had to be channeled to it. Riparian rights alone would exclude use of most of America's western lands. In addition, the equal division of riparian water, says water policy analyst Robert G. Dunbar, is a "variable right, expanding and contracting with the number of users and with the varying flow of the stream." But water flow according to the 1922 Colorado River Compact was unfortunately set at the river's highest historical flow, and is rarely if ever matched. Claims on Colorado River water far exceed normal flow, particularly claims by California and Arizona.

Beginning with heavy water needs for gold mining in California in the 1850s, westerners moved rapidly away from riparian rights to new *prior appropriation* claims based on the controversial maxim "first in time, first in right." According to Dunbar, "He who diverted water first had the prior right to it to the extent of his diversion for use on both riparian and nonriparian lands."[45] As with Lockean property rights that eastern settlers and squatters claimed because they "improved" the land, water could be diverted only if applied to beneficial use and not wasted. To this was added a proviso that was new to American land laws: when the use ceased, the right ceased. Prior rights based on "beneficial use," "reasonable use," and "greatest need" are specified today, for example, in Oklahoma's 1972 Ground Water Law. In 1980 Oklahoma's comprehensive review argued that "it required little imagination to recognize that the Legislature intended to include irrigation for the purpose of growing food and fiber as a beneficial agricultural use."[46]

"Prior appropriation" was so essential to western survival on the land that it was written into the 1876 Colorado state consititution.[47] Although the conflict first arose in California, the new legal system is known as the "Colorado doctrine." Prior appropriation, not surprisingly, dominates the western states. No one "owned" the water as a farmer or speculator or railroad or the government owned the land. Dunbar describes this departure from common law as based on "the argument of necessity."[48] This "necessity," when yoked to earlier western claims for "flexibility" regarding government restrictions (read autonomy), stands as a powerful western counterforce against nonwestern interests.

Making the Most of Scarce Water

In his 1878 report on the arid lands, John Wesley Powell argued that government policy toward the West must have one consuming objective: to distribute what little water the area had to the largest number of farmers by means of irrigation. Farmers deserved special treatment for their service to the nation. Irrigation deserved priority because it offered controlled management to provide a relatively constant flow of water where needed. It had become obvious that laws set for eastern conditions would not work. General Land Office commissioner J. A. Williamson acknowledged that "some change is necessary in the survey and disposal of the lands." Powell admitted, the "extent of irrigable land is dependent upon the volume of water carried by the streams."[49] But he optimistically claimed that "the redemption of the arid region" was ultimately an "engineering problem," which when solved would yield "bountiful crops."[50]

Powell also concluded that successful farming required tracts of land based on topography, "a system less arbitrary than that of the rectangular surveys now in vogue." The survey, harking back to a different era and a different geography in 1785, was unacceptable for western agriculture. "It is best to permit the people to divide their lands for themselves."[51] Individual tracts must be considerably larger, extending four sections (2,560 acres or 4 square miles) or better. No title would be given until settlers showed good faith by significant progress in irrigating their land. Irrigation, Powell admitted, is expensive. Wealthy landholders would invest their own capital. Poorer settlers would join together in collective irrigation districts to pool expenses and lower per-capita costs. In defense of his controversial cooperative districts, Powell drew on district or "colony" experiences in timber and pasture lands and on the much-watched community irrigation settlement at Greeley, Colorado.[52]

The issues sharpened in the drought years of the late 1880s when farmers were forced into full retreat from the zone between the 97th and 100th meridians. National irrigation congresses in the 1890s, as well as government and independent scientists, dedicated themselves to identifying the geographical line beyond which settlement was dangerous without irrigation.[53] Powell insisted in the *Century Magazine* in 1889 that as one crosses the transitional zone, "species after species of luxuriant grass and brilliant flowering plants disappear; the ground gradually becomes naked, with 'bunch' grasses here and there."[54] Powell and others warned that the region was deceptive. With rare good rains marvelous harvests were possible, but drought was normal. Crops would fail, and farms would inevitably be abandoned. Frederick H. Newell, soon to be a dominant figure in government irrigation programs, described western Kansas as a region of "periodic famine" because settlers were dreamily lured onto fertile land; but drought invaded their lives "almost imperceptibly," and too late "the settlers depart with such of their household furniture as can be drawn away by the enfeebled draft animals, the herds disappear, and this beautiful land, once so fruitful, is now dry and brown, given over to the prairie wolf."[55] William E. Smythe, an enthusiastic irrigationist, agreed. Western Kansas was a "starvation belt for non-irrigators." Even experienced dryland farmers were warned that their crops would fail in the terrible region beyond the 100th meridian.

CHAPTER 8

Water

The landowner "owns" that elusive and unstable substance, percolating water, beneath his land.

> Oklahoma Supreme Court, *Canada v. Shawnee*, 179 Okl. 53,
> 64 P.2d 694 [1936, 1937]

Water flows uphill to money.

> Old irrigationist maxim

If water flows uphill to money, it gushes uphill to politics.

> Corollary added by the governor of Wisconsin

If water flows uphill to money, and gushes uphill to politics, then the combination of money and politics in the Reclamation Act of 1902 is the nation's ultimate artesian well.

> Water historian's corollary

By the 1890s, Progressive reformers made irrigation the means to save American farmers and carry them into the twentieth century. But John Wesley Powell, the nation's foremost irrigation authority, quickly tried to cool the enthusiasm: "There is not enough water to irrigate all these lands: there is not sufficient water to irrigate all the lands which could be irrigated, and only a small portion can be irrigated." He told a national irrigation congress, "you are piling up a heritage of conflict . . . for there is not sufficient water to supply the land!"[1] Within a few years a good case could be made that the primary product of the 1902 Land Reclamation Act was not water but litigation.

Powell's mantle soon fell to William E. Smythe, never a government employee, but a newspaperman, editor, promoter, and successful lobbyist. Smythe founded the National Irrigation Congress in 1891, established the journal *Irrigation Age* in 1895, and in 1899

Fig. 17. The Ogallala aquifer (shaded area) is underground water in gravel beds replenished millennia ago from the Rocky Mountains but now cut off. As the primary source of water for Great Plains farming, it is being consumed rapidly, particularly in the southern panhandle country. Reprinted from *Geohydrology of the High Plains Aquifer*, United States Geological Survey Professional Paper 1400 B, by Edwin D. Gutentag, et al. (Washington: U.S. Government Printing Office, 1984).

wrote the bible of the movement, *The Conquest of Arid America*.[2] Smythe reaffirmed Powell's maxim that irrigation was the single solution to successful western farming. He also insisted that the federal government had the moral duty to restructure the West into an irrigated territory easily accessible to the small independent American farmer.[3] Historical land use patterns based on the eastern experience were considered irrelevant.

The Irrigation Crusade

Americans expected irrigation to save the nation's struggling small farmers. It would create "Forty Million Forty-Acre Farms." Smythe, following the lead of Powell, looked upon the farmer who worked irrigated land as a superior food producer compared with the dryland farmer of the high plains. In contrast to compact irrigated fields, eastern farmers tilled large fields "promiscuously and carelessly." Bonanza farmers along the Red River of the North were condemned for "skimming the fertility" from hundreds of square miles. In contrast, the irrigating farmer "farms a few acres and farms them well." Irrigation efficiency would bring forth a new representative American superior to Jefferson's yeoman farmer. Smythe held the prosperous midwestern prairie farmer in contempt. Farms in Illinois and Iowa were large "in order to reduce the chances of complete failure." In contrast, Smythe agreed with Powell that obtaining water through irrigation overcame the age-old uncertainty about rainfall: per-acre production would be "from two to four times as large . . . as where the dependence is on rainfall." Smythe and other irrigationists soon concluded that the 40-acre farm was probably excessive.[4] Newell wondered whether using even 20 or 10 acres was wasteful, when full attention could be devoted "to the few acres almost within a stone's throw of his [the farmer's] door." Newell acknowledged that "the idea that any man on the boundless plains would concentrate his energies on 10 acres has seemed ridiculous. Yet this . . . is making him unlearn his old habits and methods."[5] The 1895 Irrigation Congress was told that in western Kansas, where dryland farmers continued to fail, a prosperous irrigation farm "has been found . . . [on] as low as three and a half acres, although the people are new to the business." Before the 1910 Congress Smythe optimistically claimed that a hardworking family could generate $490.95 a year from one acre of land, equal to an average workingman's income. Irrigation was turning into a panacea.

Irrigated land for small-scale farming would bring better living conditions beyond the capacity of eastern or prairie farm life. A hundred homes, forming a desirable close-knit community, could exist where one or two stock ranches had covered the land. Or in a slightly more cautious view, sixteen families could prosper on a single survey section previously workable by only two or four farm families. Smythe insisted that land "hitherto fit only for cattle" would with irrigation lead "the [westward] march of civilization."[6] In a claim somewhat closer to the truth, the 1895 Irrigation Congress was told that the irrigated West would carry "a population at least as large as the present total number of inhabitants of the United States." The 1902 Congress was told that many of the forces, including loneliness, isolation, uncertainty, and poverty, that were driving Americans off the farm would be overcome. On small irrigated tracts culture would be lively, with people living "within a few rods of one another" instead of a mile or more apart. The image was utopian. In this new western culture, Americans would not continue their rush to the dirty industrial cities but would remain linked to the soil. In addition, the essential American tradition of property ownership would be protected. Proponents of the "back to nature" movement of the late nineteenth century were also pleased with the health of mind and body that rural life encouraged. Another future irrigation leader, Elwood Mead, concluded that "the agricultural society of the future in the Western valleys will realize a happy combination of town and country life—the independence which springs from the proprietorship of the soil and the satisfaction of the social instinct which comes only with community association."[7] Smythe concluded, "We shall work out here in western America the highest forms of civilization that have been seen beneath the sun."[8] But the drought passed, dryland farming recovered, and in 1909 western Kansas had less than 2,000 acres under irrigation.

Federal Intervention: The 1902 Reclamation Act

Nevertheless, no land act would dominate the western half of the United States as did the Reclamation Act of 1902. It was in large part a rescue operation for settlers already in the West, meant to salvage private irrigation operations. Pressure for federal rescue also built up because severe western drought in the 1890s came on top of the nation's worse depression yet. With lobbying on a national scale orchestrated by William E. Smythe, and with the support of President Theodore Roosevelt, Congressman Francis G. Newlands of Nevada pushed through the Reclamation Act of 17 June 1902, or Newlands Act, the most important congressional land act in the 117 years since the ordinance of 1785 had first established the public land survey of townships and sections and their transfer into private hands.

Implementation of reclamation went wrong right away. The act was intended to pay its own way and also provide low-cost water. But it was based on estimates that a typical irrigation project could be funded for $5 to $15 an acre per farmer. The first actual project estimates averaged $30.57 per acre. Costs immediately soared as high as $160 an acre and averaged nearly $85 an acre.[9] Heavily subsidized rates were not part of 1902 policy. Federal land sales in the West were to create front-end funds for irrigation construction. User charges were intended to be sufficient to recover all further costs. Government guaranteed water to settlers, but it was not cheap, and they soon defaulted on their agreements. Within twenty years, by 1923, $143 million had been invested and only $16 million recovered. Federal funds were being unexpectedly channeled into irrigation programs on an unprecedented scale.[10] Later the soil bank of the 1950s, the Payment in Kind (PIK) program in the early 1980s, and subsidies under the 1985 farm bill would experience similar unexpectedly soaring costs. Since 1928, hydroelectric projects attached to reclamation projects generated funds independent of farming-related income, but these cannot justifiably be included as part of the cost-subsidy issues. A 1978 analysis of actual reclamation costs, discovered that only 3.3 percent of the total $3.62 billion spent by the Bureau of Reclamation has been recovered from farmers.[11] Some irrigators are not even covering operating and maintenance costs, much less construction costs. In the mid-1970s, beneficiaries of federal water agreements in Kern County, California, paid $3.50 an acre-foot, while neighbors receiving water from the state authority, the California Department of Water Resources, paid $22.42. Taking into account forty- or fifty-year contracts, exemption from interest, rising water costs elsewhere, rising food prices, and inflation in general, irrigators with government water contracts will see their real costs actually decline over the next decade until their contracts are up. In contrast, state water costs in Kern County are expected to rise to about $70 an acre by the mid-1980s.[12] By 1980 government money covered between 57 and 97 percent of irrigation costs over the lifetime of a project, averaging $500 per acre per year and rising as high as $1,787.[13] Federal subsidies for the classic 160-acre farm are typically $80,000 a year, and in very dry regions as high as $286,000. The 1982 revisions of the 1902 Reclamation Act enlarged individual farm size of 960 acres, allowing a $1,715,510 annual water bonanza, and the 640-acre maximum corporate tract, allowing $480,000 annually. New York senator Daniel P. Moynihan complained that the 1982 revision represented "all that is wrong with federal involvement in water resources: chaos, arbitrariness, inequity, and waste."[14]

Did Irrigation Save the Western Farmer?

The mandate of the Reclamation Act was to help the independent farm family succeed on western arid lands. A tract of 160 irrigated acres was to be a generous base for western settlement, carry the family farm into the twentieth century, and prevent excess profits from land and water manipulation and monopoly. Smythe called it "homemaking." Theodore Roosevelt argued eloquently for "homes on the land" and "communities of freeholders," while Reclamation director Frederick Newell insisted that small farms were "fundamental to the growth and maintenance of a democratic form of government." Higher costs and poorer farmers induced another rescue with the 1914 Reclamation Extension Act. It doubled the repayment period from the original ten years to twenty, still without interest, and established a five-year grace period. Farmers still failed to meet payments while costs soared. The 1924 Fact Finding Committee report encouraged very benevolent legislation in 1926 and wrote off costs on twenty-one projects ($17.3 million, 13 percent of the total) and doubled repayment to forty years, still with no interest.

The troubles did not abate during the Great Depression. Both Franklin Roosevelt and his interior secretary Harold Ickes publicly promoted reclamation to support the small farmer. Their efforts were both reviled and praised as social planning and land redistribution.[15] The Reclamation Project Act of 1939 generously let irrigators pay only the debt they could repay (an interesting circular argument) based on farm budgets, including a ten-year grace period before an extended repayment period of fifty years, with no interest, fixed rates,

and no adjustment for inflation. These conditions, extremely beneficial for participating farmers, are still the basis for irrigation agreements running until 1996.[16] Laws and policies changed little since
the New Deal Fair Deal era until the 1982 adjustments by the Reagan
administration. For some time it had been clear that reclamation was
an ineffective force for land reform, if reform meant saving the small
farmer and keeping speculation and corporate farming in check.

The Water Picture Gets Muddied

But the Reclamation Bureau never consistently enforced the land
limitation of 160 acres.[17] Variances included the allowance of 320
acres for husband and wife. More important exemptions spread to
large federally irrigated projects, including the Colorado–Big Thompson project in 1937 and that in California's Imperial Valley in 1938.[18]
By the 1980s, the long-revered tradition of the classic 160-acre quar-
ter-section family farm finally surrendered to reality. In 1980, for
example, the Oklahoma Comprehensive Water Plan report argued
directly against the 160-acre limitation. It would "hinder water planning efforts in Oklahoma, as well as all western states."

> Essentially, this rule excludes today's average or large farm owner
> from participating in an irrigation project constructed by the Bureau
> of Reclamation. When the law was passed in 1902, farming practices
> relied exclusively on human and animal power using crude farm
> implements. The years since have brought revolutions in the farming
> industry, which require costly and complicated machines for the
> planting, cultivation and harvesting of agricultural products which
> cannot be justified by the returns on a small farm.[19]

The report noted that the average Oklahoma farm size in 1977
was 428 acres and growing, more than three times the average farm
in 1900. "Studies of farm economics set the optimum farm size in
most areas at 640 acres or more" (ironically, the original *minimum*
tract size in 1785). In Oklahoma, and across much of the arid West,
the small farmer sat on a large acreage, a fact to which federal law
seemed incapable of adjusting. "Considering the necessity of heavy
capital investment by the farmer and the emphasis on increased
food production for a starving world," Oklahoma's report argued for
"realistic modification" of the 160-acre limit. Small tracts were not
cost effective. The Reclamation Reform Act of 1982 raised maximum
tract size to 1,280 acres.

Even today irrigation agriculture accounts for almost 90 percent of water use in the West. Growth accelerated during and after World War II: irrigated acreage tripled between 1940 and 1977, covering one-quarter of the West's entire cropland today and one-half of crop value America's impressive agricultural productivity, using the least farmland and the smallest work force globally, was at midcentury the world's greatest agricultural success story.[20] Western irrigation literally did make the desert bloom, created a cornucopia of food for the nation and the world, and encouraged extensive westward population movement. Irrigation success also demonstrated the workability of the combined forces of technology and the democratic process. In 1985 the Bureau of Reclamation delivered 24 million acre-feet of water, irrigating 9 million acres that grow 55 million tons of farm products. Since 1902 the agency has spent almost $13 billion, building 700 dams, 16,000 miles of aqueducts, 35,000 miles of irrigation ditches, 275 miles of water tunnels, and 241 pumping stations.[21]

Water as a Scarce National Resource: Two Myths

Irrigation policy deliberately fostered water as a cheap resource base for private independent farming. In the past and today, the argument has been three-sided: Should water resources be used for maximum profits (the "American way"), maximum yield (global food needs), or minimum risk (to save the small farmer)? The maximum-profits course dominated private irrigation a hundred years ago. Its failure led to the 1902 act, where at first the primary objective was maximum yield. Very quickly, however, minimum risk dominated the reclamation scene: low-cost water in large volume would save the small farmer, develop the West, and guarantee cheap and abundant food to the nation. It appears that the Reagan administration is making another attempt at the maximum-profits direction, partly for ideological reasons and partly in the belief that it will work best.

It is time to dispel some traditional myths that are distorting current perceptions. One of these myths is that for decades, until recently, irrigation programs provided abundant cheap water in the West and that now this is disappearing. But the clear picture is emphatically different: *water was never, ever, cheap or abundant in the West. What was cheap and abundant in the West was federal money.* Water costs have simply been hidden elsewhere and shifted to a more difficult future as large infusions of federal money distorted real water costs. This is a troublesome three-tiered process, by which apparently abundant money produced apparently abundant water, guaranteeing abundant cheap food. As the three tiers have come apart, the potential for large-scale national and international economic and social distress has become very large.

A second myth disproved by experience is that privatization—letting water costs and allocations be controlled by free market prices, with private enterprise collecting the profits and footing the bills—is the answer to future water shortfalls. The usual term is deregulation, but the issue is a larger one comparable to the place private property has had in the history of the public lands. Had there been a free market for land sales over the past two hundred years, "bit land" ($12^1/2$¢ an acre) would have existed from the first, but prime farmland would have risen quickly into the thousands of dollars. In the case of early western irrigation, water prices would have quickly scaled so high that western growth, both agricultural and urban, might have been marginal compared with today's spectacular results.

One of the primary reasons for federal intervention over the past hundred years was the early failure of private enterprise to cope effectively on a large scale with the capital costs, research and surveys, technical development, and management of irrigation projects in the West. Federalization was from the first a bailout demanded by western entrepreneurs.[22] Most irrigation projects in arid lands have been high-risk ventures on a scale unacceptable to private enterprise. One longtime historian of reclamation observed in 1977, "The West has long benefited from a special relationship with Congress and the Federal bureaucracy, while proclaiming everlasting fealty to the gospel of 'states rights.' "[23] Government rescue of private interests in the West goes back to the Desert Land Act of 1877, which gave large rewards (subsidies) for minimal irrigation, as well as the Carey Act of 1894, which turned public domain land over to the states on condition that they sell the land at lowest cost to private irrigation companies, for their disposal at highest market prices. Despite these benefits, both acts failed to bring water to the West and hence delayed successful settlement by either the small farmer or the large producer.[24] These failures directly induced passage of the federal Reclamation Act of 1902. Today the "Sagebrush Rebellion" very often disappears behind stacks of reclamation pork barrels.

In light of the past use of water, privatization today would be not a conservative move but a radical step, creating new layers of complication without removing the old. Its effect would be to create enormous new bureaucracies, more levels of decision making, and more costs and delays.

Most drastic of the privatization arguments is the demand to detach underground water entirely from its surroundings and sell it on the open market to the highest bidder. Free sale would be a radical step away from the past. According to a 1936–37 Oklahoma Supreme Court decision, for example, water use must be controlled by "beneficial use" and "greatest need" for local "agricultural stability," set by "safe annual yield." And direct sale was expressly forbidden: "The owner of land may . . . not forcibly extract and exhaust the entire water supply of the community, causing irreparable injury to his neighbors and their lands, for the purpose of transporting and selling said water at a distance from and off the premises."[25]

However, advocates of market sales argued that the rapid urban growth of the West, and the disappearance of farmland in metropolitan regions, has sometimes left irrigation districts with "surplus water," since urban or industrial water use is almost invariably lower than that use in water-intensive farming. In August 1984 the San Diego (California) County Water Authority paid $10,000 for an option to buy Yampa (Colorado) River water from a local water conservation district. If the option was accepted, the intricate complex of laws, compacts, court rulings, and international treaties controlling water use on the Colorado River (and tributaries like the Yampa) could be compromised and collapse. Federal irrigation prices ranging from $3 to $20 an acre-foot would quickly jump to a local-use wholesale range of $100 to $200 and, some fear, rise quickly to $500 per acre-foot: "Water will start reflecting its true price."[26] Farm economists estimate that farmers who depend upon current farm price structures could absorb a maximum of $70 an acre-foot; anything more would create major dislocations in the national and international food supply. A recent plan offered by the Environmental Defense Fund argued that cash generated by surplus water could create an internal subsidy for western water districts. The plan lays primary blame for water extravagance upon farmers, as they depend on prior appropriation and the "use it or lose it" policy. A *New York Times* editorial in June 1985 supported the Environmental Defense Fund plan: "The fund wants the irrigation districts, the local government agencies that distribute water, to invest in conservation and then profit from the investment by selling the surplus. For example, an authority might line canals with concrete to reduce seepage and then auction the water saved to a distant city."[27]

The editorial claims that the Imperial Irrigation District could recover enough water to support about 2 million people, but little is said about the impact upon farming, which will persist as the nation's extreme water-intensive industry. Sale of water to the highest bidder, even where it is limited to "surplus water," can quickly shift priorities from farming and force radical production and price changes. In the developed West, if current goals are to be met, more than 90 percent of the region's water must still be directed to low-price agricultural use.

The privatization scenario goes something like this: Water in arid lands was once the *liberating* force because its low cost supported western development. Today, according to this argument, water is the *constraining* input because its price is fixed far below alternate use value. According to the best-case scenario, only surplus water would be deregulated and sold on the open market. Its price would rise dramatically through reallocation away from "misplaced" cheaper use, just as farmland sought for a shopping center has "misplaced" value if kept in farming. This argument is based on the belief that water use is very responsive to price and that little harm would be done to public interest because farmers in general are less rigid and far more elastic in their consumption than is usually acknowledged.[28]

The large-scale agricultural elasticity required for privatization is yet to be demonstrated, although water demands can be slightly reduced by various techniques, including irrigation scheduling, non-porous ditches, expensive drip irrigation, air injection, strains of wheat, soybeans, and corn needing less water, a shift to drought-resistant crops, stubble-mulch tillage and no-till planting, better weed control, and tailwater recovery. Efficiency can rise dramatically under ideal conditions, from the miserable 45 percent when drawing surface water to perhaps 75 percent with scheduled sprinkling from groundwater. Drip irrigation directly to the roots of plants claims 95 percent efficiency, but extremely high equipment costs skew the figures. Ideal conditions are unrealistic expectations and not the rule.

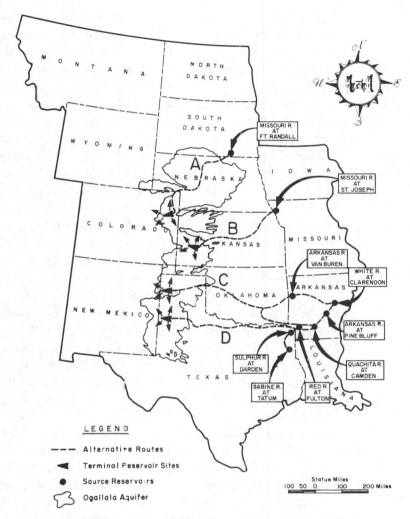

Fig. 18. At the height of the drought in the early 1980s, the U.S. Department of Commerce commissioned the United States Army Corps of Engineers to explore the transfer of outside water sources to the high-risk Great Plains. However, all plans were shelved because of high construction and energy costs as well as environmental constraints and regional opposition. Map from *Six-State High Plains Ogallala Aquifer Regional Resources Study: Summary* (Washington D.C.: U.S. Department of Commerce/High Plains Associates, 1982).

Two radical adjustments have been largely rejected. Even the Army Corps of Engineers, hardly a critic of major water projects, calculates that the cost of water imported by major multibillion- dollar transregional water projects (R. W. Beck plan, North American Water and Power Alliance [NAWAPA] project, L. G. Smith plan, among others) would be an unacceptable $320 to $880 per acre-foot.[29] Most agricultural economists and local farmers look upon any return to dryland farming as a prelude to failure. Dryland farming produces only one-third as much wheat or sorghum per acre. Oklahoma officials, for example, note that "irrigation farmers in western Oklahoma would be forced to revert to dryland farming as depleting ground water supplies become too costly to use. As a result, per-acre crop yields would decline, requiring an increase in the number of acres planted to maintain current production levels. Increased costs would reduce profit margins, placing many farmers in a tenuous financial position."[30]

Advocates of privatization note that misallocation takes place when the California Department of Water Resources measures water use in terms of maximum crop yield rather than level of profit. The issue centers on how priorities and valuation are established and misplaced. A classic example used to justify privatization is the Tehachapi basin in southern California.[31] Critics, of course, ask whether there is a point of no return, notably to maintain high yields for human and strategic reasons. Can water use depend upon pricing alone? Farmers who are customers of California's Central Valley reclamation project, which has kept abundant farming going since the mid-1930s when local wells went dry, are today faced with 500 percent water-cost increases before the end of the decade. A local water district manager noted that "the primary project purpose will be undercut if water rates are pushed so high that they drive irrigators out of business."[32] Farmers admit that $5.50 an acre-foot was "relatively inexpensive water" and that they can tolerate new $17 rates, but they say they would have to close down at the $55 predicted for 1994.

A Water Ethic: Its "Duty?"

Water is not measured and valued by price alone. There is a long history of the nonmarket function, or "duty," of water. The debate persists, as it has for the past hundred years, over "beneficial," "usufructuary," and "preferential" uses that exist outside cash markets. This was the issue in a 1954 Supreme Court case *(Farmers Highline Canal and Reservoir Co. v. City of Golden, Colo.)* when Golden, Colorado, lost its attempt to shift water from low-priced farm use to high-priced urban consumption. Nevertheless, as recently as 1980 a report of the Office of Water Research and Technology in the United States Department of the Interior downplayed these historic non-market factors that had heretofore dominated western irrigation.[33] Constraints outside the market are sometimes called externalities. A leading externality today is the food-producing farmer, the perennial low-cost user. Farmers have little flexibility, or "headroom," to absorb higher water prices. For example, a peak agricultural use price of approximately $70 an acre-foot (1977 dollars) is often mentioned (the Corps of Engineers claims $120), while acceptable urban costs can apparently go as high as $2,500 per acre-foot. A more distant externality is the limit set by food prices acceptable to the consumer: Would the public pay $7 (1982 dollars) for a loaf of bread to allow the farmer to buy irrigation water at competitive water prices? Cheap water has always been the buffer absorbing costs to keep food prices low. When this historic water duty is ignored, independent farmers become the scapegoat for their near-free water drawn from costly public reclamation projects. The Garrison Diversion Water Project in North Dakota was scaled back in 1985 from $1 billion to less than $480 million because it was considered excessive to deliver water to four hundred farms at a cost of more than $4 million an acre.[34] Complaints centered on the project's plan to irrigate new wheatland when large grain surpluses were forecast indefinitely. "Water wars" almost broke out in the 1950s during the "Little Dust Bowl." But the lessons learned during the 1930s Dust Bowl, together with reliable groundwater supplies made available by efficient technology and low energy costs, protected the plains farmer from severe hardship even if drought were to persist for a long time. Yet in the remaining decades of the twentieth century, stress levels may appear that could equal or surpass those experienced in the 1930s.

In the future, as competition for western water becomes severe, can this historic duty to keep the farmer competitive be replaced by higher food prices, more efficient (and costly) technologies, better water management (scheduling), and even a shift to alternative buffers? A strong argument can be made that externalities dominate the water-cost picture, since farmers have rarely borne the full cost of the resource they are consuming. Nor is a total shift away from this ethical duty of water likely in the foreseeable future.[35] But there is a move in the 1980s to shift priorities by offering water, which government policy developed to aid the family farmer, to whoever can afford it at market price, farmer or nonfarmer.

Important cases to watch are the revival of South Dakota's attempt to sell water for coal slurry and Arizona's reallocation from cheap agricultural irrigation to more profitable urban and industrial development. Arizona's 1980 Groundwater Management Act mandates reducing irrigated farmland from 1.3 million acres to 800,000 acres. It allows the state to buy and retire farmland that does not become irrigation efficient, regardless of the impact upon farmers or food supplies. One major citrus grower observed, "After we're all gone, where are you going to get your citrus?"[36] Governor Bruce Babbitt admitted the shift in priorities for Arizona's major canal carrying water from the Colorado River south into parched regions: "What was originally conceived as a classic reclamation project to open up new [agricultural] lands has evolved into an urban water system." Water engineer Francis Welsh attacked the lavish dollar cost and water waste: "It's an absurd project conceived at the turn of the century and designed in the 40's, and Arizona has changed since then. Its purpose was to develop the West, and God knows the West is developed."[37] Wyoming water laws in the 1970s detached water from land and permitted its transfer to alternative uses. In 1978 a New Mexico law allowed appropriators to shift water away from agricultural priorities, but a Mesilla Valley pecan farmer complained bitterly about collapsing land values: "If you don't have water, who wants the land?" Urban water prices, which farmers cannot meet, have also sparked an acrimonious feud between southern New Mexico farmers and the immediate needs of nearby El Paso, Texas. A relatively free market in water already exists in the Northern Colorado Water Conservancy District, established in 1937 to manage and distribute water from the Colorado–Big Thompson project. But the price of the water rose steeply from about $30 an acre-foot in 1962 to $1,200 in 1978.[38] One of the earliest conflicts between irrigation and population demands took place in the same region, concerning use of the Cache la Poudre River between 1874 and 1879.

Numerous "disincentives" to water conservation are built into existing laws, policies, institutions, and practices. With low prices, overconsumption has been the rule in agriculture, and the true cash value of water has received little attention. Nor is water consumption linked to crop value. In Kern County, California, for example, an acre of barley needs 1.5 acre-feet, and an acre of lower-value alfalfa needs 4.5 acre-feet. The "beneficial use" clause of the Reclamation Act, continued in succeeding legislation, which was intended to guarantee water to productive farmers, now forces 100 percent consumption of their allocation on threat of loss in future allocations of whatever is not consumed. "Use it or lose it" is still standard operating procedure even as supplies are overallocated and run low. High levels set during abundant times encourage waste, while conservation of water is discouraged.[39]

Disincentives can extend into the future: some farmers have "senior rights" to federally subsidized water, which means they will be the last to suffer if shortages increase over the next decade. Also, farmers who made water-rate agreements in the 1950s pay no interest, and no adjustment is made for inflation. This contract became one of America's greatest natural resource bargains. Their water will cost increasingly less into the 1990s.[40] Such disincentives to conservation, as they encourage groundwater mining, speed up the time when food production and agricultural survival become riskier in the nation's arid regions, and nowhere more than in the Great Plains.

It seems virtually impossible today to shut down the high water consumption required for worldwide food production even where there are unacceptably high levels of groundwater mining. Water for irrigation serves manifold economic, political, and social needs. These external demands in turn accelerate and intensify the risk of water shortages. A 1980 USDA appraisal reports a need to nearly double agricultural productivity over the next fifty years. This is possible only if current water use increases average 2 percent annually.[41] The most immediate task may be to lower the wide-ranging expectations based on unprecedented high water consumption. This changes the historic duty of water in American agriculture.

There may be far less opportunity for counterforces to make themselves felt to reduce consumption, promote conservation, and improve allocation. These counterforces include greater well and pumping efficiency, reduction of center-pivot pressures, improved on-farm conveyance systems and tailwater recovery, irrigation scheduling, alternate-furrow irrigation, and new tillage methods as well as new crop varieties, switching crops, and better know-how on plant growth and water stress, to mention some current approaches.[42] A major question is whether these counterforces can be anything more than Band-Aids on the Great Plains.

The Immediate Crisis: The Great Plains

The revolution on the northern and southern plains came in the 1930s, when the region was rescued from the Dust Bowl by the discovery of the Ogallala aquifer, underlying 174,000 square miles of the arid Great Plains. New pumping technologies and cheap energy began to tap this major national resource. But by the 1960s and 1970s, with exceedingly slow natural recharge, severe groundwater overdrafts took place at ten to twenty times replacement. Water "mining" became the rule.

In the 1940s and 1950s, irrigation expansion had centered on California and the southern Great Plains, but since the mid-1960s most rapid expansion has taken place in the northern Great Plains. In a single decade, 1950–60, groundwater withdrawals of less than 800,000 acre-feet multiplied almost four times to 2.8 million. Withdrawals more than doubled to 6.1 million in 1970 and almost doubled again in 1975 to 11.2 million acre-feet. At the same time, surface water use grew only from 2.22 million to 3.12 million in the twenty-five years from 1950 to 1975. The Sand Hills of western Nebraska are targeted as the nation's last great untapped irrigation region.[43] In contrast, the southern plains multiplied groundwater withdrawals ten times in the same period, while withdrawals in the Pacific states only doubled. By the year 2000 it is estimated that the southern Ogallala area will have previously irrigated 1.2 million acres in a water-starved condition, and an additional 616,000 arid acres in the northern and central Ogallala area. Revised 1984 estimates improved this bleak picture, estimating 40 percent more water in the aquifer and more efficient farming using only 75 percent of the 1978 levels. The crisis is thus delayed from about A.D. 2000 to 2020.

Some plains regions, such as the Texas-Oklahoma panhandle, have already run out of usable groundwater and returned to pre-1930s dryland farming, at less than half their earlier production. Yet while the water was pumped in the 1970s, per-capita personal income rose in the farmland of the Oklahoma panhandle from $3,900 to $6,200.[44] Local officials estimate 885,000 acre-feet are needed annually to maintain today's farming, and by A.D. 2040 1.9 million acre-feet, with at best 947,000 acre-feet available. North of the border, in western Kansas, pumping at half the 1977 rates will still lower the water table, which between 1950 and 1978 declined 50 to 60 feet.[45]

In the highest-risk region, the Texas high plains, the volume of water stored in the Ogallala aquifer south of the Canadian River declined to 60 percent of original capacity between 1937 and 1972, to the extent that lowered water levels and quality began to limit and reduce groundwater pumping and mining by the mid-1970s.[46] It is estimated that for a twenty-four-county area of the Texas high plains the volume of groundwater available in 1974 was 146 million acre-feet, and that this will be reduced to 85 million by the year 2000 and to 52 million by 2020.

Heavy overdrafts on the Great Plains are the only supports for today's high-yield food production. Such yields are a basic assumption of national policy and public opinion. According to the United States Commerce Department's Six States Ogallala report, "One percent of the population, living on 6 percent of the land, is producing over 15 percent of the total value of wheat, corn, and grain sorghum for the nation." The aquifer is the only major source of water for the plains, with more than 50 percent depletion in parts of west Kansas and Texas.[47] The problem is intensified because the aquifer is geologically isolated, natural recharge is unusually limited, and flow within the aquifer is slow. In a classic case of a multiplier's making the problem worse, according to a 1982 Office of Technology Assessment estimate, evapotranspiration consumes nearly 80 percent of the pumped water, ironically making the human input an accelerated version of the hydrological cycle.[48] The Second National Water Assessment of the mid-1970s estimated severe groundwater overdrafts at about 14 million acre-feet a year.[49]

Plains farmers will go to great lengths to avoid the hardships of dryland farming. In an August 1984 interview, James Mitchell, on a 317-acre farm near Lubbock, Texas, uses "low-energy precision" drip irrigation measuring out drops of water at the base of each plant. "You can almost spoon-feed a crop with them. With those old sprinklers, on a windy day you could feel the mist a quarter of a mile away. The amount of water they wasted was just tremendous."[50] Mitchell also uses surge pumps that provide water between rows of crops in timed pulses. Wasteful runoff is avoided by machine-made "furrow dikes," small mounds of dirt every few feet along irrigation rows. Electronic water monitors measure moisture in fields as well as well levels, pumping rates, and equipment efficiency. Plant strains requiring minimum water are bolstered by growth regulators, which limit water-consuming but useless foliage. As a result Mitchell's well-water levels have remained nearly constant for several years.

Another farmer in Swisher County, Texas, said he was told in 1968 that he had ten years of good irrigation left, but "it was 1976 when we bit the bullet and decided to go dryland. From 1976 to 1980 I accumulated a quarter of a million dollars in debt. . . . Every time I went to the bank, I had lost more money. . . . You might have one really good year followed by three or four bad ones." A Dallas consulting firm estimates that $5-a-pound steaks might soon cost $15 a pound, and a $20 cotton shirt will go up to $40.

Water Policy Priorities

Cheap and abundant money to produce cheap and abundant water in the arid American West solved many problems, or shelved them for several generations. This in turn allowed the family farm to continue into the modern era. In addition, this money and water gave Americans, and the world, higher levels of food production and supplies. This has been particularly true in the forty years since World War II, paralleled by a rapid increase in water mining and consumption. We have come to believe that high agricultural yields are a permanent feature of the national and international scene.

At present, as well as in the past, problems inherent in water use in the West have been deflected from water to protect the independent family farmer and agricultural expansion. Present and future water policies and allocations need to take into account the following historical developments:

1. Water is a strategic resource, no less than oil or uranium. In some critical areas it is renewable only at great expense.

2. Water allocation in the arid West continues to be predominantly controlled by "third-party" needs, or "externalities," and less by primary users or market prices. Such influence may be appropriate, but the influence of the independent small farmer has rapidly diminished.

3. When examined in direct economic terms, water has always been the low-cost support or buffer to reduce the high-risk levels of western agriculture and development. The questions are whether it can continue to play this role in the future and what force(s) could replace or supplement it, if desired. It appears that the independent farmer will be the first to go as priorities change.

4. Treated as a national natural resource, water has also been a

Fig. 19. Major man-made water systems in California. California has the most extensive water management system in the nation. From *Historical Atlas of California*, by Warren A. Beck and Ynez D. Haase. Copyright 1974 by the University of Oklahoma Press. Reprinted by permission of the publisher.

low-cost support or buffer to guarantee the nation's traditionally low food prices. Higher water prices could cause serious social and economic dislocations in the immediate and long-term future. The independent farmer is already being sacrificed to delay other changes.

In the very long perspective of ten thousand years since the dawn of agricultural civilization, an era we still live in, America's agricultural expansion into unusable arid lands by means of irrigation has made the United States the premier food producer in all of human history. As a result, accelerated water use has depleted a national resource, created a potentially high-risk economic problem with major social effects, and forced major decisions upon an unprepared nation. According to a best-case scenario, as noted above, free markets in water, together with substantially greater efficiency in agricultural consumption, could maintain food production at current levels for some decades to come, but not indefinitely. A worst-case scenario has already started in the Texas-Oklahoma panhandle and in western Kansas. In both cases, water costs rise far above the means of independent small family farmers. Priorities to sustain them into the future have been abandoned, current irrigation contracts will run out in a decade at most, and they will rapidly disappear from the western arid farmlands. The May 1983 issue of the *Oklahoma Water News* headlined a study "Fear Tested as a Persuader in Reducing Farm Water Costs."

CHAPTER 9

The California Difference

California deserves a book to itself. The state's farmland history is not the final stage in federal land policy, but instead is its contradiction. In contrast to most of the West, California entered the Union in 1846 containing over eight hundred large private estates, many the size of feudal kingdoms, ranging from 1 to 11 square leagues, or 4,426 to 48,646 acres. Some larger claims were monumental: the McNamara family asserted sovereignty over 13,314,000 acres, larger than the 11.5 million acres of the Central Valley and almost equivalent to the 14 million acres of all other private holdings together.

These baronial estates contained the most accessible and highest-quality land in the new state, but farming was casual and indifferent, a pastoral life with widely scattered herds of cattle. Production of grains, vegetables, or fruit was almost nonexistent. Not until gold fever brought a population rush did crop farming attract interest as a money-making business. In 1852 Californians had 111,000 acres under the plow, and by 1855 462,000 acres. Between 1850 and 1860, with the infusion of Anglo farmers, the number of farms rose from 872 to 18,716. But the national agrarian myth, still attached to the 160-acre quarter section for the family farm, carved out of the public domain, was not California's primary mode.

California's land was not expected to produce anything but gold. When eager immigrants, looking for a farmer's paradise, topped the Sierra passes to descend into the golden land, they were profoundly disappointed with the vast, troughlike Sacramento Valley, 50 miles wide and 450 miles long. It was yet another interminable arid desert—hot, waterless, uninhabitable—of the kind they had hastily crossed in Wyoming, Utah, and Nevada. Agricultural historian Gilbert Fite reports that one new immigrant worked his way south down the valley, lost sight of any river or distant mountain, became rattled in the midst of flat, barren cracked earth, and exclaimed, "My God! we're out of sight of land."[1] Many briefly tried their hand at gold seeking and then trudged back east or went north to Oregon's wetter Willamette Valley.

One response required radical innovation. Pioneers back in the arid lands of western Kansas, Nebraska, the Dakotas, and Texas had abandoned their eastern farming techniques for dryland farming with new winter wheats. While plains farmers doggedly (and often hopelessly) stuck with corn on 160-acre government tracts, California farmers bargained with private landowners for an average of 500 acres, which they learned to plant not in the spring but in November and December. The new life was so different that they might as well have landed on another planet. Rainfall patterns were radically different—Sacramento's rain fell between November and May—but far more predictable. Summers were equally predictable—so hot and rainless that the baked land could not be broken by a plow. To help in the disconcerting transition, the California State Agricultural Society was founded as early as 1854. By 1860 prosperous farms covered the Sacramento Valley's rich floodplain and were working their way up into the deserted foothills.

The speed with which the Sacramento Valley filled up demanded quick resolution of the landownership conflict between Spanish, Mexican, American, and private systems. Land law historian Paul W. Gates says California was filled with a "Spanish-Mexican maze of inchoate, incomplete, conditional, unsurveyed, and unlocated grants," many of which never fulfilled conditions for title. The new sovereign power, the United States, in its turn attempted to impose the cadastral survey system, "an entirely different land system which recognized only absolute fee simple titles or conditional rights whose obligations must be fulfilled before title could be issued."[2] In addition, Spanish-Mexican administration had been so loose that many large private holdings were like sovereign states, but with no fixed title. Whatever its successes in clearing up titles and conditions, the federal government never took the draconian steps that would have returned enormous private holdings to the public domain. Instead, existing private estates were sanctioned as they had not been since the first survey years in Ohio early in the nineteenth century. No state land review commission was established until 1851, and federal officials did not begin any major activity until 1853. By 1859, 227 landed estates were surveyed and titled, averaging an astonishing 17,920 acres each and covering over 4 million acres.[3]

Another opportunity for land reform had quickly passed. The ancient and revolutionary promise that public lands would be transferred directly into the hands of the independent family farmer failed to materialize in California. Scanty and less desirable public lands were not open for sale until 1857, eleven years after statehood. Throwing a bone to settlers, preemption was allowed for a brief time on the few acres of unsurveyed public land. Farm families poured into the state from the East and Midwest to squat on undeveloped land, but they found themselves under the highest risk in the history of preemption, since so much land was private and their claims could not even be located under the lax titles and descriptions of so many private ranches.

Instead of an orderly transfer of land according to government fiat, based on the survey and public auction, new settlers found they paid high prices for cloudy titles from private landholders. The conditions were right for vicious agrarian land wars. The price for good farmland owned by speculators went up rapidly since there was no competition from public land sales. The public domain was too small and too poor in quality to keep prices down. Nor were there new public regions to open. Unimproved valley land went at $10 an acre for California farms averaging 450 acres. Even when it became clear that a farmer could prosper on 80 acres in the northern Central Valley, most immigrants did not have the capital to buy land and survive until their cash crops came in. West of Sacramento, prices of improved land ran from $30 to $50 an acre. Napa Valley land sold for as much as $100 an acre and never less than $25. In contrast, foothill or mountain private land went for $2 to $4 an acre, and government land for the standard $1.25, but it was good only for orchards, with a long delay before profitable production. Settlers who planted vineyards in the cheaper uplands were warned it would take $50 an acre to bring them into production. Eastern farmers were often advised not to go beyond Kansas or Nebraska (the largest number of homesteads was in the Dakotas). Contradicting boosters who praised the agricultural wonders of California, local newspapers said they welcomed capitalists but warned other newcomers to bring a bundle of money. In 1870 the California State Agricultural Society cautioned that no cheap land suitable for grain was left in the state.[4] Governor John Bigler and the aggressive State Agricultural Society began to complain that large estates, with land held out from cultivation, were the greatest inhibition to California development. But small farmers were ignored except for their usual share of praise as salt of the earth from public officials and private state boosters.[5]

Congress refused to place limitations on privately owned acreage. Old Mexican grants were often untouched, sometimes with no signs, fencing, or blazes (or accurate maps) to show that they were any different from neighboring vacant land. Squatters sought to have California brought under the Preemption Act of 1841. The old Lockean land-use ethic came into play: thousands of acres that had never been settled by the owners deserved transfer to virtuous pioneers who transformed wilderness into productive farmland. Well into the second half of the twentieth century, the Kern County Land Company (390,000 acres), the Tejon Land Company (273,000 acres), the Irvine ranch (over 100,000 acres), and thirty-three other private preserves covering 500,000 acres in the Central Valley were legally protected from intrusion from the earliest days of statehood. Neither the state nor federal authorities displayed any desire to support the small settler, whose claims were consistently overturned by local courts and federal agencies who upheld prestatehood claims. The squatter, almost a folk hero in the Midwest and plains states, was sometimes ferociously damned in California. The eminent philosopher of the 1880s, Josiah Royce, lashed out against the "squatters' conspiracy" to bring law and order in California to its knees. He complained about the "wicked and dangerous use . . . of the current abstractions about the absolute rights of man and the higher will of God."[6] The absolute autonomy of private property was to be protected at all costs.

Slightly more successful than squatters were homesteaders on scarce public land. California farming had the attraction of consistently good weather and fewer insect infestations than the Midwest or plains lands. Farmers quickly discovered that over 60 percent of original homestead entries before 1880 were made final by 1885, in sharp contrast to between 40 and 50 percent in midwestern and plains states.[7] For a total of $200 a settler could prove up a preemption, enter a homestead, and gain clear title to 320 acres. Yet California was so distant for eastern farmers, and workable public land was so scarce, that fewer homesteads were entered there in the 1860s than in a single year in Minnesota. At the same time, California's largest speculator, William S. Chapman, paid cash for 631,000 mostly public, seemingly worthless acres.

Since a few large speculators monopolized California's best farmland, their private land-use practices took the place of federal land policies. William S. Chapman's views were perhaps more liberal and certainly more candid than most. He was openly paternalistic, considered himself a benevolent capitalist in the mold of Andrew Carnegie's "gospel of wealth," and would be praised by conservatives today for his commitment to "privatization" of public policy.[8] Between 1865 and 1871 Chapman paid cash for more than a million acres, mostly apparent wasteland in the public domain. While he benefited extravagantly from the government policy of rapid transfer of public land into private hands, he also complained about the social dislocations and economic imbalances of the system that kept small farmers from acquiring good land and prevented them from making a living. While his own self-interest surely prevailed, he early promoted settlement colonies for farm families, crop experimentation to suit local climate and soil conditions, and irrigation as California's primary opportunity for farmland expansion. In 1875 he capitalized the Central Colony in Fresno County by donating 4,000 acres divided into 192 20-acre tracts. He urged profitable cash crops for the colony: planting alfalfa for cattle feed and importing muscatel grape cuttings from Spain.

Chapman also saw a future for wheat on California's vast desert lands if irrigation could expand on a scale previously unknown. In 1871 he had established the Fresno Canal and Irrigation Company and took the lead in forming the major San Joaquin and Kings River Canal and Irrigation Company, which anticipated in concept and engineering the twentieth-century Central Valley project. Gerald Nash argues that Chapman "filled a void created by the many imperfections in the systems of land distribution devised by the State and Federal governments."[9] In a long letter to San Francisco newspapers in 1868, Chapman defended his vast holdings, acquired at prices as low as the government's standard $1.25 an acre. But these lands "were thought to be worthless, for they were during the dry season an apparently barren worthless plain, without trees, and without water." But they could become prosperous wheatlands if entrepreneurs like himself risked their development. He admitted he was a speculator, but the lands could never have been settled by independent farmers or produced wheat at a tenfold greater rate without his risk venture. "This land is not of the kind which invites the class of settlers who usually enter land by preemption. It is better calculated to be cultivated in larger tracts at present, than in farms of 160 acres each. It is calculated, at present, for *making money* by raising wheat on a large scale, by men who can use six or eight mule-team with gang-plow and seed sower."

But California's golden age of farming seemed short-lived. Crops unexpectedly began to fail when droughts repeatedly hit the Central Valley and San Joaquin Valley in 1863 and again in 1864. Farmers had barely recovered when once more the rains did not fall in 1871 and in 1876–77. Settlers abandoned the state for the certain rains of Oregon and Washington. New immigrants were told to stay back in Minnesota and the Dakotas or in eastern Kansas and Nebraska; the lands were not worth the arduous crawl across mountains and deserts.[10] In addition, good farmland was long gone even in the unlikely case that the new settler brought at least $2,000 for land purchase and had deep pockets while waiting for an orchard or vineyard to mature into productivity. California was never a paradise for the small struggling farmer, but it remained extremely profitable for the middle-class commercial farmer who had cash reserves for the bad times and the strong entrepreneurial skills to run a business operation.

But in a legendary turnaround, Californians "invented" millions of acres of new farmland through extensive irrigation. By 1880 complaints grew that existing farmland had been filled up; the rest was a desert wasteland. The only way a newcomer could remain was to buy existing improved farmland at high prices. Irrigation and water diversion for a "hydraulic civilization" had existed since Spanish and Mexican settlement. But the difference would be in scale, technology, and capitalization. This "new" farmland had only distant connections with the historical land survey policies. Despite public pronouncements from state and federal officials, the small independent farmer was given few inducements to settle there even when irrigation came to dominate California agriculture. Instead, water was carried to private undeveloped land to enhance land values and multiply productivity. When water reached unimproved arid land, prices skyrocketed from $5 an acre to $100–200. Where once a tract was so barren cattle could not graze on it, a constant flow of water guaranteed up to three harvests a year. Where dryland farming produced wheat and barley, irrigation offered more profitable orchards and vineyards on far less acreage. In contrast to the national trend, the average California farm decreased in size. This misled officials, farmers, and the public into heady predictions about the rescue of the cash-poor small farmer. But the new agriculture would be highly capitalized, intensively mechanized, and dedicated to California's specialty—fruits and vegetables directly tied to the commercial marketplace.[11]

California's land became only one element among many instead of the controlling factor, as land had been treated under the old survey and sale policy. As early as 1872 the California legislature tried to persuade Congress to trade land for technology by granting public land to capitalize private irrigation companies. Wealthier independent farmers had been diverting streams in the 1850s and 1860s to grow grapes and fruit trees on about 50,000 acres around Los Angeles and Sacramento. Larger enterprises used irrigation companies to build dams, water gates, and canals. By 1874 the scale of irrigation had grown to the extent that the San Joaquin and Kings River Company built and managed a 40-mile canal from the San Joaquin River. Such irrigation projects were so profitable for both company and farmer that by 1877 over six hundred irrigation ditches served almost 202,000 acres. Two years later almost 293,000 acres were artificially watered. Over a million acres of new farmland came into production by 1889, compared with the widely accepted preirrigation "limit" totaling approximately 10 million farmable acres. In addition, by 1889 groundwater supplied over 38,000 acres.[12]

But few farm families in California could afford their own dams and canals. They had neither the cash for independent systems nor the necessary management skills. The San Joaquin and Kings River Canal and Irrigation Company advised prospective settlers in the 1870s that individual farmers "are too poor to carry out the necessary canals and ditches by themselves, and require the cooperation of capitalists."[13] To the surprise of many, California's push toward widespread irrigation depended upon land reform, which tried to relieve the poor farmers' plight by advocating collective agricultural communities using a combination of private water companies and the new state irrigation districts. Californians repeatedly looked to Colorado's successful Greeley irrigation colony as their model. Irrigation spokesmen included William E. Smythe and Elwood Mead.[14] Smythe believed western farming potential would be fulfilled only through new social institutions. He may have been more radical than he realized when he doubted the validity of the independent farm family situated on its own piece of land. Instead Smythe worked to bring small settlers into agricultural communities less vulnerable to steep price swings and economic cycles. "We must show the poor man how he can afford to get married . . . and become a home owner."[15] Even the Salvation Army worked to set up 20-acre farmer communities based on irrigation systems.

Elwood Mead condemned the poor performance of earlier unplanned national land policies. Federal land laws were not dedicated to aiding the independent farm family. They distorted America's farm potential, drove the nation's young people from the sacred land into profane urban factories, encouraged speculation, extreme land prices, soil depletion, and un-American tenancy, and forced patriotic, hardworking farm families into failure. With irrigation technology as the new physical base, farmers would be encouraged to settle in communities rather than on isolated, high-risk homesteads. Here they would benefit from cooperative village life—stores, churches, schools, and local markets.[16] Many new settlers found it difficult to surrender their precious personal autonomy and hard-earned independence to collective enterprise. On the other hand, the capacity to earn a better living with a 20-acre orchard than a 640-acre Kansas wheat farm was a stunning achievement. In the process of creating new farmland by irrigation, American farming was reinvented in the watered valleys of California. Mead's plan would eventually break on the anvil of fee-simple ownership and the unyielding national commitment to landowning, autonomous farming as the symbolic center of American life. Interest nevertheless ran high enough to persuade Californians in 1917 to legislate 110 farm allotments on 6,239 acres for an irrigation community at Durham in Butte County. Despite early success, the community collapsed during the farm recession of the 1920s.

Wherever the water came, land prices went up. Even local booster newspapers warned new settlers about the shock of seeing unimproved, previously arid land snapped up at $100 an acre instead of the usual $5, and nothing went for the government's $1.25. Improved land under the vine could be sold for $300 to $500 for a single acre, equivalent to a quarter or half section on the plains. This was still more money than many dismayed arrivals ever had in their hands at one time.

One innovative boom town was Ontario, a few miles east of Los Angeles. It prospered by pioneering the mutual ownership of water by individuals and the community, new engineering techniques, the use of groundwater to back up surface irrigation sources, and effective water conservation, all of which transformed a desert landscape into profitable orange groves.[17] An 1881 irrigation colony, the Etiwanda Water Company, discovered that the land values of its small 1,200-acre property depended entirely on extensive water rights, not on the land itself. This discovery of the cash value of water rights became the model in 1882 for the San Antonio Water Company, a mutual company whose landowners valued their water shares to 15,000 acres more than the acres themselves. The economic success of the company depended on complex, sophisticated hydraulic engineering—moving the water—as much as on good farming techniques. Tunnels, concrete pipes, wells, and hydroelectric power for pumping to control and direct both surface and underground water would soon make available a minimum of 390,000 gallons of water each month for each 10-acre orchard.[18] A careful balance sheet for the community concluded that to settle successfully on 10 acres for five years a farmer needed $1,500 for the land, $750 for a thousand trees, annual costs of $250 to $300, incidental expenses of $500, and interest charges of $1,200. This total commitment of $5,300 would produce no income for the first three years and only $500 in the fourth, but in the fifth year the trees would yield two hundred oranges per tree (market value of $10 per thousand) and generate an income of $2,000. There would then be yearly orchard costs of $300, incidental expenses of $100, and interest charges of $240. Net income would be about $1,360, enough to return a frugal farmer's original investment in less than five years. By 1894 Ontario's colony had 2,500 settlers; each farm prospered at between 10 and 20 acres for a total of almost 7,700 acres. Undeveloped land with water rights soon sold for $200 an acre and established orchard land for $1,000 an acre.

Federal land laws never accomplished their objectives in California. As irrigation projects spread over the landscape, they drowned federal policies in their successes. This rejection of the survey system became law in California when in 1887 the Wright Act created a new land system: irrigation districts. The legislature, in C. C. Wright's words, "created a special government for the one purpose of developing and administering the irrigation water for the benefit of the people."[19] California farmland policy became dedicated to one cause: to distribute water as widely as possible onto fertile but dry valley flatlands.

California's agricultural institutions would be built around irrigation districts with coercive powers instead of traditional townships and sections. Earlier, development corporations could purchase land, dig ditches, form mutual irrigation companies, and sell land and stock to settlers, but they could not force local farmers to participate in a major irrigation project. The Wright Act, using the needs of San Joaquin farmers as its model, created sovereign powers attached to a board of directors of a specific irrigation project. Irrigation project bonds were secured by taxes on all the farmland within a district, making even the most rebellious farmer a reluctant participant. A district could be formed by two-thirds of the electorate in the area. Such comprehensive and coercive powers were confirmed by an 1896 United States Supreme Court decision, *Fallbrook Irrigation District v. Bradley.*[20.]

In contrast to the limited resources and lack of management know-how of independent farmers, the collective resources amassed by irrigation districting made the system spread rapidly and successfully. The half-million-acre Imperial Valley district is a classic case of the districting process as it combined private interests and public policies. Private money had been poured into the Imperial Valley desert in anticipation of using Colorado River water. The irrigation district was created to protect this high-risk enterprise. This combination succeeded in making the valley a major food producer. Although farmers feared the dictatorial powers of the irrigation district manager and his board, they had easier access to credit and capital, large-scale technological resources, far more political leverage, a common labor pool, and cooperative marketing strength. The irrigation district became a new political, economic, social, and geographical entity. By 1920 California had 71 irrigation districts.[21] By 1969 seventeen western states contained 469 irrigation districts covering 7.2 million acres.

The spread of intensive commercial farming based on irrigation set California farmers apart from their counterparts elsewhere in the country. California became famous for specialized intensive farming: fruit orchards, vineyards, nut farms, and vegetable tracts. By the mid-1880s trainloads of produce reached the Midwest, the East Coast, and even some foreign markets. The 1899 report of the Department of Agriculture announced that 64 percent of the cash value of California farming came from noncereal commodities. Wherever irrigation took hold, fortunes were made because individual farmers needed less land. Many of the old large tracts of 400 to 2,000 acres and upward were divided up.[22] The capacity to make a satisfying living on 5 to 40 acres was not simply advertising rhetoric but a working reality. Those who owned larger acreages—the average California farm in 1900 was perhaps 150 acres—could create a fortune. In this agricultural revolution, land became less the controlling factor, and proper management of resources like water and capital and new technologies, such as mechanization and plant science, helped guarantee success. In the process, the average farm in places like Los Angeles and Fresno counties was half as large in 1900 as in 1880. This contradicted the midwestern and plains trend toward larger farms, where settlers struggled to make ends meet with 320 acres or more under wheat or corn.

It is not surprising that when Nevada congressman Francis G. Newlands urged national irrigation legislation, he based it on a maximum of 80 acres per landowner, preferably limited to homesteaders. Congressional rhetoric still claimed to be dedicated to the well-being of the small farmer. "The aim . . . is to prevent monopoly of every form, to open up the public domain to actual settlers who desire homes, and to disintegrate the monopolistic holdings of land that prevail on the Pacific coast and in the intermountain region."[23] But the 160-acre or 320-acre limitation for participation in government irrigation projects written into Newland's Reclamation Act of 1902 was excessive for California because of small profitable farms of 5 to 40 acres. But among long-established large-scale farmers, reclamation policies were still another intrusion of the survey philosophy. In 1933 the secretary of the interior released users of Colorado River water in California's Imperial Valley from the limitation. Farm size rose between 1944 and 1960 to 5,000 acres and more. This "excess lands" provision would trouble California irrigation programs into the 1980s.[24]

The 1902 act was welcome where the resources of private companies or state resources could not match the need for large-scale irrigation projects. Donald Worster concludes that federal intervention to "make the desert bloom" through the Bureau of Reclamation was instrumental in making "California the most powerful agricultural region on the planet—the home base for what has become an international agribusiness empire."[25] Such government action was a rescue operation to avoid the economic collapse of private interests, to guarantee their profits, and to limit conflict between special interests. By the dark days of 1917, reclamation seemed positively humanitarian. A local Bureau of Reclamation official urged speedy federal intervention: "More than a million acres face an acute irrigation crisis. . . . Between 40,000 and 50,000 acres of producing lands have been abandoned, and 200,000 acres are in the process of gradual reversion to desert. Another 400,000 acres in the fertile Sacramento–San Joaquin Delta are menaced by intrusion of salt water from San Francisco Bay."[26] Over the next forty years, water would pour onto California farms from the Central Valley project, from the generous allotments of Colorado River based on optimistic flow predictions of the 1922 compact, and from future-be-damned groundwater mining.[27] After twelve years of planning, in 1933 California scheduled dams on the upper Sacramento River, with canals and pumps moving surplus water to over a million acres in the San Joaquin Valley. But the $170 million cost in the midst of the depression put the project in the hands of the Bureau of Reclamation in 1935 for large-scale integrated development to be completed over the next twenty years. By 1964 California contained more than 20 percent (2.3 million acres) of all Bureau of Reclamation projects. But private and state programs still accounted for 5.3 million more irrigated acres.

California's success with abundant water on parched land demonstrated the validity of John Wesley Powell's cautionary vision of the West and then went far beyond it. Irrigation districts, successful commercial farms on minuscule acreage (compared with midwestern needs), the perpetuation of baronial estates—all tied to the Central Valley Project and interstate use of Colorado River water—created an enduring physical and institutional structure akin to the great hydraulic civilizations of the Nile Valley and the Fertile Crescent and of India and China. Donald Worster says Californians today participate not only in "factory farming" but in an entire "social order founded on the intensive management of water."[28] The result is a form of modern consumerism: once a great deal of water became available, there had to be created an above-normal demand for its use, which took place through California's intensive agriculture and urban growth. The mass consumption of water is symbolized by flooded vegetable fields in the countryside (and by a swimming pool in every urban backyard). The farmer's measure in California has never been land, but always water. Back in 1878 Powell argued for irrigation not only because more land could be made productive, but also because limited water resources could be controlled and managed. To make a fickle resource into a reliable controlled supply was the farmer's ancient dream. In California the dream became a reality.

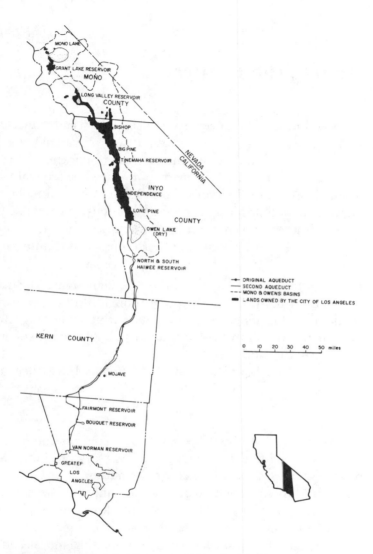

Fig. 20. Los Angeles—Owens River aqueduct. A classic water conflict between agricultural and urban use persisted as Los Angeles captured farmland
and water rights on the Owens River valley far to the north of the city. From
Historical Atlas of California, by Warren A. Beck and Ynez D. Haase. Copyright 1974 by the University of Oklahoma Press. Reprinted by permission
of the publisher.

CHAPTER 10

Rescuing the Farmer

There was a kind of homogeneity in the quality and value of the land of [the old Northwest Territory]. It was all valuable for agriculture and habitation, but in the western portion of our country it is otherwise; . . . One region is exclusively valuable for mining, another solely for timber, a third for nothing but pasturage, and a fourth serves no useful purpose whatever. . . . the homestead and preemption laws are not suited.
1880 Report of the Public Lands Commission

The day [28 June 1934] on which the President signed the Taylor Act, which virtually closed the public domain to further settlement, laid in its grave a land policy which had long since been dead and which walked abroad only as a troublesome ghost within the living world.
Rexford G. Tugwell, *Scribner's Magazine*, 1936

In January 1909 the National Conservation Commission published in three large volumes an exhaustive inventory of United States natural resources. It was backed by the authority of Gifford Pinchot, the leading conservationist of the day and chief forester of the United States, and by President Theodore Roosevelt.[1] The report unexpectedly announced that the useful public domain was almost gone. No longer should settlers be urged upon the land, as had been national policy for generations. Already the historian Frederick Jackson Turner used census statistics in 1893 to announce the closing of the frontier. Turner's "frontier thesis" had always emphasized "the advance of the more steady farmer" on the public domain rather than the trapper, miner, or cowboy. Turner was one of the first to trouble himself about the future of this "representative American" with the demise of open western lands.[2]

In the beginning the land all Americans held in common totaled an astonishing 1.44 billion acres.[3] By 1909 the National Conservation Commission reported that 387 million acres were left open to entry, much of it wasteland useless for farming. Twenty years later, in 1929, this was down to 190 million acres, made up of 30 million acres of desert wasteland and 160 million acres of grazing land. In 1956 the federal government reported that it had no farmland left to sell or give away. The commission also noted in 1909 that 235 million acres had been taken off the market since 1872 and put into perpetual reserves in national parks and national forests. By 1956 these reserves were down to less than 180 million acres. In addition, over the years 224 million acres had been donated to the states for internal improvements, 73.5 million to war veterans as military land bounties, and 131 million acres to private railroad companies to guarantee construction and profits. Only a disappointing 147 million acres of free land had gone to homesteaders since 1862. By way of comparison, over 170 years almost half a billion acres (455.5 million) had been sold to private interests. This was mostly in cash sales ranging from $2.50 an acre down to 12$1/2$¢. The remaining public lands included Indian holdings, military ranges, wildlife preserves, and miscellaneous tracts.

The Problem of Classification

The 1909 National Conservation Commission, following the conservationist precepts of Gifford Pinchot, urged Congress and the president to establish a long-overdue classification of the remaining public lands. With a reforming zeal popular during the Progressive Era, it called for radical revision of policies ranging back to 1785 and 1796. The land survey, for example, had treated all public lands west of the Pennsylvania-Ohio line identically. A section in southeastern Ohio was the same entity of property as a section in western Nebraska or southern Missouri. Instead the commission proposed dividing the public domain into distinctive timber, mineral, desert, and farm units. It implied that the egalitarian tendency of the venerable survey system was at fault; the landscape was not all the same but had different values and diverse uses. Pinchot's "best possible use" seemed elitist and implied restrictions on the owners' free choice to use their land for highest profit. The argument that "best possible use" and "highest price" might not coincide would become the center for major conflicts in the twentieth century. By midcentury the ideals of classification, and the resulting land-use limitations, would also be damned as "takings" that reduced the value of private property. Western landholders feared classification as an intrusion into their venerable flexibility.

When settlers moved across the level prime farmland from Ohio through Iowa in mid-nineteenth century, it seemed that many survey tracts were roughly interchangeable. But midway across the nation, as farmers edged out of the midwestern grasslands onto the arid plains, the picture unexpectedly changed. A badly chosen survey tract could bring a farmer into harm's way. Most farm families were provident enough to salt away sufficient cash to survive for three to five years, but farming arid lands demanded stronger resources. Rain did not follow the plow. Between 1890 and 1900 some Great Plain counties lost more than half their population. "Within the memory of many of us the lands of eastern Weld County [Colorado] have been settled and abandoned twice—the settlers starved out. . . . Eastern Weld County has been settled for the last time."[4] The Dust Bowl of the 1930s, so far as it was man-induced, was in no small part the result of a half-century of settlement on tracts badly designed for arid-lands geography and climate.

Earlier attempts at dividing the public lands according to land use held little promise. When land office inspectors were ordered in 1905 to enforce the irrigation standards of the Desert Land Act, they found they had no land-quality rules. The only informal distinction was between surveyed and unsurveyed land, and that became ambiguous with the rise of preemption and homesteading. Back in 1878 Interior Secretary Carl Schurz had sought to separate and save the nation's timberlands in the Timber Cutting Act of 1878. The Timber and Stone Act of 1878 had jurisdiction over surveyed land unfit for cultivation but containing valuable timber or stone. But no specific test for unfit farmland was included in the public laws. Western defenders of "flexibility" knew that classification and division of public lands would restrict opportunities for speculation.

John Wesley Powell had also urged comprehensive and scientific classification to distinguish between useful and useless land in the West. He was joined in this crusade in 1880 by the Public Land Commission, which called for universal land classification, major divisions being arable, irrigable, timber, and mineral. Land would also be distinguished by its physical geography. Was the climate humid or dry? Was there access to water for irrigation? Following such classification, settlers would be directed toward one type of land, lumbermen to another, miners to still another, and some land would be off limits because it was useless. Already homesteaders in the 1890s were being doomed to failure when they depended upon 1785 survey standards alone. The *Laramie Boomerang* in 1907 noted that the homesteader is made "a cordial invitation to come in and make himself welcome . . . [where there is] no prospect save that of starvation."[5] Although traditional farming had reached its useful limits on the plains, dryland farmers might still succeed on the right piece of land, and the small stockman could prevail on land where the dryland farmer would fail. And Americans believed that should the common man fail to work out his own salvation the government would come to his aid. In 1888 Congress passed legislation to identify and "segregate" arid regions needing only irrigation for good farming. But no specific guidelines were provided. The important omnibus General Revision Act of 1891, which tried to clean up and harmonize thousands of laws and regulations, did not provide for any classification program. Congress continued to try to legislate new farmland through the Carey Act of 1894, which promised the states gifts of reclaimable land if they would separate it out from hopeless land. The Geological Survey could do a rough classification, but no department of government had adequate resources for a skillful separation according to soil types, vegetation, farmland carrying capacity, or irrigation potential. By the end of the century, most of America's workable farmland was already gone. Reclamation boosters, however, preached the virtual invention of 100 million acres of new farmland.[6]

Land Classification and Settlement in Conflict

But in a 1903 report the Public Lands Commission still reflected the power of frontier farming to move public opinion: "to affect the largest practicable disposition of the public lands to actual settlers." But it also sought to control where settlers went. It urged discriminate "best" use of well-defined land types for "the fullest and most effective use of the resources of the public lands." This could exclude the yeoman farmer from large "inappropriate" tracts. Farmland within forest reserves was to be made available, but large arid grasslands were excluded from sale to farmers. The western farmers' magaine, the *Denver Field and Farm*, found no conflict in a 1906 editorial: "We should put the whole West to its best use and fill it with people."[7] Other western publications looked upon classification as a repressive control over free entry to all land. Idaho senator William Borah complained in 1910 that classification was a newfangled "modern doctrine" that went against tradition: "A state which has her agricultural lands locked up is not on an equality with the state which can devote them to raising foodstuffs for her people." To settle on all the public domain was a basic American right. "It is a violation of the Constitution to withhold them from our use. . . . We ask Congress not to adopt a policy, therefore, which will take from us the means by which we must live and thrive, the means by which our citizens are to prosper and our state to grow and take its place with the older states of the Union."[8] In 1912 Borah told the Senate it must not only protect free entry into western lands, but aggressively aid settlers. Western interests rightly feared that land classification would block off large desert regions into permanent empty zones. The rage over classification depended upon whose ox was being gored. Westerners fought to preserve the dogma of flexibility, but cattleman Senator Harvey Ferguson of New Mexico took advantage of the move toward classification when he insisted that over 330 million acres of western land were not suitable for traditional farming or for irrigation settlement, had no forest or mineral interests, and hence belonged exclusively to cattle grazing.[9]

Soil Depletion and Farmer Failure

As the debates ranged though the halls of Congress, newspaper editorial offices, and Grange halls in the early twentieth century, the farmland being wrangled over was washing and blowing away. The crisis arose paradoxically with the success of dryland farming on the plains about 1900. It gave farmers a bounty of winter wheat to raise their standard of living even in years of limited rain.[10] Deep plowing, summer fallowing, and marketable grain were a good combination to give the plains farmer some security. Mechanization made life easier—first steam tractors and then Ford's inexpensive gasoline tractor. Most farmers put their incomes into more land and machinery. The chief of the Bureau of Soils reflected the national mood when he said in 1909, "The soil is the one indestructible, immutable asset that the nation possesses. It is the one resource that cannot be exhausted, that cannot be used up."[11] The Great American Desert seemed bested by technology, new strains of wheat, and the frontier farmer's true grit. But the soil of the Great Plains is "fossil" soil, easy to use up with intensive farming but slow to be replaced. Soon 6,000 years of nutritious deposits had been mined out of a possible 14,000 years' accumulation. It takes between 250 and 1,000 years to build one inch of topsoil. Modern accelerated monoculture agriculture began consuming the "indestructible" resource to keep farmers going. They were cannibalizing their own resource.

With record acreages and record wheat prices (up 250 percent to $2 a bushel) during World War I, American agriculture had its golden age. Even as prices started their precipitous collapse after the war in 1919, plains farmers were in the midst of the infamous "plowup" of 17 million marginal acres.[12] The additional acres put to work by the new machines would transmute wheat into cash to carry them through difficult years. But the soil, more exposed by row crops and small grains closely planted for the sake of desperately needed high yields, began blowing and washing away. The first nationwide estimate of soil erosion was not published until 1928, and the first intensive inventories were not reported until after 1933.[13] In the meantime "black blizzards" of dust storms ran across the plains in the 1920s as well as the more notorious 1930s.[14]

Despite the rapid collapse of the farmland as well as the farmer by the 1930s, a national response did not begin until dust from the storms literally settled on Congress in 1935. By adroit maneuvering, Hugh Hammond Bennett, director of the new Soil Erosion Service, held off a congressional hearing vote on his agency's work until a dust cloud from an Oklahoma storm hit Washington and blotted out the sun. He then told the worried legislators that erosion had already decimated 282 million acres of cropland and rangeland and was at work on another 775 million acres. "A hundred million acres of the best cropland we have is finished. . . . it will be impossible to maintain permanent prosperity over large areas of the United States." Later in 1935 Bennett persuaded Congress to pass the Soil Conservation Act, which marked a definitive change in national policy toward America's farmland. No longer would attention center on settling independent farmers on virgin lands. Existing farmland must be held at a soil quality high enough to guarantee high yields indefinitely. (A similar environmental quality standard would in 1969 be called "no significant deterioration." See chap. 11.)

New Deal Rescue Programs

Franklin Roosevelt's New Deal gave its immediate attention not to soil conditions, but to the desperate straits of the resident farmer. Interior Secretary Harold Ickes and Agriculture Secretary Henry Wallace, together with Henry Morgenthau and Rexford Tugwell, insisted the federal government had power to intervene and relieve the deeply distressed small farmer, in trouble since the collapse of farm prices in 1920.[15] The slogan of the New Deal—Relief, Recovery, and Reform—could be directly applied to agricultural needs. Ickes had already concluded that western farmers must not be tempted onto 25 million submarginal acres to repeat the disastrous World War I plowup. The government must actively intervene by forcibly retiring marginal lands, even when they were in private hands. Ickes discovered that none of the three thousand federal land laws authorized him to intervene into private property for the public good. Ickes, like a Mesopotamian tetrarch, ordered a national classification by dividing the national land into crop lands, range lands, forest lands, and mineral lands. Ickes also acted forcefully on the remaining public domain—now mostly 173 million acres of grazing land—by turning it into permanent public lands like the national forests.[16] The remains of the 1785 survey had simply disappeared.

In the 1930s over one-quarter of all Americans still lived on the farm. The dedicated farm family hard at work on its own land still represented an American ideal. But prices for farm goods dropped to less than half between 1929 and 1932; net income fell by 70 percent. To his credit, Agriculture Secretary Wallace sought long-term answers when he made conservation of soil into national policy. An early policy of "no significant deterioration" toward farmland was institutionalized with the creation of a new reformist agency, the Soil Conservation Service.[17]

But conflicting priorities of saving the small farmer versus saving the soil spilled over into interagency squabbling between Agriculture and Interior, competing federal and state self-interest, and the old but hardly forgotten impasse between private property and public interest. In early 1936 the Supreme Court stepped in with a landmark property rights decision when it declared the Agricultural Adjustment Act unconstitutional because the act "coerced" farmers by penalizing them for "incorrect" planting or refusing to reduce their crop acreage to control production. This was a "taking" of income and freedom of action on private property: "The price of such refusal is the loss of benefits. The amount offered is intended to be sufficient to exert pressure on [the farmer] to agree to the proposed regulation; . . . the plan [is]. . . to keep a non-cooperating minority in line. This is coercion by economic pressure. The asserted power of choice is illusory."[18] The federal government could not intervene directly into private land-use decision making.

Within six weeks Congress bypassed the Court with the Soil Conservation and Domestic Allocation Act of 1936, which combined soil conservation and aid to farmers by paying farmers an average of $10 an acre to shift from "soil-depleting" to "soil-conserving" crops.[19] In a tidy distinction, "class I payments" under the act raised farm income by rewarding farmers for acreage limits, while "class II payments" fostered soil recovery by "soil building" through terracing, planting cover crops, and planting trees. With visions of perpetual dust bowls and the specter of a food-supply failure, momentum grew to support soil protection even when it meant repudiating old farmer values. The Wheat Conservation Conference, a lobby put together by wheat producers, told Congress that "society has suffered an irreparable loss. . . . as a result of rugged agricultural individualism."[20] Not only had the family farmer collapsed, but the erosion of farmland meant "incalculable . . . social loss." Independent farmers did not serve the nation's interest with cheap and abundant food when they abused their land.[21] The mood swung from saving the farmer to saving the soil

Federal Intervention into the Private Sector: Land-Use Planning

By 1937 Congress took a radical step. It would create new land units: soil conservation districts. These districts overlapped the jurisdictions of other legal land entities including farmers' platted sections. By 1939 thirty-seven soil conservation districts covered more than 19 million Dust Bowl acres. With the authority it had in these districts, the Soil Conservation Service encouraged contour plowing, terracing, strip cropping, fencerows, and other techniques to rebuild misused land. A Civilian Conservation Corps team terraced land in southeastern Colorado in 1936, and when between 1.05 and 2.33 inches of rain fell in May, terraced land had over 41 inches of moisture penetration compared with only 11 inches on unterraced land.[22] Today, 2,950 conservation districts cover almost all private farmland in the United States, with authority over farmland management and property owners' decisions.[23] Farmland was for the first time aggressively separated from forest, range, and mineral lands. Equally important, the reorganization of America's private farmland into soil conservation districts allowed for division of land and land-use restrictions according to quality. In place of four or five original classes, there are now at least eight, with important subdivisions. In the 1980s the classes listed below were the basis for the Important Farmland Survey of the Soil Conservation Service.[24] It is tempting to wonder how America's farmland would have looked had the districts and classification appeared in 1785 and 1796 instead of the survey, plat maps, and public auction.

Class I—soils with few limitations that restrict their use.

Class II—soils with moderate limitations that reduce the choice of plants or require moderate conservation practices.

Class III—soils with severe limitations that reduce the choice of plants or require special conservation practices, or both.

Class IV—soils with very severe limitations that reduce the choice of plants, or that require very careful management, or both.

Class V—soils not likely to erode but with other limitations on their use that are impractical to remove.

Class VI—soils with severe limitations that make them generally unsuitable for cultivation.

Class VII—soils with very severe limitations that make them unsuitable for cultivation.

Class VIII—soils and landforms with limitations that nearly preclude their use for commercial crop production.

The Soil Conservation Service quickly became an aggressive land reform agency with a sense of mission. Congress had already in 1936 put teeth into no significant deterioration of farmland by paying farmers to take land out of soil-depleting crops. Unlike so much reform and relief legislation for farmers in American history, the acts of 1935, 1936, and 1937 had immediate and positive results. They lowered day-to-day farm operating expenses. They improved yields. They exchanged cash for land taken out of production.

No significant deterioration became national policy for a federal government that recognized that the national soil was finite. The frontier was closed, the lands were sorted out into classes, and federal intervention for the sake of rational planning, wisest-use development, and resource protection became the norm for America's private farmland. Institutions to keep America's farmland intact were in place. In effect, the New Deal had established a three-tiered land-management program: reduction of soil-depleting crops, maintenance of farmland at levels of no significant deterioration (status quo), and attempts at "soil building" or recovery. Much of the New Deal legislation that created the Soil Conservation Service and gave it authority over the nation's farmland has been continued into the 1980s.[25]

Despite farmers' weakened hold on public policy, Interior Secretary Harold Ickes risked the label of commissar when he proposed that the nation's poor farmers be taken off their marginal or worn-out land and relocated on good farmland to make a fresh start. Ickes conceived that a new public domain and a new social order were yoked together, just as they had been back in 1785 and 1796. Half the nation's farms had failed as money-making ventures. Roosevelt established the controversial Resettlement Administration in 1935. Some citizens condemned "un-American" cooperative farm communities that might result rather than individual farm sites, but the plan also retired marginal farmland, resettled farmers on better land, and lent money for land and equipment. Within a year more than 200,000 almost helpless farm families were given a new start. Agriculture Secretary Henry Wallace proposed that the federal government return 31 million acres of abandoned farmland to the public domain. President Roosevelt set up the Land Retirement program to buy back exhausted land from farmers; he joined Ickes in relocation plans. But Dust Bowl historian R. Douglas Hurt concludes, "As a humanitarian program, designed to improve the standard of living among those who sold their lands by relocating them on better farms, the resettlement portion of the land utilization program was a failure."[26] Even as the public domain grew slightly, the historic policies of survey and sale were brought to an official close with

Colorado congressman Edward I. Taylor's 1934 Grazing Act. It set aside the last of the public lands into permanent national holdings, mostly as "grazing districts" that would total 142 million acres by 1936. In fact, President Roosevelt upstaged the Taylor Grazing Act with his executive order of 26 November 1934, which, as of 5 February 1935, took the remaining public domain—165,695,000 acres—off the market. Roosevelt made the order on the authority of the act of 25 June 1910 in which Congress had given the federal government the right to withdraw public land for soil conservation and watershed protection.[27]

The 1930s were soil conservation's golden age. In the 1940s the food demands of World War II pushed aside land-saving projects. Instead American farmers threw themselves into high gear to save the world with wheat. Global food needs and high prices, together with new technologies and guaranteed government intervention (new policies and new money), allowed the not-so-independent farmer to endure and prosper even on the arid plains. Hope also revived with new techniques: terracing, contouring, summer fallowing, and holding dry soil with row crops, list furrows, and shelterbelts. Postwar pro-farmer government programs followed the New Deal mold. High production built large surpluses in the 1950s. The Soil Bank program of 1956 established precedents when it created *acreage reserves* set aside from their normal wheat, corn, cotton, peanuts, rice, and tobacco crops. Longer-term *conservation reserves* retired land for three to ten years and included rewards for entering the program and penalties for breaking contracts. The reward-penalty system was called "cross compliance."[28] Suspicion once again built up among farmers that their interests had been set aside. The policy of encouraging fewer people on larger tracts of farmland, with large acreages retired, was "systematically destroying the fabric of North Dakota's small community life," said a congressman from that state.[29]

The 1950s brought a "little dust bowl," followed by a decade of adequate rain that encouraged more extensive land plowup. Drier years in the early and middle 1970s are reminders of the historical aridity of the Great Plains. Farming over fifty years since the 1930s was never self-sufficient but is based instead upon enormous external inputs. Government and commercial interventions include widespread use of fertilizers and insecticides, new tillage techniques, intensive capitalization, and government land-use planning. New conditions in the future may wipe out these precarious advances and revive questions about the staying power of Great Plains farming. Evidence exists for a long-term global warming trend that would increase desertification on the plains. Each period of drought between 1870 and 1940 has been more intensive and more widespread. In addition, growing concentrations of carbon dioxide (CO_2) in the upper atmosphere could intensify this drying trend. Using the model of a "greenhouse effect," climatologists have made computer runs predicting that a rise of three degrees Celsius in global temperature would turn the middle of the American continent into a true desert region, unable to sustain significant food production. Past misconceptions about the breadbasket of the world might be repeated.

Not until 1946 were the offices of land surveyor and registrar abolished. The land they were to survey and register had long since disappeared. The same act created the Bureau of Land Management in the Department of the Interior. It became responsible for 778 million acres of the public domain, none of which were classified as farmland. The government seemed to be out of the farmland sale business. But the government, said the president of the American Livestock Association, had "gobbled up" 24.5 million private acres in 1937–39 and was sniffing at 100 million more. In Janurary 1961 President John F. Kennedy's new interior secretary, Stewart Udall, withdrew 177 million acres (aside from Alaska's 300 million acres) of "unreserved public domain lands" for reclassification. In a step that would have astonished generations of Americans struggling to carve farmland out of wilderness since 1785, the 1964 Wilderness Act set aside fifty-four permanent areas "where the earth and its community of life are untrammeled by man, where man himself is a visitor who does not remain."[30]

Classification continued with the 1964 Public Land Law Review Commission; in comparison with the 1880 commission, it now had to review almost five thousand land laws still on the books and tens of thousands of policies and regulations. Reclassification was tied to multiple use and public sale; there must be irony in the authorization to sell tracts of land up to 5,120 acres but only to promote the orderly growth of western cities. A 1970 report, following the policy of "highest and best use," mixed with multiple use and with democratic "general public" use, proposed that the size of farms be controlled not by a federal authority, but locally.[31]

The report continued to take apart the survey tradition. Whenever the government sold land, it should charge the market price to discourage speculation. And the report seemed fated to urge once more the repeal of the Homestead Act and the Desert Lands Act. It also promoted no significant deterioration by holding public land users responsible for environmental damage. Arid lands acquired by the government in the 1930s were to be mantained at levels that would prevent future dust bowls.[32]

In 1977 the nation's pro-environment and anti-exploitation mood encouraged Congress to pass the Soil and Water Resources Conservation Act (RCA).[33] Already no significant deterioration had been legislated and tested in the courts.[34] The RCA was to appraise and regularly review the status of soil and water even though they were in private hands. Additionally, it was to develop means to safeguard and even improve these privately held resources. By 1979 the Carter administration admitted loggerhead conflicts between farm income programs, still intended to perpetuate the small farmer, and soil conservation planning, intended to regulate land use for environmental quality rather than profitable yield alone.[35] Farmers began to complain of government intrusion into their private property rights. The chairman of the House Agriculture Committee said RCA's strategy was "coercive." Land restoration should be "based on cooperating with and assisting landowners in their own voluntary efforts—not on trying to blackjack people into compliance." Property rights were to be sustained at almost any cost to the public interest.

The cycle of false prosperity around both world wars was repeated in 1972 with the large-scale sale of wheat to the Soviet Union. Great Plains farmers, who had paid heed to the admonitions of the Soil Conservation Service and had terraces, contours, shelterbelts, and rotation patterns in place, were now exhorted to plant all their lands "from fencerow to fencerow." By 1974, 24 million more acres were harvested.[36] Terraces, shelterbelts, rotation schedules, diversified crops, and other conservation plans came apart. More farmers turned to monoculture, planting only wheat, soybeans, or corn. Farmers were praised for their spectacular production and the boom in export sales. Their incomes rose satisfyingly, farmland values skyrocketed, farmers borrowed to buy quality land and sophisticated equipment, and American agriculture experienced a second golden age until the collapse in 1980.

One critical observer told the *New York Times* in October 1980,

"We've become like a third world country, mining our natural resources in order to pay for our imports."[37] The switch from saving the farmer to saving the soil was complete. Despite the nostalgia about the independent farm family that still fills the Sunday supplements of city newspapers, the image of Jefferson's virtuous and admirable yeoman farmer tilling the good earth is a broken myth. Instead of being praised for their heroics, farmers trying to make ends meet today are reviled as "sodbusters." Former USDA official Don Paarlberg said farmers were caught by surprise: "sometime during the early 1970s . . . we had lost control of the policy agenda."[38] Sodbuster bills against the apparently willful misuse of marginal land for speculative profit have worked their way through the legislative maze in 1982, 1983, 1984, and 1985, only to lose their way each time. But support of sodbusting penalties has built up in the 1980s. In one case 15,000 acres of eastern Colorado rangeland was plowed up in thirty-six hours, since nonirrigated cropland is worth twice as much as rangeland. In 1982 Weld County, also in eastern Colorado, began to require permits for plowups. When rangeland was plowed and planted in wheat in Petroleum County, Montana, the county created a series of strong regulations. South Dakota, with the most 1862-style homesteads of any state, passed a Blowing Dust and Fragile Lands Act to prevent sodbusting. Pending federal legislation would deny price supports, crop insurance, and other benefits to farmers who plow land known to be prone to erosion or other degradation. Such farmers would be "socially unacceptable." The new pro-land mood meant that for the first time in American history some farmers were condemned as abusers and not stewards of the land. Often yoked to federal sodbuster legislation are "conservation reserves" that would use tax dollars to pay farmers to retire vulnerable cropland—as much as 30 million acres—for up to fifteen years. A reserve would cost the government $40 an acre compared with today's typical $140 per acre for government subsidies.

Sodbusting legislation is a radical turnabout from previous American land laws. As Sara Ebenreck, a philosopher specializing in agricultural and land-use issues, observed, the primary objection is that punitive sodbusting laws go against the ideal of autonomous property ownership in America. Plowup people fall back on their "constitutional right" to do what they please with their land.[39] The complaint about public interference also covers most soil conservation legislation since the New Deal in the mid-1930s. Sodbuster legislation is usually justified, however, on the basis that society has the right, and even the duty, to protect land as the national food base. Contending rights, including those of the independent family farmer, are falling by the wayside. In April 1985 the *Wall Street Journal* reported that even with plowups, the independent farmer is going the way of the dinosaur, with "sweeping" and "abrupt change in land ownership."[40]

CHAPTER 11

"No Significant Deterioration" Farmland

"No significant deterioration." These words, almost casually set in the preamble to the 1970 Clean Air Act, caused a major brouhaha between government officials, smokestack industry spokesmen, and environmentalists that has not yet been laid to rest. Even if the air in a specific region is superior to the most rigid federal standards now in effect, ordered a federal judge in 1972, there can be no significant deterioration of its quality. The judge determined that the Clean Air Act created the duty not only to clean up ("enhance") polluted air, but also to maintain ("protect") the quality of existing clean air, even if it is already superior to the highest standards.[1]

"No significant deterioration." The phrase can also be applied to the third phase in federal treatment of western farmland during the accelerated changes in the twentieth century. Federal land policy first worked toward the speedy and undiscriminating turnover of public domain into private hands. This first phase lasted from 1785 well into the twentieth century. It was not officially terminated until the Taylor Grazing Act of 1934. The second phase, which overlaps the first, began during the Progressive Era. It was based on the realization that the public lands were finite and centered its attention on land classification. But it did not gain momentum until the creation of the Soil Conservation Service in 1935. The third phase has hardly begun: aggressive government action to protect prime farmland as a strategic national resource, at theoretical levels of no significant deterioration. The direction and success of this third phase are unclear.

There is almost universal agreement that conversion of prime farmland, a national resource, to nonfarm uses is undesirable. This is reflected in punitive erosion penalties included in the 1985 federal farm bill. An early version of Aldo Leopold's "land ethic" may be at work here: highly productive farmland, with its bountiful yields, is still regarded as a primary American asset.[2] In turn, those who practice farming are particularly virtuous. "It seems a sin to put all that fine cornland under the shopping center!" The independent, hardworking productive farmer is still also idealized as the "representative American." "Isn't it a tragedy to drive them off the land?"[3]

In the cutthroat world of economic survival, and the politics generated by economic survival, America's stupendous food production has far-reaching ramifications. It is a low-cost consumer resource. It is powerful leverage serving national and global self-interest. In recent years prime farmland has been reemphasized as the ultimate fallback resource for food production. This stands in sharp contrast to traditional government policy to expend farmland to shore up the independent farmer. As a result, American land policy commitments are being rapidly discarded. The massive subsidies anachronistically offered in the 1985 farm bill will in time taper off and put farmer and farmland at higher risk. Independent family farmers will no longer have government protection—virtually guaranteed since the 1930s—for the higher risks they take. This safety net is disappearing simultaneously with their decline in numbers from one in four Americans in 1935 to one in forty in 1985.

In addition, the walls of protection surrounding private farmland as representing absolute rights of private property are being dismantled. For more than a century, the debate has been whether society's "right" to control farmland for the common good invades landowners' freedom and right to profit. The question here is the "duty" of farmer and farmland (like water) to the public interest and its impact upon American traditions of property rights and individual freedom of action. Over the past two decades in particular, regulations controlling farmland are being put in place. Such controls will affect not only farmland but also, in ever-expanding circles, independent family farmers, their corporate equivalents, food production and prices, consumers' standard of living and quality of life, regional growth, national priorities, and international relations. The survey method of turning the frontier public lands into private hands, dating from 1785 and 1796, had its own debatable plan to regulate American development. Most policies new to the twentieth century repudiated survey policies. New farmland structures overlap or simply ignore the survey. In the broad sweep of American history, attention has shifted from how the farm family *gets* its farm to how it *keeps* its farm.

Pennsylvania Coal Company v. Mahon

In 1878 the Pennsylvania Coal Company sold off a parcel of its land but reserved the rights to an underground seam of coal. About 1920 a new owner, Mahon, whose name would become famous in the annals of property law, took the coal company to court to halt subsidence of the surface land and damage to his house. He claimed not only that his property was unlivable, but that subsidence had reduced its market value. The coal company was "taking" Mahon's property value. The case went to the United States Supreme Court, where *Pennsylvania Coal Company v. Mahon* became the first modern test of the "taking" of individual private property by outside interests. In time, the taking principle would involve government "police power" used to protect common or public good against private property interests. Justice Oliver Wendell Holmes admitted to an ambiguous middle ground between private property and public interest: "If regulation goes too far it will be recognized as a taking." But America's farmers did not own their land or its potential wealth unrestrictedly. Justice Louis D. Brandeis, in his opinion, stressed public interest: "Restriction imposed to protect the public health, safety or morals from dangers threatened is not a taking," even if "it deprives the owner of the only use to which the property can then be profitably put."[4] Using the arguments in *Mahon*, state and local courts allowed "taking" even when it substantially reduced the fair market value of property. The question remained, however, whether this violated the Fifth Amendment, which stated that no property can be taken for public use without just compensation.

Historically, the 1785 survey (and its modifications) made the government indifferent to the private cash value, or even any public "duty," of American farmland. But during the 1930s the federal government took special interest in farmland protection. Today in rural regions where farming is the dominant way of life, court decisions have generally supported keeping farmland as farmland. For example, agricultural "down zoning" took place in 1976 when 842 acres were reclassified by a court from residential to farm/forest. The court said this was not a taking because the land could be put to profitable/beneficial use for farming. But this direction invades the landowner's right to sell property freely to a developer at much higher prices. All Illinois court disallowed permanent farmland, since it bore "no real or substantial relation to the public health, safety, morals, comfort, or general welfare." A 1978 United States Supreme Court case argued simply that no private party, whether an individual or a corporation, was compelled to absorb the primary costs of preserving the public or common good. Contradictory court cases may mean that more clear-cut policy must come from legislation.

Intense pressure persists to make farm property into farmland waiting to be something else. Farm property tends to be treated as empty, "unused" land, with striking parallels to the original 1785 viewpoint toward the frontier public domain. Indeed, farmland has acquired a two-tiered price level: as farmland at below market cash value, and nonfarm use for shopping centers, suburban housing tracts, service stations, and highways, typically at several times farm value. The intrinsic economic value for farmland as farmland has its own rules set by soil quality, terrain, climate, water availability, access to transport and markets, geographical location, size and scale, and market demand as well as by competing investments, property tax rates, loan capacity, and long-term cropping potential. Farmland waiting to be developed carries a price based on proximity of encroaching development, access to public services like water and sanitation, population growth and mobility, topography and stability of soils, and whether development is commercial, industrial, or residential.

Tax Relief to Hold Land for Farming

Farmers have perennially complained that though food production has buttressed the common good, they have not received their fair share of resulting national prosperity. This debate about "parity" has rung through Congress and the Department of Agriculture since the benchmark years of 1909–14.[5] In fact, their lower than average standard of living, based in part on lower land values, meant that individual farmers subsidized the well-being of the rest of the nation. In this light it was argued that the best way to keep farmers working on their land was to give them tax relief. Maryland in 1956 and Florida in 1959 assessed productive farmland at lower agricultural rates even when surrounding land was being developed for nonfarm use bearing higher taxes. By 1969 eighteen more states followed suit. By 1980 tax relief had succeeded so well, and was so acceptable, that

only Georgia and Kansas had not granted farmers preferential assessment. This 1950s notion that farmland ought to be taxed according to
agricultural use and not highest (developed and subdivided) value is
part of the historical debate about the nation's duty to give preferential treatment to the American farmer. Opponents have complained
that preferential treatment, as always, is an indirect subsidy that is
paid in higher costs elsewhere. This is sometimes called the loss of
income by third parties.

As land-value differences build up, farmers feel extreme pressure
because they generally have few liquid assets. American farmers are
habitually land-rich and cash-poor. Their annual cash flow can be
very large, but very little stays in their hands—2 percent to 6 percent,
less than the interest on a government savings bond. They are traditionally more affected by property values than most Americans.
Taxes that would seem merely high to local homeowners become
impossible for farmers because of the acreage they require. Without differential protection, their per-acre annual land costs would be
higher than their per-acre income. Farmers sell off their land to pay
taxes or debts, not for agricultural or personal reasons.

Tax incentives have been adopted as the first line of defense for
high-yield prime farmland. Of the forty-eight states with some tax
relief, seventeen today also authorize *preferential assessment* of eligible farmland.[6] This usually means that land regularly under crops
is taxed on agricultural or "current use" value instead of "fair market
value." Wisconsin and Michigan also link tax levels to farm income.
Twenty-eight states tack on *deferred taxation* plans to preferential
assessment. If farm owners themselves in time convert the land to
nonfarm use, they must pay some or all of the deferred taxes. This
prevents preferential assessment, intended to save local agriculture,
from being used as a very beneficial investor's shelter until prices go
higher. Texas requires that the owner be an individual and not a corporation. Nebraska applies the tax break only to land zoned exclusively for agriculture. Other states require minimum farm income
per acre, a recognized history of regular farming, or a minimum term
for on-site family farming. Five states attach *restrictive agreements*
to tax breaks. These are enforceable agreements that farm owners
must keep their land in recognizable agricultural use. Six states
enforce special taxes if there is a land-use change, ranging as high
as 20 percent in Maine.

Tax breaks have definitely helped to hold prime farmland in production. Data from New York, New Jersey, Maryland, and North Carolina suggest that tax-induced sales have gone down significantly.[7] But as prices soar, when the shopping center or industrial park appears across the county road, tax incentives become less attractive. There are also many farmers who do not want to be locked into agricultural use alone. Tax reductions may only postpone briefly the transfer of working farmland away from agricultural use. In practice, tax reductions have today become part of a larger package of legislation and policies for the protection of farmland. One major drawback is tax revenues lost to the local municipality. There is no doubt that lower taxes for farmers create involuntary subsidies from other parts of the tax base. Nonfarm landowners justifiably complain of a tax-based "taking" of part of their property value and a loss of "equity." A taxpayers' rebellion might result, as in New York's Dutchess County in the 1970s, where residents argued that too much land stood protected in agricultural districts. Nonfarm taxpayers called for a moratorium to avoid further erosion of the property-tax base. In the great American tradition of land-law manipulation, some developers buy up farmland long before they need it, rent it out for farming, reap significantly lower taxes, and make high profits when the time is ripe for development.

Agricultural Districts

One farmland safekeeping method dates only from 1965, but it was anticipated by timberlands, irrigation districts, grazing districts, and soil conservation districts. In six states, beginning with California in 1965, farmland owners can now organize themselves into *agricultural districts* exclusively for farming. By 1980 districting protection was also available in New York, Virginia, Maryland, Illinois, and the Twin Cities area in Minnesota. New York's program is compulsory; land can be included within an agricultural district without the owner's agreement. The other programs are voluntary. New York's program, legislated in 1971, is also the most successful, with almost 6 million acres in agricultural districts, or about 60 percent of the state's farmland. There are 411 districts in the state, containing a total of approximately 17,500 farms, and the average acreage per district is about 14,500 acres.[8]

Agricultural districting sets important precedents because it measures and organizes land not according to political entities like counties, or along the survey geometry of townships and sections, but according to the agriculturally significant qualities and features of the land. New York authorizes agricultural districts of at least 2,000 acres, based not on owner initiative but on farmland identified as unique and irreplaceable. New York owners can also band together to petition for districting protection when faced by an immediate crisis. This is usually the threat of rapidly rising property taxes or the danger that eminent domain will be invoked for a superhighway, power plant, airport, or industrial park. New York's first district was formed in Schoharie County in response to plans for a reservoir with hydroelectric capacity. Virginia and Illinois require that a district include at least 500 acres with common borders. Land is evaluated by soil type, quality, and farm improvements, owners' commitment to profitable farming, land conservation patterns, and external factors like local development plans. Maryland's law, for example, accepts only land that is "outstanding in productivity" and is "of significant size." Most districts are created for eight to ten years with renewals.

One wonders how American society would have been reshaped had agricultural districting been established in 1785 instead of the cadastral survey and public auction. Jeffersonians would have been delighted, while Hamiltonian speculators would have been outraged. In states where districting is available, it identifies a geographical zone of active farmland and exercises comprehensive controls to preserve its status. According to the Department of Agriculture's 1981 National Agricultural Lands Study (NALS), agricultural districts give farmers preferential treatment because (1) market value is consistent with agricultural land use; (2) antifarming "nuisance" ordinances against smells, noise, and appearance are prohibited; (3) tax assessments for costly urban-scale utilities are prohibited; (4) nonfarm intrusions into productive farmland, such as highways, industrial sites, and public facilities, are limited; (5) nonfarm tax assessments are restricted; (6) nonfarm pollution of air, water, and land is restricted; (7) land speculation based on farm conversions is limited or eliminated.[9] Local governments approve districting reluctantly, since it limits the tax base for favored sewer, water, and road projects. Business and development interests oppose agricultural districts as archaic irrelevancies belonging to a preindustrial past; at best, ma-and-pa farms are due for supermarket takeovers.

But state legislators can be persuaded to look favorably on agricultural districting because there is little direct spending by the state for administration or land costs. As the controversy over farmland preservation has become a major issue, legislators have become newly sensitive to pro-farm or anti-farm special-interest groups. The Farm Bureau finds districting attractive because it protects against eminent domain takings and "overregulation" of agriculture by nonfarm special interests. Home builders' associations, municipal associations, and public utility companies in Illinois, for example, argue that agricultural districting limits their freedom of action, raises consumer prices, and dilutes their capacity to generate profits for shareholders. Beneficiaries also have duties: farmers protected by districting are supposed to be environmentally responsible. They are to use effective soil and water conservation management to preserve the agricultural value of the land, to minimize degradation, and to make appropriate improvements.

Agricultural districts are popular among farmers.[10] A 1977 New York survey of the attractions of districts evoked typical responses. One-third said they kept down taxes and assessments; 31 percent said districting prevented conversion to nonfarm uses; 11 percent reported the preservation of farmers' solidarity; 10 percent, interestingly enough, believed districting prevented excessive government interference in farmers' affairs through ordinances and regulation. In other reports, farmers in agricultural districts felt far safer in their ability to hold large tracts of land indefinitely, despite low cash liquidity and external nonfarm pressures. They felt insulated from the threat of the spread of superhighways, obnoxious landfills, reservoirs, recreation projects, and claims upon their land through eminent domain. They felt less helpless against outside power and wealth and more in control of their own destinies, and perhaps the destinies of future farm generations. In one New York case, when a taking project was defeated, the local county extension agent observed, "Without the agricultural districts framework to work around, and the support of the Agricultural Resources Commission . . . it would have been pretty difficult for individual farms to battle." Hard lobbying, local initiative, and participatory democracy have become the rule rather than the exception. The Livingston County agent commented that the district farmers are "not at all afraid to call their Congressman or write the Governor. . . . the different state agencies have gotten to the point that they respect the group."

Agricultural districting increased the opportunity for the farmers to make an adequate living in a more congenial political and economic setting than they had usually experienced during two hundred years of western expansion under the 1785 statute. However, there may be no ultimate protection from the lures of very high prices for alternative uses. Increased profitability from farming, conferred by tax relief, districting, and other protective measures, did delay selling off the family operation. But farming has so consistently been a low-profit operation that it may never be competitive with non-farming activity. At best agricultural districting can be an agent of delay. One New York official in the Department of Environmental Conservation recently concluded that "agricultural districts are not a preservation tool *per se*. They are just trying to make it more feasible to remain in farming." One author of the 1971 legislation reported that districts "help to facilitate the coexistence of farming and non-farming. They give farmers the option of continuing to farm if they want to. We'll make sure that they won't be taxed or regulated out of existence."[11] A state farm bureau advocate realistically concluded that the "developer may offer big money, but we can hope that it's not taxes or government regulations that will force the farmer to sell."[12] Agricultural districting appears best suited where speedy action is needed to preserve existing rural areas and where land costs have not begun to rise from urban pressures. It is also possible that agricultural districting is more successful in New York and other eastern states than in the survey regions of public domain states because eastern farmland is likely to be organized along agriculturally sound borders rather than by the gridiron survey system.

The Right to Farm

For most of American history, no one had to worry about "the right to farm." Well into the twentieth century, city dwellers had gardens, chickens, horses and stables, and even a family cow. In the country the primary objective of land laws, westward expansion, and national "manifest destiny" was to fill empty land with virtuous, hardworking, independent family farmers. But as twentieth-century city people moved into suburbs in established rural areas, they tried to shut down their farm neighbors through "nuisance ordinances." A working farm, no matter how modern, entails smells, noises, long working hours, dust, pesticides, and polluting animals and offensive equipment. Santa Cruz County in California requires that nonfarm owners, homeowners, or other residents be informed that they live in a protected agricultural preserve zone:

> This subdivision is adjacent to property utilized for agricultural purposes, and residents of the subdivision may be subject to inconvenience or discomfort arising from the use of agricultural chemicals, including herbicides, pesticides, and fertilizers; and from the pursuit of agricultural operations, including plowing, spraying, pruning and harvesting which occasionally generate dust, smoke, noise and odor. Santa Cruz County has established agriculture as a priority use on productive agricultural lands, and residents of adjacent property should be prepared to accept such inconvenience or discomfort from normal, necessary farm operations.[13]

The "impermanence syndrome" hit farmers on the outside edges of expanding metropolises; they were made to feel like the outsiders and interlopers. Nonfarming distractions were enough to lead to premature departure and sales of land at distressed prices. But nuisance ordinances were reversed, and "right-to-farm" laws now stand on the books of at least seventeen states. Beginning with New York's 1971 districting law, farming cannot be "unreasonably restricted," nor can farm buildings or farming practices be disallowed except for public health or safety. North Carolina's 1979 right-to-farm law aggressively defends traditional barnyard conditions:

> It is the declared policy of the State to conserve and protect and encourage the development and improvement of its agricultural land for the production of food and other agricultural products. When non-agricultural land uses extend into agricultural areas, agricultural operations often become the subject of nuisance suits. As a result, agricultural operations are sometimes forced to cease operations. Many others are discouraged from making investments in farm improvements. It is the purpose of this Article to reduce the loss to the State of its agricultural resources by limiting the circumstances under which agricultural operations may be deemed to be a nuisance.[14]

The statue goes on to speak eloquently about the virtues of farming for society's well-being.

Agricultural Zoning

Tax relief, agricultural districts, and right-to-farm laws are attempts to hold off costs and pressures when nonfarm development intrudes. They are indirect forces preventing conversion of farmland. *Agricultural zoning* has become the most common direct-action local initiative to save farmland. Between 1970 and 1980, 104 counties and 166 municipalities in twenty-three states turned to agricultural zoning to save farmland. But there may not yet be sufficient experience to demonstrate that agricultural zoning works. It has usually been part of a larger planned scheme by a state, county, city, or local community. And zoning programs are not all identical. Some are voluntary, as in Wisconsin. Others are mandated, as in Oregon. Most are custom-made to serve the interests and needs of local conditions.

Agricultural zoning may be the most important method of regulating the use of private land. It is also the most controversial, because it appears to interfere with the stout American tradition promoting independent property rights. Most agricultural zoning in the past was open-ended, often a catchall district, and easily allowed nonfarm exceptions, such as nonfarm "country homes." But most "new generation" zoning, such as in Washington Country, Wisconsin, specifies (1) aggressive protection of farmland; (2) prohibition of nonfarm disruptions of regular farming activity; (3) maintenance of public utilities on a "farm service" level only; (4) inducements to sustain food production despite its low profitability.[15] In addition, such protective zoning can also (1) put a freeze on overall land use patterns; (2) restrict nonfarm development to land unsuitable for crops and livestock (based on terrain, soil conditions, drainage and flooding, plant cover, and tract location and size); (3) recover land lost to erosion, misuse, or flooding; (4) guarantee "open space" needed for farm operations; (5) regulate "improvements" such as roads and utilities; (6) protect environmental resources such as clean water; and (7) reserve the best soil types for highest-quality food production.[16] "New generation" agricultural zoning intentionally works toward long-term protection. In the 1970s this received political and public support. As a result, Soil Conservation Service class I and II land, once zoned, is not being taken out of agricultural use. When protection controls have proved weak, local initiatives have often intervened to preserve large blocks of farmland.

Ineffective Protection Plans

Aside from zoning, right-to-farm laws, agricultural districts, and tax relief, there have been some spectacular failures. Traditionally, private ownership of farmland has included all interests and rights. But litigation and manipulation of farmland have often created separable interests and rights, such as preemption "floats" in Missouri or homestead "relinquishments" on the Great Plains. The perpetual struggle over water rights transformed western landholding. The *Mahon* case involved a company's reserved coal mining rights on private property. More recently, there have been attempts to encourage farmland preservation by separating and selling "development rights" apart from "agricultural use value." These purchase of development rights (PDRs) are comparable to the detachable coupons in today's "zero-coupon" bonds. And as with the initial low cost of zero-coupon bonds, after PDRs are sold, farmland descends to its fundamental agricultural use value and cannot be threatened by development. But no market has emerged in the eastern states—New York, Maryland, Massachusetts, New Jersey, and New Hampshire—where PDRs were developed.[17] Among the public domain states, only Washington has offered PDRs, in King County. When local governments have moved to save farmland by purchasing PDRs, the costs have been prohibitive, up to thousands of dollars an acre. The intent of the PDR is to allow local farmers to keep working their land but at the same time reap the cash benefits they would have received had they sold to developers. Cost alone can make the PDR plan unworkable.

Private Preservation Efforts

A private enterprise alternative has also attracted interest in these laissez-faire times. Instead of large-scale public intervention to protect private farmland, a number of private land trusts across the countryside have selectively targeted "crown jewel" farmland tracts under pressure to convert to nonfarm use. As nonprofit organizations they solicit contributions, generate private grants, and in some cases receive public funds to make loans to threatened farmers, or under emergency conditions they step in to buy farmland away from developers. These land trusts follow the highly successful tactics established by the nationwide Nature Conservancy, or by regional groups like the Western Pennsylvania Conservancy, for private acquisition of wilderness or natural sites, which are then given to state and local governments. The American Farmland Trust and the American Land Resource Association are nationwide. Local groups include the Mesa County (Colorado) Land Conservancy, the Montana Land Reliance, the (San Francisco) Trust for Public Land, the Lancaster (Pennsylvania) Agricultural Preserve Board, and the statewide Massachusetts Farmland and Conservation Trust.[18] A 1984 "case no. A-7100" of the American Farmland Trust (AFT) tells contributors about the 1,200-acre Williams family ranch in Colorado, with class III and IV soil. According to the report:

> The Blue River Valley in Colorado is ideal for cattle ranching. The combination of irrigated valley hayfield and mountain summer pastureland has made this an important agricultural area for many generations. In fact, AFT already holds a 3,500 acre conservation easement nearby. The Williams family has recently been approached by developers of a ski resort. Mr. Williams grew up on this ranch, which has for generations been a cow-calf operation—raising and breeding cattle. He and his wife have to put their life-savings into this ranch. They've had some rough years, but they have made a go of the ranch, and want to continue this traditional way of ranching. They want to stay on the land and hope their neighbors remain ranchers . . . not skiers.

By the end of 1984 AFT had acquired an agricultural conservation easement for the Williams's "crown jewel" farm.[19] Another American Farmland Trust case reports on the 114-acre Zendor farm in Michigan, growing corn and alfalfa on class II soil.

> This Michigan widow wants to *give us* her family farm. Working alongside her husband, Mrs. Zendor produced corn and alfalfa for silage on this farm. The Zendors have no heirs, but they both felt very strong about keeping this farm in production. . . . she doesn't want to sell the farm for development. She'd rather give it to AFT so we can find a farmer who will keep the land in production.[20]

The Reagan administration's ideological drive to shrink the role of government in agriculture and land management has already stimulated private farmland trusts and conservancies to try alternative strategies. In 1981 there were five hundred trusts with 250,000 members in control of 675,000 acres, an increase in number of trusts by 40 percent since Reagan took office.[21] Affluent individual conservationists have been urged to buy land, set stringent development restrictions, and then resell it. In New York's Catskills, an older region with few agricultural zoning laws, already invaded by developers, Laurence Rockefeller acquired 4,000 acres for restricted resale. The Beaverkill Conservancy bought up 5,000 acres with similar limits. Resale losses could be made up in tax benefits. In eastern Pennsylvania, the nonprofit Brandywine Conservancy took advantage of liberal limited partnership incentives to acquire 5,300 acres of the old King ranch as quickly as the land went on sale. Brandywine sets limits of one house for each 33 acres, restricts pesticide use on farmland, and bans plowing within 100 feet of creeks, yet the tracts were sold immediately. But a Conservancy officer muses, "After time passes, there are going to be people who will want to forget about the restrictions, and do whatever they please with their land." Unlike a national park, there are no rangers to prevent abuses.

The most effective farmland preservation still appears to come through the soil and water conservation districts, set up fifty years ago in the Department of Agriculture. In a 1979 survey, 775 of the 2,950 districts reported action to prevent loss of farmland to metropolitan development. But while the districts have long promoted farmland conservancy techniques, they are public entities and must avoid politically sensitive activity.

State and Regional Farmland Protection

California's 1965 Williamson Act gave local city and county governments the right to form restrictive "agricultural preserves" under ten-year renewable contracts with local landowners. Originally, only prime class I or II farmland in active production was included, measured by physical characteristics and market value of agricultural production. Each acre had to generate $200 annually, based on a complicated test.[22] In an important step, each city or county had to develop a comprehensive local land-use plan with means of enforcement. Benefits include tax breaks and protection from utility "public improvements" or eminent domain takings. The state committed funds to cover a part of lost local taxes and administrative costs. Recently state costs averaged $12 million a year. By 1980 over 16 million acres were under Williamson Act contracts, with 5 million acres defined as prime farmland. Within fifteen years 40 percent of California's eligible prime land had been included. About a million acres were considered under development jeopardy. Half of the state's land under direct threat is still not covered. Critics blame this lack of coverage on the voluntary nature of the act.[23]

In Wisconsin, from 1977 to 1982, farm owners could contract directly with the state to receive state income tax credits if they kept their lands in agricultural use. After October 1982 such benefits were tied to local town or county agricultural preservation programs or zoning for agriculture. According to Wisconsin's Farmland Preservation Program, each county seeking state benefits is required to appoint a technical advisory group to map, plan, and identify qualifying farms. A minimum 35-acre tract is measured by soil type, current and future productivity, and appropriate management practices. Most counties do not just measure farm operations on cultivated land with high-quality soil, but treat each property as an entire economic unit, akin to the classic family farm. Buildings and inhabitants must be substantially connected with on-site agricultural activities.

Before the 1977 act, only four Wisconsin counties had enacted agricultural zoning. By March 1980, after twenty-seven months of the act, more than four-fifths of the state's farmland was under the program. One reason for extensive acceptance was strong local participation in defining eligibility, based on minimum size, farm profits, soil quality, and inclusion of complete farm units. Complaints about the loss of control over private property—that planning and zoning were unacceptable infringements on property rights—came from only two counties, Clark and Wood, rural regions in the middle of the state. One Wisconsin official observed that "once the farmers began to receive their rebates, all debate over private property rights stopped. . . . Farmers no longer care to debate the land use implications of the bill. All they want us to do is to help them fill out the income tax rebate form."[24] In 1979 Wisconsin spent $1.33 an acre to protect its best farmland. The state has 10.8 million acres of class I and class II land. A protection program to include all this land would cost between $7 and $10 an acre.

Mandatory farmland preservation still goes against farmer individualism, the dominant American tradition of free enterprise, and the total autonomy of property owner. Voluntary programs do not force participation. This encourages political peace but leaves large tracts of prime farmland unprotected. Seventeen states have strictly voluntary programs. Twenty-eight have deferred tax programs. Only two states compel binding agreements prohibiting nonfarm development. Only four states have costly PDR programs, and these are small, measuring at the most $5 million a year. Political liability is also reduced by sending land-use planning down to the local township or county level. But California's Williamson Act demonstrates significant weaknesses in voluntary programs. Only 50 percent of California's prime land is enrolled in scattered patterns of protection. When farmland has high development potential, landowners are reluctant to limit their options. Wisconsin attempted to avoid scattered preserves by disallowing tax credits in its second post-1982 phase unless local governments establish agricultural zoning or preservation plans. As a result protected farmland acreage in Wisconsin matched that in California in a third of the time, twenty years since 1965 in California and eight years since 1977 in Wisconsin.

With its limited size and unusual conditions, the state of Hawaii has since 1961 had the strictest and most comprehensive land-management plan in the United States. It is like looking into America's future. Since Hawaii has only four counties, power is centralized at the state level. The state provides for education, welfare, health, and housing instead of leaving them to local governments. Agricultural preservation was an important factor in the 1961 Land Use Law because of the primary importance of the sugar and pineapple industries (these have since been surpassed by tourism). Large corporate farmland owners strongly supported the legislation, to keep farmland at low cost levels against the increasing intrusions of powerful and wealthy land speculators. In addition, the 1961 law sought comprehensive land-use management to limit urbanization and protect the "Hawaiian way of life."

With a 1963 amendment, all land in Hawaii was classified into urban, conservation, rural, and agricultural districts. Of agricultural districts it was said that "the greatest possible protection shall be given to those lands with a high capacity for intense cultivation."[25] But USDA Soil Conservation Service soil classifications were not part of the criteria. Standards for farmland, or for reclassification to nonfarm use, were not established. By 1975, facing growing criticism that the Hawaii Land Use Commission had been releasing too much land for development, the state legislature attempted to set specific criteria.

The effectiveness of Hawaii's 1961 land-use law is debatable, since in the first twenty-three years more than three-quarters of all petitions for nonfarm use were granted. There were even housing developments called "agricultural subdivisions." The urban district grew by 30,000 acres, or 25 percent, including some of Oahu's most fertile land. But in general the Land Use Law led to more compact urban growth and less chaotic and extensive development of farmland.

The Department of Agriculture's 1981 report, the National Agricultural Lands Study, called Oregon's Land Use Act of 1973 "a system of planning and regulation which is more comprehensive and more tightly integrated than any other in the United States."[26] Oregon made working or workable farmland its highest priority. Local zoning is the foundation of a larger integrated comprehensive program.

A 1973 Oregon law set up the Land Conservation and Development Commission, responsible for planning and managing statewide, city, county, and special agricultural districts. Agricultural land receives highest priority for preservation, since it is "environmentally sensitive." The Land Use Act of 1973 treated agriculture as a total economic and human entity, combining farmer, farming, and farmland. Farming is defined as an important societal activity deserving protection and tax incentives. Priority is given to fostering the conditions needed for economically successful farming.

Other key features of the act include decentralized local planning and zoning, a court system weighted in favor of farmland preservation, and a powerful independent lobby, 1,000 Friends of Oregon. Oregon's policies are clearly and intentionally tilted in favor of agricultural land protection and farming as a way of life. According to statute, "Agricultural lands shall be preserved and maintained for farm use consistent with existing and future needs for agricultural products, forest and open space. These lands shall be inventoried and preserved by adopting exclusive farm use zones."[27] All class I–IV soils not already in nonfarm use must be zoned "exclusive farm use." State policy argues:

> Open land for agricultural use is an efficient means of conserving natural resources that constitute an important physical, social, aesthetic, and economic asset to all the people of this state. . . . The preservation of a maximum amount of the limited supply of agricultural land is necessary to the conservation of the state's economic resources and the preservation of such land in large blocks is necessary in maintaining the agricultural economy of the state and for the assurance of adequate, healthful and nutritious food for the people of the state and nation.[28]

Oregon policy is also expressed on the threat of nonfarm development:

> Expansion of urban development into rural areas is a matter of public concern because of unnecessary increases in costs of community services, conflicts between farm and urban activities and the loss of open space and natural beauty around urban centers. . . . Exclusive farm use zoning . . . substantially limits alternatives to the use of rural land . . . and justifies incentives and privileges offered to encourage owners of rural lands to hold such lands in exclusive farm use zones.[29]

A key feature is the "Urban Growth Boundary," which locates and separates land vulnerable to development ("urbanizable") from long-term farmland. The Boundary draws a line around urban fringes and identifies agricultural lands. This separates markets for urban land from markets for farmland, instead of the usual commingling and confusion. In Yamhill County in the Willamette Valley, Oregon, over 90 percent of class I–IV lands are in Exclusive Farm Use Zones. In 1980 almost 12 million acres of private land came under this zoning, about two-thirds of all potential Exclusive Farm Use lands.[30]

By the summer of 1985, among states first organized according to the survey, Colorado defeated a bill for a statewide agricultural land conservation program, but Nebraska amended its constitution to guarantee that farmland will be taxed on its agricultural value rather than "highest and best use." Minnesota funded seven more pilot farmland preservation programs patterned on the Twin Cities metropolitan model. Illinois added teeth to its 1982 Farmland Preservation Act. Among eastern landmark states, New York now has 9.2 million acres covered by agricultural preservation districts, second only to California's 15 million acres, while Wisconsin runs third with 5.7 million acres. Maryland continues to experiment with PDRs, now covering 29,000 acres; Massachusetts has preserved 13,500 acres with PDRs.[31]

Prospects

The preservation of high-quality, productive farmland—and the independent family farmer—is at a crossroads.[32] Evidently the traditional American way of voluntary participation is not effective often enough. But compulsory land reform implies the undemocratic picture of a peasant population receiving confiscated land as a handout from a dictatorial central government. Compulsory zoning and districting, with their new and unsettling implications, have emerged as consistently successful modes of protection. But even mandatory programs still depend upon political realism. They become workable only if there is a strong local consensus on the importance of protecting farmland and farmers.

Voluntary programs have usually failed because individual farmers refuse to relinquish their independence. This encourages a self-defeating fragmentation and eventual failure. In addition, when some farmland is withheld voluntarily, the surrounding tracts, available for development, become scarce and premium-priced, thus penalizing (and tempting) the volunteers. Although mandatory programs may appear undemocratic and militate against free choice, all farmland owners are treated equally. All have the same burden of limited options, offset by tax reductions and other benefits. Paradoxically, mandatory programs cannot succeed without widespread grass-roots political support. Most obligatory programs accept built-in limits, often set by the standards of the Soil Conservation Service. In addition, most regulations contain political safety valves to cover valid opposition, changing economic and development conditions, and even the right to break contracts if penalties are accepted.

Effective farmland protection in the current political climate and before the end of the twentieth century requires

> restrictions on private ownership;
> least cost to the public;
> use of private nonprofit conservancies;
> use of local standards and management;
> protection of equity for all parties;
> long-term quasi-permanent restrictions;
> a public "land ethic."

Less clear is the continued role of the two historical actors in American farmland development

> "big government" financing and regulation;
> "small farmer" ability to prosper (or survive) on protected lands.

Continued attempts to create an agricultural structure that would make protected farmland a benefit instead of a liability include leveraged real estate transfers, a revival of farmland-only preemption, combinations of development rights, conservation easements and deed restrictions, and co-opting of Soil and Water Conservation Districts. Attention has also been called to land freezes and land banks in Canada, as well as France's SAFER or preemption program.[33]

According to a 1980 Louis Harris poll for the USDA, almost two-thirds of the public is more committed to "the owner's right to do what he wants to with his property" than to "the public's right to make sure that the best farmland is used only for producing food." This is on a collision course with the willingness of Carter's Democratic presidency (on ideological grounds) and Reagan's Republican administration (on grounds of cost effectiveness) to use police power for regulation.

Historical evidence suggests that mandatory conservation has its limits. In the long run no farmland protection program can overcome the pressure of extremely high prices. Long-term preservation, much less permanent protection, is still unlikely under either voluntary or mandatory plans. America's prime farmland still depends upon a strong public awareness and powerful political resolve.

CHAPTER 12

Treated like Dirt: The Future of America's Farmers and Farmland

Agricultural output is becoming less a function of natural factors and more a function of the degree to which cost-effective technology is utilized. High land values today no longer mean farm prosperity; rather, like expensive machinery or chemicals, they just mean high production costs.

Dennis Avery, agricultural specialist with the State Department

If you let the market do it, we'll keep destroying the soil until we run out of food. . . . The public ought to pay a farmer to take care of his soil.

James B. Gilliford, State of Iowa conservation official

The mid-1980s were the best of times. Food production on the American soil had not leveled off as experts feared but had continued to soar. The record 1.8 billion bushels of wheat in 1978 was unexpectedly topped by 1981's 2.8 billion bushels, compared with 1.1 billion in 1949.[1] The Malthusian Armageddon was once again shunted into the distant future.

They were also the worst of times. Another decade of fence-to-fence farming made soil erosion and depletion worse than the 1930s. Ironically, because of large scale and long-term surpluses, total net farm income, in constant dollars, hit its lowest levels since 1933. Income per farm was the lowest in twenty years, and 13 percent interest rates on borrowing drove many farmers into unacceptable debt.[2]

The Best of Times

Americans do not comprehend what a benevolent standard of living has been created for them as ordinary natural resources—water and land—are transformed into food. Today Europeans spend up to 50 percent of their income on food while Americans spend less than 20 percent. In 1800 it took 5 acres of cropland and 250 hours of labor to produce 100 bushels of wheat. In 1985, 100 bushels needed only 3 acres and 4 hours of work. The reason has been the industrial revolution down on the farm, including the mechanization of work, chemical fertilizers and pest control, scientifically evolved strains of efficient foods, irrigation technologies, and industrial management. As a result, fewer than 3 percent of American workers produce enough food to comfortably supply the nation at low cost, with very large surpluses in storage or sent overseas.[3] Prime farmland across the midwestern and western food belt is so productive and exists in such excess that it is treated as the nation's limitless resource—America's ultimate safety valve. Experts at the Center for Agricultural and Rural Development at Iowa State University and at the Washington-based Resources for the Future reported in 1982 that American farmland, used at current levels, was more than sufficient to serve national food needs and global export levels for the indefinite future.[4] For example, of 61 million irrigated acres, only 32 million were essential to meet the nation's needs in the year 2000.

Not only is there a very large surplus of cropland, but more is available "on demand," since former cropland that has reverted to forest or pasture (in Pennsylvania and other formerly agricultural eastern states) can be put back into production within a year. This rapid recovery might not be possible if it required the return of the traditional resident farmer, but it is easily within the management skills of large enterprise. In addition, "new" cropland can be created with irrigation, mechanization, new crops, deforestation, and other efficiencies. Even with existing farmland being converted to urban development at the rate of 100,000 acres a year, food supplies will not be jeopardized, and the level of surpluses can be easily maintained. A worst-case projection by Sandra S. Batie and Robert G. Healy in the February 1983 *Scientific American* reports a 22-million-acre loss by the year 2000, but more than a 150-million-acre reserve.[5] The Department of Agriculture estimates that the United States has 540 million acres of arable land. Since 1920 cropland in actual production has run no more than 390 million acres. During the banner years, 1950 to 1970, output doubled while cropland in actual production declined from 380 to 325 million acres.[6] Americans have a large farmland cushion based on exceptional per-acre productivity, large surpluses, and unused acreage. Future technological breakthroughs are likely, including a doubling of irrigation efficiency and development of drought-resistant, salt-tolerant plants. The picture is historically so rosy that the American public has judged that much farmland has no intrinsic value but exists simply as "farmland waiting to be something else."

The Worst of Times

A more cautious view is presented by, among others, Lester R. Brown of the Worldwatch Institute. In a November 1981 article in *Science,* he reports that the loss of momentum since the remarkable two decades between 1950 and 1970 has created food insecurity and greater pressures on the world's cropland.[7] The surpluses and prosperity of the 1950s and 1960s were rare and are unlikely to be repeated. Since then the balance between production and need has been unexpectedly threatened by the 1970 corn blight, massive Soviet wheat purchases beginning in 1972, the energy crisis since 1973, semipermanent drought across Africa and Asia in the 1970s and 1980s, and the accelerated degradation of good and marginal farmland around the globe. At one point in 1980 the world had less than a forty-day food reserve, the lowest since World War II. Worldwide grain production per person, which had climbed 14 percent in the 1950s, rose only 5 percent in the 1970s. In Africa in the 1970s, per-capita grain production declined 14 percent, the first such case since World War II.

Batie and Healy agreed with Brown about the loss of momentum and pointed to growing global risk as water, energy, erosion, and technological innovation costs go up.[8] Farmland will get less bang for the bucks. As a result, crises caused by droughts or blights or similar threats cannot be met as readily by new crops or cheap water. Nor can farmland weakened by erosion be continually revived by fertilizers or mechanization. The American public may look back upon 1950–70 as the age of cheap and abundant food, just as farmers looked back nostalgically to the good old days between 1900 and 1920. At issue is the twentieth century's intensive consumption of prime farmland.

Farm Policy Has Not Kept up with Change

Government policy toward farmland and farmers did not change significantly over the fifty years between 1935 and 1985.[9] Even though the experts, politicians, and farmers acknowledged the shift to agribusiness, federal policy treated American agriculture as if it still depended largely upon the family farmer. The 1985 farm bill still sought to compensate American farmers for their chronically low annual income owing to food surpluses, and contrarily, to encourage high food production to guarantee the American public abundant food at low prices.

But though policy did not change significantly over fifty years, American agriculture changed dramatically. The changes were manifold and startling. Farmland, for example, lost its central place in American agriculture. The independent, self-sufficient farm family is losing its protected status as "primary farming" moves elsewhere. American preeminence in food production is eroding as revolutionary changes sweep Third World agriculture. Farm policy itself turns, more often than not, on "externalities"—consumer needs, foreign policy, and deficit spending. The result is the abandonment of the small landed farmer who, it was claimed, was the object of federal farm policy for two hundred years. The result is also indifference to disappearing farmland, since there is so much of it. However, in an era of little pressure to produce food at capacity, American agricultural policy has an extremely opportune "window" to improve the chances of both farmers and farmland.

The Disappearing Small Landed Farmer

But in the process the vaunted independent American farmers are also disappearing from the center of agricultural policy. Their very productivity has drastically reduced their numbers and simultaneously dissolved the once-invincible farm lobby.[10] The government rescue that began during the Great Depression and established such a successful "safety net" that farmers prospered until the 1970s, may not be repeatable. National priorities have been shifting almost imperceptibly yet decisively toward sustained food production and farmland preservation and away from small farmers. The inefficiencies of independent farmers, their lack of staying power in hard times, and the decline of their political influence make them the first object of sacrifice.

In large part, the divergence between saving farmers and saving farmland has been created by economic cross-purposes. Today's farmers, tied tightly to credit and prices, need high yields from their land to keep themselves afloat. It is almost impossible to plan ahead, much less set aside cash, for more than a year or two. Farmers must have enough income from their remaining land before they indulge in long-term conservation. Less-productive field rotation and summer fallowing are forgotten under today's conditions of low prices and high interest payments. In addition, tenant farmers, "suitcase" farmers who live in nearby towns, speculators, and other absentees treat the land as a short-term profit base. Iowa's Department of Soil Conservation director James B. Gilliford insists, "If you let the market do it, we'll keep destroying the soil until we run out of food."[11] Another disincentive for conservation by local resident farmers comes from their capacity to compensate for the decline in soil quality through efficient machinery, higher-yield crops, and greater use of fertilizer and pesticides. There always seems to be another profitable technological fix around the corner. Gilliford concludes that "the public ought to pay a farmer to take care of his soil." American agriculture has its own Scylla and Charybdis: independent farmers have been encouraged by the USDA to be the most productive ever in human history; the USDA thus finds it necessary to reduce production by paying farmers (in cash or cash-equivalent grains) not to grow crops on large parts of their acreage.

Today's Policy Trend Contradicts Historical Patterns

For most of its two hundred years, land policy had one stated objective: to locate American citizens on their privately owned tracts of farmland. Here they could apply commonplace skills to building homes and working the land. These independent farmers had a safe haven from risks because they owned the land they lived on. Their private property was to make them self-sufficient enough to weather most temporary crises, man-made or natural. In a large number of cases, the system succeeded. American farmers were idealized not only for their proud independence but also for their resilience under adversity.[12] And it was universally believed that whatever befell them, personal ownership of land would always carry them through to better times.

It was recognized that the farmers who over time edged onto the western frontier of settlement would have a particularly hard time and deserved privileged status. Then, after settlement had covered most arable land, American farmers were to live in a widely admired golden age of prosperity. In large degree this utopianism came true between 1900 and 1920. Today's concept of parity is still measured by this era. But while the rest of the nation continued to grow in the 1920s, farmers entered a time of chronically low prices for their crops, and the global depression of the 1930s drove them to collapse. Radical farm support programs created in the 1930s were justified by the farmers' importance to national well-being. Controversial economic planning was often wrapped in the flag. Farmers must not fall so deeply into debt as to lose their land or the American dream would be lost. Government farm programs over the past fifty years centered on keeping resident farmers in safe ownership of their land. Even today it is not this stated policy that has come under severe criticism but its soaring cost, from $1 billion in 1980, $15 billion in 1985, and $30 billion in 1986.

Farming: A Perennial Decentralized "Cottage Industry"?

Land policies in the past made American farming into a "cottage industry" by stressing private ownership, living on the property, and owner operation. This is more the creation of public laws and policies since 1785 than the inherent superiority of the independent property owning farm family. The midwestern integrated farm communities that centered on German immigrant groups, for example, have endured longer and more successfully. Many other agricultural styles might have worked more effectively than the small family farm had they been given equal opportunity.

This autonomous cottage farming is failing across the nation, despite the herculean efforts and investments made to save it over the past fifty years. Historical momentum leads toward large-scale centralized operations, familiarly known as agribusiness. This shift toward industrialization of farming can be compared to the demise of "ma-and-pa" neighborhood grocery shops after World War II and the move toward supermarkets across the nation. Or parallels can be drawn with the early steel industry, which at first depended upon locally produced iron "pigs" but rapidly moved toward centralized and integrated factory mills. The same was true of textiles in England in the eighteenth century, where the term "cottage industry" first appeared.

An argument in favor of cottage industry has made some headway. Americans have a vast surplus of farmland. Even without the benefits of new engineering, fertilizers, pesticides, and equipment, the nation could produce enough food at a lower yield per acre. Well-managed, low-technology farms using limited fertilizer and pesticide and borrowing little (thus with little or no debt) might be sufficient to feed the nation and allow for some export. This is the argument advanced by advocates of "organic farming" and "sustainable agriculture." But the sustainability argument often describes an ideal farm style that would indefinitely benefit land, farmer, and consumer simultaneously. This view is based on Frederick Clement's theory of ecological "climax" (i.e., organic farming on a small scale is ecologically the best) and its "stasis," which has been effectively criticized by Henry Cowles's contrary claim that constant dynamic change is a sign of a healthy ecosystem.[13] Aside from inherent problems in cottage farming, American agriculture has been deeply and probably irrevocably committed to a scientific, industrial, and government infrastructure in which low prices and high production have the highest priority. Despite more than fifty years of experience, government policy has yet to balance farmland use and farmers' employment against food production and acceptable prices.

As noted in an earlier chapter, agriculture is at best a high-risk operation. The impact of bad climate can never be entirely eliminated. Insect infestations cannot be completely controlled. New threats from monoculture blights like the corn failure in the 1970s, and the increased rate of soil erosion where row crops dominate, add to farmers' vulnerability. Chronic price fluctuations are only partly buffered by commodity supports, and the uncertainty of future government price supports itself creates additional uncertainty for farmers. When cottage farming is not treated in an isolated manner, but is compared with the larger economy, it loses much of its appeal. The large resources of industrial operations are required to carry agriculture through bad times.

The traditional policy answer to agricultural risk has been to spread the harm into wider circles of government and society. Hence the taxpayer has been asked to keep the farmer from economic collapse. Another answer is to admit that American agriculture cannot remain a cottage enterprise in a high-risk industry. Despite rhetoric to the opposite, today the low-capital cottage farmer is disappearing from the food-production economy. The important distinction is that food production can be protected from excessive risk, but autonomous family farming cannot.

Triage: Saving Only the "Primary Farmer"

Unless some dramatic rescue appears from an unexpected source, the prospect for the family farm is dismal for the rest of the 1980s and into the 1990s. Government policies, virtually unchanged in 1985, continue to funnel funds toward large-scale profitable operations, and in the process they hasten abandonment of the mid-size and small operator. In 1980 the USDA identified its "primary farm" as having over $40,000 in gross sales. These 575,000 farms have efficiencies of scale that produce almost 80 percent of total farm output although they make up less than 20 percent of all farms. As J. B. Penn notes, "These farms will most likely influence the effectiveness of the commodity programs as now structured, and they will be the largest beneficiaries of the program benefits."[14] The largest type of primary farm is the cash grain farm producing almost three-quarters of all wheat, corn, and soybeans. On this basis only 115,000 farms, identified as large enough and situated in appropriate geographical settings, have a crucial strategic status. Primary wheat farmers average 800 acres harvested. Primary corn and soybean farmers average 430 acres. Primary wheat farmers do best in Kansas and North Dakota, and corn and soybean farmers fare best in Illinois and Iowa. Successful primary farming is mostly in grain, which produces more than 80 percent of sales for farms grossing over $40,000. When prices were at their highest in 1974, primary cash grain farms averaged a return of approximately 20 percent on income and equity. In 1979 a wheat or barley farmer would do best in the northern plains on 1,500 acres with gross sales of $105,000. A corn or soybean farmer would do best in the corn belt on 640 acres grossing $145,000.

In a 1985 case study, an Iowa corn farmer who farmed 800 acres had a total investment of $516,000 with a $189,000 debt. After harvest he netted $24,100 from 200 acres of corn, $8,800 in corn subsidy, $5,180 from 185 acres in soybeans, and $2,400 for cattle on 200 acres of grazing land, for a total net agricultural income of $40,480. If he had had an average corn yield of 95 bushels an acre instead of the bumper crop of 150 and no government subsidy, his net loss on his corn acreage would have been $5,300 with total net farm income reduced to $26,380.[15]

Government policy is now directed toward these primary farmers at least until 1990. Totally discounted are "rural farm residences"—44 percent of all farms—with sales of less than $5,000. "Small farms"—34 percent of all farms—grossing $5,000 to $40,000, have been largely bypassed by federal funding policies. If present trends continue, the failure of the small independent farmer will take place on a massive scale by 1990. In light of low grain prices and high surpluses, much farmland will be on the market at attractively low prices. This will lead to a cheap buy-up by investors and industries with deep pockets. A onetime opportunity would also exist for government agencies and private conservancies to intervene to create large farmland reserves.

The "Window of Opportunity" before 2000

American agriculture in the 1980s is working at half-capacity. Technology continues to expand the carrying capacity of American farmland. Wheat, corn, and soybean production in 1985 surpassed supposedly impenetrable "natural limits" set by agricultural experts as recently as 1980. It was expected that all of America's prime, average, and marginal farmland would be under high productivity stress by 1985, but land is still not the limiting factor.[16] Nevertheless, human ingenuity cannot entirely remove limits on a nation's biological support system. Although chemical fertilizers have effectively compensated for the loss of soil nutrients, soil structure deteriorates under the extreme pressures of long-term row farming, with few remedies. The land becomes more expensive to work both mechanically and chemically.[17]

The 1990s ought to see the end of the chronic surpluses that have long depressed farmland values and discouraged conservation strategies.[18] American food production is likely to come into greater demand globally, causing domestic consumer food prices to rise. Pessimistic estimates made for 1980 may simply be delayed a decade: 0 percent domestic productivity growth, with 8 percent annual world demand and 1 percent domestic demand, would raise real prices received by farmers between 1 and 3 percent a year, compared with the 1–2 percent annual average decline since World War II. The value of prime American farmland may go higher than ever, both in productivity and in cash value.

The crisis expected by 1980 did not materialize. But the move toward crisis management of farmland taught a classic lesson in the fragility of America's farmland base that should not be comfortably cast aside. Conservative predictions about world population growth by A.D. 2000, together with a worldwide pace of soil erosion that far surpasses that in the 1930s and inherent limits on crop per acre, should encourage highest priority planning for future farmland use. Before American farmland feels this pressure in the 1990s, American society has an unexpected "window of opportunity" for farmland management. If the traditional "duty" of American farmland is high productivity of cheap and abundant food for the consumer, then another priority must be land preservation. The opportunity rests in the difference between land realistically needed for today's food production goals and the nation's bounty of surplus good farmland.[19] Almost 50 million acres of cropland were idled in the United States during the late 1960s and early 1970s, but the "sales quota" mentality returned the land to production between 1974 and 1977. Even in 1980 as many as 65 million acres, one-quarter of the nation's farmland resource base, was held out of production to keep American and world agricultural supply and demand in approximate balance.[20] The Reagan administration's free market ideology, which idled no land in 1981 and 1982, was upset by the collapse of the farm economy in 1983, resulting in the largest and most expensive idling in American history—over 70 million acres. 1980 estimates concluded that another 65 million acres, half the resource base, could have been held out without profoundly affecting either domestic or foreign markets. Five years later, in 1985, farmland came under less pressure as foreign demand continued to fall while per-acre domestic productivity rose.

The "window of opportunity" could avoid future global crisis. When drought hit the North American grain belt in 1983 it meant a reduction in surpluses and a rise in food prices. But under heavier pressures, as early as the 1990s a grain-belt drought could translate into widespread hunger and the threat of global famine. Without grain and farmland reserves, could the United States intervene with

food aid where famine threatened, as it did following monsoon failures in India in 1964 and 1965, when the nation allocated almost
20 percent of its wheat crop for two successive years?[21] But without
enforceable guidelines about farmland quality, 17 million acres of
marginal land are needlessly in crops today. This land is eroding so
rapidly that it should be entirely withdrawn from production.[22] Its
crop capacity is virtually exhausted. It is beyond cost-effective support from more fertilizer or no-till farming.[23] In the past, policy has
encouraged land consumption instead of preservation.

American farmland is no longer a simple, safe haven that will protect the resident farm family from all conceivable threats. Nor has the
family farmer been the representative American since the turn of the
century. Historical land-use priorities—to keep independent farmers
on their privately owned tracts, which they personally worked—are
often at war with contemporary policies intended to guarantee abundant food at low prices and provide cheap surpluses for international
leverage and the trade balance. Farmers and farmland are integrated
into a complex large-scale economic structure. The issues are also
complicated by different and contrary policies about farmland and
farmers. Is the central issue "food policy," as the Department of
Agriculture insists, or "farmer policy," as Congress instinctively
argues, or the high-production "agricultural policy" demanded by
agribusiness, or "farmland preservation" as piously claimed by conservationists and environmentalists? Americans have historically
used farmland to create private property, cheap and abundant food,
and the virtuous independent farmer. But all of these are on a collision course. All of them have invested too much in both the mythical
symbol and the hard-cash value of good land as a safe national haven.
American farmland policy has a long history of misplaced concrete-
ness, outdated response, and contradictory interests that ignore new
farmland "uses."

The Prevailing Frontier Ethic

American farmland policy is still closely connected to the patriotic pieties of frontier individualism and Manifest Destiny. Congressional rhetoric still reflects the lasting public faith in the independent farmer, who remains a persistent national hero. Federal

protection of farmland is still tied to a Lockean land-improvement ethic of private property, reminding Americans of the hard times of clearing the wilderness and carving out a homestead. But the revolutionary change in agriculture over the past fifty years may no longer require private ownership, on-site residency, and the fabled (and flawed) owner-operated farm. Their past ability to produce an abundance of cheap food for the nation gave farmers high status and preferential treatment in American society. But if high productivity is a final objective of national policy, it is being achieved largely without the survival of traditional independent farming. The enduring value Americans have long attached to homesteading by the owner-farmer may have become irrelevant.

It is hard to shake off the mystique of private landownership and of residency and operation by farmers. But the sacred and bountiful land plays a diminished role in both food production and American farm life. Compared with its earlier preeminence, today farmland is but one factor among many, including fertilizers and pesticides, genetic engineering, the efficiencies of costly equipment, bank credit, government policies, and international markets. In an earlier day, farmers' capacity to prosper on the land was reminiscent of primitive subsistence agriculture, tied more to basic farming skills and tools, muscle power, and hard work than to ready cash and borrowing power. Self-sufficiency was traded long ago for total integration into national and worldwide economies. Today high productivity is essential, but the self-sufficient autonomy of farmers and their land has long since disappeared. No longer does the two-hundred-year-old tradition prevail; citizens are not secure on their personal tracts of land.

In a contradictory turn of events, even as American farmland became less significant for crop production, it became the farmer's "land of many uses." Farmland became the foundation for loan equity, the measure for government subsidies and tax breaks, the ultimate source of ready cash, and offered staying power for the heavily leveraged modern farmer. Historically the cash value of farmland did not affect daily or seasonal operations. It was treated as a neutral or "free" entity, to be excluded from the fickle marketplace. But today farmland is treated as a multilayered capital and debt resource that must be regularly managed to serve the owner's needs on the marketplace.[24]

The Ethics of Modern American Agricultural Policy

Government farm policy for the past fifty years has been defined
primarily as an ethical question: it was the moral "duty" of the nation
to save its independent farmers because of their historical service to
the nation. By analogy, they were veterans of extended "farm wars"
who deserved respect and benevolence. The farm policy ethic was
summed up in 1980 by USDA economist John E. Lee:

> Many of the USDA's current major programs had their roots in the
> twenties and thirties, when there were over 6 million farms, mostly
> small and mostly poor. Agriculture was considered "disadvantaged"
> relative to much of society. Farmers were considered high-risk borrow-
> ers, so capital was limited and expensive. Overproduction, depressed
> prices, and depressed incomes appeared chronic. Except in wartime a
> plentiful food supply was not a major policy concern. Thus, policies
> were initiated to address the perceived problems: to make credit avail-
> able at competitive or low costs, to reduce the inherent risk in farming
> through crop insurance and price stabilization, and to enhance income
> through price supports and other means.[25]

Congressional debates over the 1981 and 1985 farm bills translated
this moral duty into a "fairness doctrine." According to this ethic,
since the marketplace has not provided the farmer with sufficient
rewards, he needs federal assistance to guarantee his rightful share
of national prosperity. In addition, it was widely taken on faith that
farming involved not only a material standard of living but also
an entire way of life. The rhetoric of farm bill debates in Congress
demonstrates that Americans believe their traditional and perhaps
unique agricultural way of life cannot be surrendered without some
undefinable societal loss. As is true in most cases of government
policy, the real issue is a matter of ethics and values, often defined
by powerful lobbies.

A second moral issue centers on the "land ethic" doctrine. This
is more than the seemingly esoteric but hotly debated environmental question, "Do trees have [intrinsic] rights?" The greatest environmental pressure today upon any American natural resource is
on farmland. The ethical question focuses upon soil depletion as a
result of intensive monoculture production and extreme erosion.
Soil depletion involves the loss of "soil health" and subsequent
poor harvests. A realistic agricultural "land ethic" is not a romantic

preservationism wishing to return farmland to its prehuman natural state. Instead, it is a real-world "sustainability doctrine" using natural, technological, societal, and economically practical means to guarantee (and even upgrade) the "health" of American farmland by balancing food production with soil-quality maintenance. The checkered history of the Soil Conservation Service over the past fifty years is a history of the agricultural land ethic.

A third moral imperative—plentiful food—is based on a long-term global perspective. It also includes a painful immediacy—tens of millions of people today experience the specter of starvation, which is more than the failure of markets and distribution. The question is not only food supplies for the people of the Sahel or Bangladesh, but also the world food picture by A.D. 2000 or 2020. Although Cassandra-like doomsaying has been discounted—the full-land-use scenario made in 1980 did not materialize—even the most hopeful predictions expect extreme pressure on food supply in less than a generation. A "food security doctrine" would overwhelm the fairness doctrine or the land ethic doctrine.[26] Farmers, for example, might have difficulty protecting their traditional interests. The debate between ethical doctrines would be considerable. According to the USDA's 1980 analysis, "A goal of adequate food supplies may be given higher priority than assuring equitable distribution of economic benefits . . . [or instead] the progress in equity could be judged by the body politic to be worth the cost of reduced assurance of adequate food supplies."[27]

Under a food-security doctrine, farmland would be treated less as autonomous private property than as a national strategic resource with its own unique "public utility" status. Yet investment capital from the private sector would be needed for intensive/extensive development of farmland. This would require competitive economic returns on land both as private property and as a renewable productive resource. The conflict between the attractiveness of farming as an occupation and farmland as a business investment would not disappear under a food-security doctrine. What might be reduced is managerial freedom for both the independent farmer and agribusiness industry. Little is left today of an open commodity market, but this might be further diminished. Policy would require extensive controls over the farmland real estate market; some regulations are already in place with farmland districting and agricultural zoning. Farmland would receive more intensive regulation and management

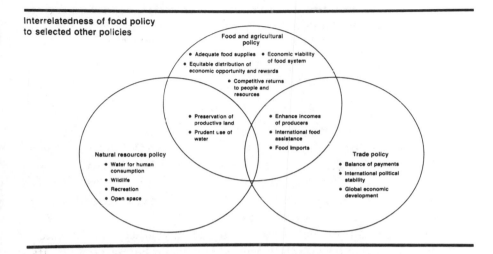

Fig. 21. Interrelatedness of food policy to selected other policies. From "Food and Agricultural Policy: A Suggested Approach," by John E. Lee, in *Agricultural–Food Policy Review: Perspectives for the 1980's* (Washington, D.C.: U.S. Department of Agriculture AFPR-4, 1981).

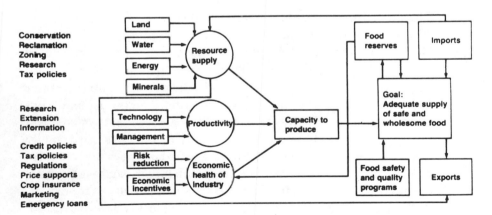

Fig. 22. Program linkages to the goal of food security. From Lee, *Agricultural–Food Policy Review*, USDA, 1981.

as a strategic resource needing physical protection, conservation of quality, and efficient productivity.

1980 *Agricultural–Food Policy Review*

Other than during World War I and World War II, a plentiful food supply has not been a major American policy concern. A "deliberate food policy," however, was examined in the 1980 USDA background documentation for the 1981 congressional farm bill.[28] If food production took priority, it would require new allocation of resources. A land ethic doctrine would be essential not as an end in itself, but to secure land and water resources to provide food for generations to come. Agricultural technology development would not be dedicated to efficiency and profitability alone but would be measured by its contribution to the environmental quality, to effective farm institutions, and to nutritional objectives. Consumers would be encouraged to balance their food consumption—less meat and more grains—to protect natural resources. Links to foreign trade and foreign policy not only would include the types of surpluses available—wheat, soybeans, corn—but would also factor in the domestic cost of excessive exports—soil erosion of the resource base.

Learning Lessons from OPEC

The United States should treat itself as the OPEC of the world's food. Although the international food picture has improved, it is still the United States that has consistently produced very large surpluses of grains available for foreign trade, to correct regional losses, and for humanitarian service. Americans have always taken pride in their technological mastery, industrial production, and cornucopia of consumer goods. For decades the United States was the equivalent of an OPEC of steel and industrial goods. This dominance has faded rapidly over the past quarter-century. In a turnaround that is not yet completely understood, the United States began to ship overseas a natural resource—food—for a far larger dollar value than any other export. And this primary export is based on the simplest and most direct of all the raw materials a sovereign nation possesses—land, water, and climate. Nor have these connections been properly assessed.

America's domination of global grain surpluses raises fears that the rest of the world might be held hostage to its economic and political interests. The United States is more powerful than OPEC has ever been in its potential monopoly of a far more essential resource.[29] American (and Canadian) wheat feeds the world. American grain supports much of the world's milk, meat, and eggs. Between 1950 and 1980 exports from the heartland grew fivefold, from 23 million metric tons to more than 130 million, based less on increased acreage than on higher per-acre productivity. Today this dominance is symbolized by American soybean production, which is over 60 percent of the world's total and two-thirds of soybean export. Yet soybean acreage was marginal in the 1950s and grew eightfold between 1960 and 1980.

Dependence upon the Middle American Grassland

The world has an "unhealthy dependence" upon the North American breadbasket for basic staples such as wheat, corn, and soybeans.[30] Ranging north and south across the middle third of the United States and into Canada, this grassland turned monoculture is vulnerable, since, as Brown notes, "the United States and Canada are affected by the same climatic cycles and . . . heavy dependence on any two countries for grain gives these governments extraordinary political power.[31] As the plains enter higher-risk conditions, projected food production will become more vulnerable in the immediate future. The accelerated disappearance of the independent farm family from the grassland has yet-unknown ramifications. The preceding chapters on the farming of arid and semiarid regions, mistaken assessments of farming conditions, patterns of settlement and removal, and boomer farming among other invasions have made the grassland a classic case of mismanagement and inefficiency. Yet despite these disadvantages, the region is a global breadbasket.

But excessive global dependence on the food production of the American heartland could be disastrous. The region is burdened with a risky climate tending more toward drought than sufficient rainfall for wheat or corn or soybeans. Insect infestations have periodically created havoc. New factors include increased blight or insect risk as fencerow-to-fencerow monoculture holds sway, as in the corn blight of the early 1970s. Wheat surpluses are under pressure as production declines with the falling water levels of the Ogallala aquifer, the only significant regional irrigation resource. Climatologists look with apprehension to the expected increase in global temperature owing to the carbon dioxide "greenhouse effect." The American Midwest might be profoundly affected early in the twenty-first century and reduced to a desert region. Miscalculated USDA actions in 1983 also combined human intervention and global climate: government policy encouraged the idling of large acreages which, together with an unexpectedly severe drought, changed the predicted worldwide grain surplus into a potential deficit. Record idled acreage in 1972 also contributed to global food shortages in 1974. The new United States acquired a prime farmland region in the 1803 Louisiana Purchase and turned it into the breadbasket of the world; but the days of the bountiful American heartland may be numbered.

In addition, as Americans become aware of land and water as precious national resources, they may be less willing to exploit them at current levels. Lester Brown wrote in 1984,

> Countries that rely on North American food should take heed of the philosophical debate emerging within the United States about the wisdom of mining the nation's soils to meet the ever-growing world demand. . . . Some argue that it makes little sense to sacrifice a resource that has been a source of economic strength since colonial days merely to buy a few billion barrels of oil. . . . the current generation of farmers has no right to engage in the agronomic equivalent of deficit financing, mortgaging the future of generations to come.[32]

Food Was Never Cheap

Not only is farming a high-risk venture for the nation, it is also costly. Prices for wheat, corn, and soybeans are only apparently low. Indirect but real costs must be factored in. When many resources—land, labor, capital, government subsidies and planning, borrowing from future generations, and scientific, technological, and industrial investment—are entered into the equation, the result is disequilibrium. Based on new economic inputs devised as a result of the energy crisis since 1973, it is clear, for example, that the total units of energy applied to agriculture do not return an equivalent amount but present a significant net loss. American farming is not the resource base to subsidize other nonfarming arenas of national life. In the light of energy exchanges, the nation's intensive high-technology food production is not a surplus. However, Americans may be willing to accept this negative feedback loss because of the convenience it affords, the foreign policy leverage it creates, and even its ability to keep the independent farmer's life-style afloat. On the other hand, it provides neither sustainability nor equilibrium. In particular, the consumer reaps great benefits from the current disequilibrium while the farmer has been severely penalized. For a time the rise in farmland prices carried the farmer toward equilibrium. For fifty years the American taxpayer has covered some of the disequilibrium through farm-support programs. Policy has also encouraged more extreme disequilibrium by farmland and water exploitation, which will reduce future productive capacity and environmental quality. The cost of using resources needs to be internalized in higher prices. Using the criteria of equilibrium reached through economies of scale, government policy today measures its success by its service to the "primary farmer."[33] But there is little connection between this primary farmer and the self-sufficient family farmer the ordinance of 1785 claimed to serve.

Notes

Preface

1. See the conclusions reached in Lester R. Brown, *State of the World 1984* (New York: W. W. Norton, 1984), p. 181.

2. See Patrick M. O'Brien, "Global Prospects for Agriculture," in *Agricultural–Food Policy Review: Perspectives for the 1980's* (Washington, D.C.: USDA, ESS AFPR-4, 1981), pp. 3, 13–14, 19.

3. Milton H. Ericksen et al., "Commodity Programs and Policies," in *Agricultural–Food Policy Review*, p. 109.

4. O'Brien, "Global Prospects," p. 19.

5. J. B. Penn, "The Changing Farm Sector and Future Public Policy: An Economic Perspective," in *Agricultural–Food Policy Review*, pp. 31–32.

6. See John E. Lee, "Food and Agricultural Policy: A Suggested Approach," in *Agricultural–Food Policy Review*, pp. 136 ff.

7. See *Agricultural Statistics 1984* (Washington, D.C.: USDA, 1985), pp. 4–5; compare with O'Brien, "Global Prospects," p. 14.

8. Austin S. Fox and Kenneth C. Clayton, "Agriculture's Production Potential," in *Agricultural–Food Policy Review*, pp. 70 ff.

Introduction

1. See the excellent discussion in Hildegard Binder Johnson, *Order upon the Land: The U.S. Rectangular Land Survey and the Upper Mississippi Country* (New York: Oxford University Press, 1976), pp. 170–78; see also N. J. Thrower, *Original Survey and Land Subdivision* (Chicago, 1966), pp. 98–99.

2. Quoted in Johnson, *Order upon the Land*, p. 128.

3. Johnson, *Order upon the Land*, p. 4; see also pp. 28 ff. and 119 ff.

4. Johnson, *Order upon the Land*, p. 231.

5. See N. T. Newton, *Design on the Land: The Development of Landscape Architecture* (Cambridge: MIT Press, 1973), pp. 210–17 and passim.

6. Roy M. Robbins, *Our Landed Heritage: The Public Domain, 1776–1970*, 2d ed. (Lincoln: University of Nebraska Press, 1976), p. 28.

7. Quoted in Johnson, *Order upon the Land*, p. 151.

8. Johnson, *Order upon the Land*, p. 151.

Chapter 1

1. See the discussion in Hildegard Binder Johnson, *Order upon the Land: The U.S. Rectangular Land Survey and the Upper Mississippi Country* (New York: Oxford University Press, 1976), pp. 21–24.

2. This subject is the central theme in Peter S. Onuf, *The Origins of the Federal Republic: Jurisdictional Controversies in the United States, 1775–1787* (Philadelphia: University of Pennsylvania Press, 1983); see also Jack N. Rakove, *The Beginnings of National Politics: An Interpretive History of the Continental Congress* (New York: Alfred A. Knopf, 1979), and Gordon Wood, *The Creation of the American Republic, 1776–1787* (Chapel Hill: University of North Carolina Press, 1969).

3. *U.S. v. Perchman*, 7 Peters 61 (1834).

4. Merrill Jensen, "The Creation of the National Domain," *Journal of American History* 26 (1939): 323–42.

5. See Ray H. Billington, *Westward Expansion*, 4th ed. (New York: Macmillan, 1974), pp. 197–201; Paul W. Gates, *History of Public Land Law Development* (Washington, D.C.: Public Land Law Review Commission, 1968); see particularly chap. 3, "State Cessions of Western Land Claims," pp. 49–58.

6. Gates, *History of Public Land Law*, p. 57.

7. Onuf, *Origins of the Federal Republic*, pp. 15, 33, 190–200, 207.

8. E. J. Ferguson, *The Power of the Purse: A History of American Public Finance, 1776–1790* (Chapel Hill: University of North Carolina Press, 1961); Forrest McDonald, *The Formation of the American Republic, 1776–1790* (Baltimore: Penguin Books, 1965), pp. 51–52.

9. Lewis C. Gray, *History of Agriculture in the Southern United States before 1860*, reprint ed. (Gloucester, Mass.: Peter Smith, 1958), 2:626.

10. Quoted in Gates, *History of Public Land Law*, pp. 69–70.

11. Archer B. Hulbert, "Washington's 'Tour of the Ohio' and Articles of 'The Mississippi Company,' " *Ohio Archeological and Historical Quarterly* 17 (October 1908): 431–88; Charles H. Ambler, *George Washington and the West* (Chapel Hill: University of North Carolina Press, 1936); Roy B. Cook, *Washington's Western Lands* (Strausburg Va.: Shenandoah, 1930).

12. A. M. Sakolski, *The Great American Land Bubble: The Amazing Story of Land-Grabbing, Speculations, and Booms from Colonial Days to the Present Time* (New York: Harper, 1932), p. 48.

13. Thomas P. Abernethy, *Western Lands and the American Revolution* (New York: Appleton-Century, 1937); John Bakeless, *Daniel Boone* (New York: William Morrow, 1939); William S. Lester, *The Transylvania Colony* (Spencer, Ind.: S. R. Guard, 1935); Robert L. Kincaid, *The Wilderness Road*, reprint ed. (Middlesboro, Ky., 1973; originally published 1957).

14. Jack M. Sosin, *Whitehall and the Wilderness* (Lincoln: University of Nebraska Press, 1961); see also Sosin's "The Yorke-Camden Opinion and American Land Speculators," *Pennsylvania Magazine of History and Biography* 85 (January 1961): 38–49. Alfred P. James, *The Ohio Company* (Pittsburgh: University of Pittsburgh Press, 1959); Shaw Livermore, *Early*

American Land Companies (New York: Oxford University Press, 1939); Wood, *Creation of the American Republic,* pp. 344–89; and Frederick Jackson Turner, "Western State-Making in the Revolutionary Era," *American Historical Review* 1 (1895–96): 70–87, 251–69.

15. Richard B. Morris, *Studies in the History of American Law, with Special Reference to the Seventeenth and Eighteenth Centuries* (New York: Columbia University Press, 1930), pp. 73–125; Gray, *History of Agriculture in the Southern United States,* 2:618–20.

16. Useful summaries of colonial land policies include A. C. Ford, *Colonial Precedents of Our National Land System as It Existed in 1800,* Bulletin 352 (Madison: University of Wisconsin, 1910); Marshall D. Harris, *Origin of the Land Tenure System in the United States* (Ames: Iowa State University Press, 1953); see also J. Franklin Jameson's chapter "The Revolution and the Land" in his 1926 *The American Revolution Considered as a Social Revolution,* reprint ed. (Boston: Beacon Press, 1956), pp. 27–46; Abernethy, *Western Lands and the American Revolution:* and Henry Tatter, "State and Federal Land Policy during the Confederation Period," *Agricultural History* 9 (1935): 176–86.

17. See Billington, *Westward Expansion,* pp. 53, 54, 56, 57, 59, 60, 92–94.

18. John R. Stilgoe, *Common Landscape of America* (New Haven: Yale University Press, 1982), p. 77.

19. James T. Lemon, *The Best Poor Man's Country* (Baltimore: Johns Hopkins University Press, 1972), pp. 42–70.

20. See Billington, *Westward Expansion,* pp. 94–101.

21. Stilgoe, *Common Landscape,* pp. 43–99; Douglas R. McManis, *Colonial New England: A Historical Geography* (New York: Oxford University Press, 1975), pp. 46–72.

22. See Stilgoe, *Common Landscape,* pp. 100–104.

23. Stilgoe, *Common Landscape,* pp. 100–101.

24. Payson Jackson Treat, "Origin of the National Land System under the Confederation," in *American Historical Association Annual Report for 1905* (New York: American Historical Association, 1905), 1:231–39: Johnson, *Order upon the Land,* pp. 42–46; Gates, *History of Public Land Laws,* pp. 61–67; Stilgoe, *Common Landscape,* pp. 99–107; Ford, *Colonial Precedents;* and the observations in Vernon Carstensen's introduction to his edited collection of essays, *The Public Lands: Studies in the History of the Public Domain* (Madison: University of Wisconsin Press, 1963); J. B. Jackson, "The Order of a Landscape," in *The Interpretation of Ordinary Landscapes,* ed. D. W. Meinig (New York: Oxford University Press, 1979), pp. 153–63.

25. Quoted in Gates, *History of Public Land Laws,* p. 62.

26. Johnson, *Order upon the Land,* p. 43.

27. Johnson, *Order upon the Land,* p. 39; Gates, *History of Public Land Laws,* p. 62.

28. Quoted in Gates, *History of Public Land Laws,* p. 64.

29. *Journals of Congress,* 20 May 1785, pp. 118–21.

30. Quoted in Gates, *History of Public Land Laws,* p. 66.

31. Quoted in Malcolm J. Rohrbough, *The Land Office Business: The Settlement and Administration of American Public Lands, 1789–1837* (New York: Oxford University Press, 1968), p. 10.

32. McDonald, *Formation of the American Republic*, pp. 164–65.

33. McDonald, *Formation of the American Republic*, pp. 166–75.

34. *Journals of Congress*, July 1787, 32:334–43, 33:399–401.

35. McDonald, *Formation of the American Republic*, pp. 206–7.

Chapter 2

1. Quoted in Clinton Rossiter, *Seedtime of the Republic* (New York: Harcourt, Brace, 1953), p. 254.

2. Quoted in Rossiter, *Seedtime*, p. 275.

3. This self-righteous profiteering was hardly restricted to Virginia. See Forrest McDonald's review of rampant Connecticut speculation in *The Formation of the American Republic, 1776–1790* (Baltimore: Penguin Books, 1965), pp. 107 ff.

4. See the discussion in William B. Scott, *In Pursuit of Happiness: American Conceptions of Property from the Seventeenth to the Twentieth Century* (Bloomington: Indiana University Press, 1977), pp. 6–7.

5. Quoted in Rossiter, *Seedtime*, p. 72.

6. Quoted in Rossiter, *Seedtime*, p. 78.

7. Quoted in Rossiter, *Seedtime*, p. 78.

8. See the excellent discussion in Eugene C. Hargrove, "Anglo-American Land Use Attitudes," *Environmental Ethics* 2, no. 2 (Summer 1980):125–48.

9. Thomas Jefferson, "A Summary View of the Rights of British America," in *The Portable Thomas Jefferson*, ed. Merrill D. Peterson (New York: Viking Press, 1975), p. 133.

10. Quoted in Scott, *Pursuit of Happiness*, p. 37.

11. Quoted in Scott, *Pursuit of Happiness*, p. 38.

12. J. Franklin Jameson, *The American Revolution Considered as a Social Movement*, reprinted ed. (Boston: Beacon Press, 1965; originally published 1926), pp. 34–35.

13. Quoted in Scott, *Pursuit of Happiness*, p. 41.

14. Scott, *Pursuit of Happiness*, pp. 44–49.

15. Seven colonies (New Hampshire, Rhode Island, New York, New Jersey, Virginia, North Carolina, Georgia) made landholding the absolute requirement, the famous "forty-shilling freehold." But the standards varied widely. South Carolina required "a freehold at least of fifty acres of land, or a town lot" or equivalent. Maryland set qualifications at "real or personal property above the value of five hundred pounds current money." Massachusetts asked for "a freehold estate" with a liberal "annual income of three pounds, or any estate of the value of sixty pounds." In Pennsylvania, anyone who had wealth enough to pay taxes owned the franchise. Other colonies accepted alternatives to owning land, such as the personal property

of a city merchant or the payment of taxes by a Massachusetts fisherman. But virtue lay in the land. Governor William Berkeley in Virginia was instructed in 1676: "You shall take care that the members of the assembly be elected only by *freeholders*, as being more aggreeable to the custom of England, to which you are nigh as conveniently you can to conform yourself," Quoted in Rossiter, *Seedtime*, p. 19; see also pp. 425–29, 447.

16. See Scott, *Pursuit of Happiness*, p. 42.

17. Quoted in Hargrove, "Anglo-American Land Use Attitudes," p. 140; see also Scott, *Pursuit of Happiness*, pp. 39–40.

18. The word *land*, without further elaboration, appears in the Constitution only in article 3, on judicial powers, where final government jurisdiction had been traded away from the Senate to the Supreme Court during the Constitutional Convention.

19. *Journals of the Continental Congress, 1774–1789*, Vol. 19 (1912), 214–22.

20. The first paragraph of section 3 provides for the the admission of new states, none of which are to be carved out of existing states. Reading between the lines, these new states would have to be created from undeveloped federal territory. Lack of originality in 1787 is also shown by the 1781 Articles of Confederation article 9 declaration that "no state shall be deprived of territory for the benefit of the United States," inserted by Robert Henry Lee to protect state claims west of the Appalachians. But in new states carved out of the Northwest Territory, the ordinance of 1787 kept the territorial lands in federal hands.

21. *Journals of Congress*, May 1785, p. 118; italics mine.

22. *Journals of Congress*, July 1787, p. 91.

23. But Hildegard Binder Johnson, *Order upon the Land* (New York: Oxford University Press, 1979), p. 48, disagrees: "When the first Congress under the Constitution assembled in March 1789, the Ordinance of 1785 was allowed to lapse and with it land legislation," and the survey and sale legislation was reestablished in 1796.

24. *Journals of Congress*, June 1787, pp. 85–93.

25. John Locke, *First Treatise of Government*, in *Two Treatises of Government*, ed. Peter Laslett, ix.92 (New York: Mentor Books, 1965), p. 247.

26. See for example, Marcus Cunliffe, *The Right to Property: A Theme in American History* (Leicester: Leicester University Press, 1974); see also Ralph H. Gabriel, *The Course of American Democratic Thought* (New York: Ronald Press, 1956).

27. Henry Steele Commager, *The Empire of Reason: How Europe Imagined and America Realized the Enlightenment* (New York: Anchor/Doubleday, 1977).

28. James Harrington, *The Oceana and Other Works* (London: T. Becket et al., 1791), pp. 94–103, passim (author's copy); Scott, *Pursuit of Happiness*, pp. 24–30.

29. Lawrence Meir Friedman, *American Law* (New York: W. W. Norton, 1930).

30. Scott, *Pursuit of Happiness*, pp. 30–35.

31. Thomas Jefferson, *Notes on the State of Virginia,* in *Portable Thomas Jefferson,* ed. Peterson, p. 217.

32. Scott, *Pursuit of Happiness,* pp. 34–35.

33. Quoted in Scott, *Pursuit of Happiness,* p. 36.

Chapter 3

1. Quoted in Malcolm J. Rohrbough, *The Land Office Business: The Settlement and Administration of American Public Lands, 1789–1937* (New York: Oxford University Press, 1968), p. 14.

2. Murray Benedict, *Farm Policies in the United States, 1790–1950* (New York: Twentieth Century Fund, 1953), p. 3.

3. Quoted in Beverley W. Bond, Jr., "The Foundations of Ohio," in *The History of the State of Ohio,* ed. Carl F. Wittke (Columbus: Ohio Historical Society, 1941), 1:349–95.

4. Quoted in Rohrbough, *Land Office Business,* p. 17.

5. *Annals of Congress,* 4th Cong., 1st sess., 5:411; see also p. 339.

6. Quoted in Rohrbough, *Land Office Business,* p. 18.

7. Quoted in Eugene C. Hargrove, "Anglo-American Land Use Attitudes," *Environmental Ethics* 2, no. 2 (Summer 1980):140.

8. Jefferson to James Madison, 28 October 1785, in *The Portable Thomas Jefferson,* ed. Merrill D. Peterson (New York: Viking Press, 1975), p. 397.

9. The following discussion is indebted to the excellent analysis in Rohrbough, *Land Office Business,* pp. 17–25.

10. *American State Papers, Public Lands,* 3:459; Paul W. Gates, *History of Public Land Law Development* (Washington, D.C.: Public Land Law Commission, 1968), pp. 121–22; Albion M. Dyer, *First Ownership of Ohio Lands* (Boston: New England Historic Genealogical Society, 1911), pp. 53–57.

11. Summaries based on data in Gates, *History of Public Land Law,* p. 128.

12. William D. Pattison, "Beginnings of the American Rectangular Survey System, 1784–1800" (Ph.D. diss., University of Chicago, 1957), pp. 200–204.

13. See Randolph C. Downes, *Frontier Ohio* (Columbus: Ohio Historical Society, 1935), pp. 74–78, 116–17; see also *Annals of Congress,* 6th Cong., 1 April 1800, pp. 210, 652.

14. See the statistics gathered by Gates, *History of Public Land Law,* pp. 132–34.

15. See the statistical tables collected in Gates, *History of Public Land Law,* pp. 132–34.

16. See Edith McCall, "Upheaval on the Mississippi," *American History Illustrated,* October 1984, pp. 18–21.

17. See the assessment of local newspaper accounts and land office records in Rohrbough, *Land Office Business,* pp. 106–7.

18. Quoted in Rohrbough, *Land Office Business*, p. 132.

19. Morris Birkbeck, *Notes on a Journey in America from the Coasts of Virginia to the Territory of Illinois* (Philadelphia: M. Carey, 1819), pp. 25–26.

20. Quoted in Rohrbough, *Land Office Business*, p. 90.

21. See the excellent discussion in Rohrbough, *Land Office Business*, pp. 137–79.

22. Quoted in Rohrbough, *Land Office Business*, pp. 141–42.

23. Gates, *History of Public Land Law*, pp. 141–43.

24. Payson Jackson Treat, *The National Land System, 1785–1820* (New York, 1910), pp. 144 ff.; Rohrbough, *Land Office Business*, p. 156.

Chapter 4

1. *New York Times*, 4 November 1984.

2. "Anecdotes of Major Daniel Ashby," in *Glimpses of the Past*, publication no. 8 (Columbia: Missouri Historical Society, 1941), p. 105.

3. Quoted in Malcolm J. Rohrbough, *The Land Office Business: The Settlement and Administration of American Public Lands, 1789–1837* (New York: Oxford University Press, 1968), p. 15.

4. W. H. Smith, ed., *Papers of Arthur St. Clair* (Cincinnati: R. Clarke, 1882), 2:3; see also John D. Barnhart, *Valley of Democracy: The Frontier versus the Plantation in the Ohio Valley, 1775–1818* (Lincoln: University of Nebraska Press, 1953), pp. 128–31.

5. *Annals of Congress*, 12th Cong., part 1, p. 1031.

6. Quoted in Rohrbough, *Land Office Business*, p. 93.

7. James Daniel Richardson, ed., *A Compilation of Messages and Papers of the Presidents* (New York: Bureau of International Literature, n.d.), 1:572.

8. C. E. Carter, ed., *Territorial Papers of the United States*, 19 January 1816, 8:373–74.

9. Achille Murat, *A Moral and Political Sketch of North America* (London, 1833), p. 62.

10. Quoted in Roy M. Robbins, *Our Landed Heritage: The Public Domain, 1776–1970*, 2d ed. (Lincoln: University of Nebraska Press, 1976), p. 66.

11. Quoted in Rohrbough, *Land Office Business*, pp. 92–93.

12. See particularly Gordon T. Chappell, "John Coffee: Surveyor and Land Agent," *Alabama Review* 14 (1961): 180–95, 243–50.

13. The standard history is Rohrbough, *Land Office Business*.

14. Robbins, *Our Landed Heritage*, pp. 60, 62.

15. Paul W. Gates, *History of Public Land Law Development* (Washington, D.C.: Public Land Law Commission, 1968), pp. 167–69.

16. Quoted in Charles R. Tuttle, *An Illustrated History of the State of Iowa* (Chicago, 1876), pp. 102–3; see also Gates, *History of Public Land Law*, pp. 157–60.

17. George C. Duffield, "An Iowa Settler's Homestead," *Annals of Iowa*, 3d ser. 6 (October 1903): 213.

18. See the extended discussion in Rohrbough, *Land Office Business*, pp. 220–70.

19. Robbins, *Our Landed Heritage*, pp. 59–65.

20. Gates, *History of Public Land Law*, pp. 165–66, 176.

21. Quoted in Gates, *History of Public Land Law*, pp. 171–72.

22. Quoted in Gates, *History of Public Land Law*, pp. 172–73.

23. Russell L. Berry, *The Scully Estate and Its Cash-Leasing System in the Midwest* (Brookings: Department of Economics, South Dakota State University, 1966); Allan G. Bogue, *Money at Interest: The Farm Mortgage on the Middle Border* (Ithaca: Cornell University Press, 1955); and see Gates, *History of Public Land Law*, pp. 179–80, 403, 406.

24. Thomas S. Berry, *Western Prices before 1861* (Cambridge: Harvard University Press, 1943).

25. James Flint, *Letters from America*, in *Early Western Travels, 1748–1846*, ed. Reuben G. Thwaites (Cleveland: A. H. Clarke, 1904), 9:180.

26. *Collections of the State Historical Society of Wisconsin* (Madison: State Historical Society of Wisconsin, 1900), 3:475.

27. Roy M. Robbins, "Preemption—A Frontier Triumph," *Journal of American History* 18 (1931): 331–42; also chap. 5 in Robbins, *Our Landed Heritage*.

28. *American State Papers, Public Lands* (Washington, D.C.: Gales and Seaton, 1825–37), 5:401.

29. Quoted in Rohrbough, *Land Office Business*, pp. 203–4.

30. Quoted from Fitz's General Land Office Report in January, 1831, to Commissioner Graham, in Rohrbough, *Land Office Business*, p. 212.

31. Quoted by Rohrbough, *Land Office Business*, p. 207, out of his comprehensive study of the voluminous records of the General Land Office.

32. Quoted from Fitz's General Land Office report in January 1831 to Commissioner Graham, in Rohrbough, *Land Office Business*, p. 212.

33. See the data gathered by Rohrbough, *Land Office Business*, p. 219.

34. Quoted in Robbins, *Our Landed Heritage*, pp. 75–76.

35. *Congressional Globe*, 26th Cong., 2d sess., pp. 420–21.

36. Quoted in Robbins, *Our Landed Heritage*, pp. 90–91.

Chapter 5

1. Quoted in Lewis C. Gray, *History of Agriculture in the Southern United States in 1860* (Gloucester, Mass.: Peter Smith, 1958), 1:452.

2. *American State Papers, Public Lands* (Washington, D.C., 1832), 5:401.

3. *Congressional Globe*, 33d Cong., 1st sess., 13 April 1854, pp. 906–59.

4. See the statistical studies in Paul W. Gates, *History of Public Land Law Development* (Washington, D.C.: Public Land Law Commission, 1968), pp. 182–86.

5. *Annals of Congress*, 18th Cong., 1st sess., 1824, p. 583.

6. *Statutes at Large*, 10:574.

7. See Gates, *History of Public Land Law*, pp. 187–88, 194–96.

8. See the statistical data in Gates, *History of Public Land Law*, p. 188.

9. Roy M. Robbins, *Our Landed Heritage: The Public Domain, 1776–1970*, 2d ed. (Lincoln: University of Nebraska Press, 1976), p. 175.

10. Quoted in Gates, *History of Public Law*, p. 187.

11. See Frederic Cople Jaher, *Doubters and Dissenters: Cataclysmic Thought in America, 1885–1918* (New York: Macmillan/Free Press, 1964).

12. Quoted in Robbins, *Our Landed Heritage*, p. 84.

13. See the analysis by Gates, *History of Public Land Law*, pp. 390–93, and Greeley's constant but inconsistent influence as reviewed by Robbins, *Our Landed Heritage*, pp. 98–105 passim.

14. Horace Greeley, *Hints toward Reforms* (New York: Harper, 1853), pp. 317–18.

15. See Robbins, *Our Landed Heritage*, p. 171.

16. Data in Gates, *History of Public Land Law*, pp. 394–96, 401–2.

17. See the important new research in Michael J. O'Brien et al., *Grassland, Forest, and Historical Settlement: An Analysis of Dynamics in Northeast Missouri* (Lincoln: University of Nebraska Press, 1984). Detailed studies of specific Kansas and Nebraska county settlements include Addison E. Sheldon, *Land Systems and Land Policies in Nebraska* (Lincoln: Nebraska Historical Society Publications, 1936); Yasuo Okada, *Public Lands and Pioneer Farmers* (New York: Arno Press, 1979; originally published 1971); Allan G. Bogue, "Farmer Debtors in Pioneer Kinsley," *Kansas Historical Quarterly* 20 (May 1952): 84–87; and John A. Caylor, "The Disposition of the Public Domain in Pierce County, Nebraska" (Ph.D. diss., University of Nebraska, 1951).

18. See the statistical data in Gates, *History of Public Land Law*, pp. 398–401 passim.

19. Quoted in Gates, *History of Public Land Law*, p. 462.

20. See the important contemporary interpretations by Henry N. Copp, *Public Land Laws . . . with the Important Decisions* (Washington, D.C.: Henry N. Copp, 1875), and *The American Settler's Guide: A Popular Exposition of the Public Land System of the United States*, 2d ed. (Washington, D.C., 1882).

21. Hamlin Garland, *A Son of the Middle Border* (New York: Macmillan, 1917, 1919), pp. 301–17.

22. Gates, *History of Public Land Law*, p. 479, gives extended attention to Humphrey's 1931 memoir of high plains farm life.

23. Gates, *History of Public Land Law*, pp. 395–96.

24. John Ise, *Sod-House Days: Letters from a Kansas Homesteader, 1877–1878* (New York: Wilson-Erickson, 1937), p. 19.

25. Gates, *History of Public Land Law*, p. 416.

Chapter 6

1. Randolph G. Downes, "Thomas Jefferson and the Removal of Governor St. Clair in 1802," *Ohio Archeological and Historical Publications* 36

(1927): 62 ff.; *Annals of Congress*, 7th Cong., 2d sess., 22 February 1803, pp. 584–86.

2. See the details in William E. Peters, *Ohio Lands and Their Subdivisions* (Athens, Ohio: W. E. Peters, 1918).

3. See the Ph.D. dissertation by Harry N. Scheiber, "Internal Improvements and Economic Change in Ohio, 1820–1860" (Cornell University, 1962); and see Paul W. Gates, *History of Public Land Law Development* (Washington, D.C.: Public Land Law Review Commission, 1968), pp. 346–50.

4. Gates, *History of Public Land Law*, p. 350.

5. John Bell Rae, "Federal Land Grants in Aid of Canals," *Journal of Economic History* 4 (November 1944): 167 ff.; *Congressional Globe*, 25th Cong., 2d sess., 5 July 1838, pp. 428 ff.

6. Quoted in Leo Marx, *The Machine in the Garden: Technology and the Pastoral Ideal in America* (New York: Oxford University Press, 1964), p. 207.

7. Quoted in Marx, *Machine in the Garden*, p. 194.

8. Quoted in Marx, *Machine in the Garden*, p. 208.

9. See the data gathered by Gates, *History of Public Land Law*, p. 373.

10. Walt Whitman, "Passage to India," in *Leaves of Grass*, 1892 ed. (New York: Bantam Books, 1983), p. 330.

11. John Bell Sanborn, *Congressional Grants of Land in Aid of Railways*, Bulletin no. 30 (Madison: University of Wisconsin, 1899); and the companion piece, Lewis H. Haney, *Congressional History of Railways in the United States to 1850*, Bulletin no. 211 (Madison: University of Wisconsin, 1903).

12. See Paul W. Gates, "The Railroad Land-Grant Legend," *Journal of Economic History* 14 (Spring 1954): 143–46.

13. *Congressional Globe*, 31st Cong., 1st sess., 29 April 1850, pp. 844–45.

14. See George Rogers Taylor and Irene D. Neu, *The American Railroad Network, 1861–1890* (Cambridge: Harvard University Press, 1956).

15. Gates, *History of Public Land Law*, pp. 360–62.

16. Richard C. Overton. *Burlington West: A Colonization History of the Burlington Railroad* (Cambridge: Harvard University Press, 1941).

17. Oscar O. Winther, *The Transportation Frontier: Trans-Mississippi West, 1865–1890* (New York: Holt, Rinehart, Winston, 1964), particularly chap. 7.

18. Richard A. Bartlett, *Great Surveys of the American West* (Norman: University of Oklahoma Press, 1962).

19. Gates, *History of Public Land Law*, p. 374.

20. See the data gathered by Gates, *History of Public Land Law*, p. 279.

21. See Paul W. Gates, *Fifty Million Acres: Conflicts over Kansas Land Policy, 1854–1890* (Ithaca: Cornell University Press, 1954), pp. 153–93.

22. Quoted in Addison E. Sheldon, *Land Systems and Land Policies in Nebraska* (Lincoln: Nebraska State Historical Society, 1936), p. 91.

23. See the analysis and data gathered by Gates, *History of Public Land Law*, pp. 366–69.

24. Gates, *History of Public Land Law*, p. 378.

25. Quoted in Gates, *History of Public Land Law*, p. 380.

26. Quoted in Gates, *History of Public Land Law*, p. 440.

27. John B. Rae, "Commissioner Sparks and the Railroad Land Grants," *Mississippi Valley Historical Review* 25 (September 1938): 211 ff.

28. The academy's deliberations and congressional responses are analyzed and documented in A. Hunter Dupree, *Science in the Federal Government: A History of Policies and Activities to 1940* (Cambridge: Harvard University Press, 1957), pp. 194 ff.; Wallace Stegner, *Beyond the Hundredth Meridian: John Wesley Powell and the Second Opening of the West* (Boston: Houghton Mifflin, 1953), pp. 232–42, 284–87; Roy M. Robbins, *Our Landed Heritage: The Public Domain, 1776–1970*, 2d ed. (Lincoln: University of Nebraska Press, 1976), pp. 311–14; Gates, *History of Public Land Law*, pp. 422 ff.; Harold H. Dunham, *Government Handout: A Study in the Administration of the Public Lands, 1875–1891* (New York: DaCapo Press, 1941).

29. Milton Conover, *The General Land Office: Its History, Activities and Organization* (Baltimore: Johns Hopkins Press, 1923).

30. *The Existing Laws of the United States of a General and Permanent Character and Relating to the Survey and Disposition of the Public Domain* (Washington, D.C., 1884).

31. *The Public Domain: Its History with Statistics* (Washington, D.C., 1884).

32. *Land Office Report, 1886*, p. 43.

33. *Land Office Report, 1885*, p. 50.

34. J. H. Hawes, *Manual of United States Surveying* (Philadelphia: J. B. Lippincott, 1868); John R. Stilgoe, *Common Landscape of America, 1580 to 1845* (New Haven: Yale University Press, 1982), pp. 100–101. See also the description of nineteenth-century field instruments in François D. Uzes, *Chaining the Land: A History of Surveying in California* (Sacramento: Landmark Enterprises, 1977), pp. 1–38.

35. Vernon Carstensen, "Patterns on the American Land," *Surveying and Mapping* 36 (December 1976): 303–9; see also a summary of complaints laid before the Public Land Commission in Gates, *History of Public Land Law*, pp. 420–22.

36. Gates, *History of Public Land Law*, p. 477.

37. *Congressional Record*, 51st Cong., 2d sess., 28 February 1891, p. 3615.

38. Gates, *History of Public Land Law*, pp. 484–86.

Chapter 7

1. John Wesley Powell, *Report on the Lands of the Arid Region of the United States*, reprint ed. (Boston: Harvard Common Press, 1983; originally published 1879), pp. 38–39.

2. *Scientific American* 63 (20 December 1890): 384–85.

3. *North American Review* 153 (October 1891):385–404; *Nation* 53 (22 October 1891):1373; *Scientific American* 65 (5 September 1891):144–53.

4. See John Opie, "America's Seventy-Year Mistake; or, How We Got Fooled by Good Weather in Difficult Country," in *Proceedings of a Seminar on Natural Resource Use and Environmental Policy* (Ames, Iowa: North Central Regional Center for Rural Development/Iowa State University, 1982), pp. 27–56.

5. John L. Allen, "Exploration and the Creation of Geographical Images of the Great Plains: Notes on the Role of Subjectivity," in *Images of the Plains: The Role of Human Nature in Settlement,* ed. Brian W. Blouet and Merlin P. Lawson (Lincoln: University of Nebraska Press, 1975), pp. 3–12; Waldo R. Wedel, "Some Early Euro-American Precepts of the Great Plains and Their Influence on Anthropological Thinking," in *Images of the Plains,* ed. Blouet and Lawson, pp. 13–21.

6. The classic study is still W. Eugene Hollon, *The Great American Desert, Then and Now* (New York: Oxford University Press, 1966).

7. Quoted in Wedel, "Precepts of the Great Plains," p. 15.

8. Quoted in Allen, "Exploration and Geographical Images," pp. 8–9.

9. Quoted in David M. Emmons, "The Influence of Ideology on Changing Environmental Images: The Case of Six Gazetteers," in *Images of the Plains,* ed. Blouet and Lawson, p. 126.

10. Quoted in Emmons, "Changing Environmental Images," p. 129.

11. David F. Costello, *The Prairie World: Plants and Animals of the Grassland Seas* (New York: Thomas Y. Crowell, 1969), pp. 37, 38, 51; Robert G. Athearn, *High Country Empire: The High Plains and Rockies* (Lincoln: University of Nebraska Press, 1960), pp. 179–91.

12. Quoted in Terry G. Jordan, "Between the Forest and the Prairie," in *Geographic Perspectives on America's Past,* ed. David Ward (New York: Oxford University Press, 1979), p. 53.

13. See Wallace Stegner, *Beyond the Hundredth Meridian: John Wesley Powell and the Second Opening of the West* (Boston: Houghton Mifflin, 1953).

14. Athearn, *High Country Empire,* pp. 185, 192; Gilbert C. Fite, *The Farmers' Frontier, 1865–1900* (New York: Holt, Rinehart and Winston, 1966), chaps. 6–7.

15. See Costello, *Prairie World,* and the extraordinary *Pasture and Range Plants* (Bartlesville, Okla.: Phillips Petroleum, 1963).

16. Quoted in Paul Horgan, *Josiah Gregg and His Vision of the Early West* (New York: Farrar, Straus and Giroux, 1979), p. 48. See also Fite, *Farmers' Frontier,* pp. 20–22, 96–97.

17. Gilbert extrapolated his views from his "special study of the drainage-basin of Great Salt Lake," chap. 4, "Water Supply," inserted as a corrective to Powell's pessimistic *Lands of the Arid Region,* pp. 57–80.

18. Quoted in Powell, *Lands of the Arid Region,* p. 71.

19. Powell, *Lands of the Arid Region,* pp. 57–80.

20. Powell, *Lands of the Arid Region,* p. 91.

21. Quoted in Hollon, *Great American Desert,* pp. 145–46.

22. Walter Prescott Webb, *The Great Plains* (New York: Ginn, 1931), pp. 377 ff.; Hollon, *Great American Desert*, pp. 153–54.

23. Emmons, "Changing Environmental Images," p. 125.

24. Quoted in Athearn, *High Country Empire*, p. 185.

25. Powell, *Lands of the Arid Region*, pp. xxiv, 1.

26. Powell, *Lands of the Arid Region*, p. 9.

27. Fite, *Farmers' Frontier*, pp. 106 ff.; Webb, *Great Plains*, pp. 343 ff.

28. Fite, *Farmers' Frontier*, pp. 125 ff.

29. Athearn, *High Country Empire*, pp. 212 ff.

30. Roy M. Robbins, *Our Landed Heritage: The Public Domain, 1776–1970*, 2d ed. (Lincoln: University of Nebraska Press, 1976), p. 218.

31. Quoted in Robbins, *Our Landed Heritage*, pp. 219–20.

32. Indispensable to any review of the history of western land reclamation, its related policies and controversies, and its impact is Lawrence B. Lee's exemplary essay and bibliography, *Reclaiming the American West: An Historiography and Guide* (Santa Barbara: ABC-Clio, 1980).

33. Robbins, *Our Landed Heritage*, p. 297.

34. Lee, *Reclaiming the American West*, p. 13n; Wells A. Hutchins, "Background and Modern Developments in Water Law in the United States," *Natural Resources Journal* 2 (1962): 416–41; George Thomas, *The Development of Institutions under Irrigation* (New York: Macmillan, 1920); Ray P. Teele, *The Economics of Land Reclamation in the United States* (Chicago: A. W. Shaw, 1927).

35. Lee, *Reclaiming the American West*, pp. xii, 12.

36. Paul W. Gates, *History of Public Land Law Development* (Washington, D.C.: Public Land Law Review Commission, 1968), pp. 498–501.

37. Robbins, *Our Landed Heritage*, pp. 342, 362–63; Gates, *History of Public Land Law*, pp. 503 ff.

38. Quoted in Gates, *History of Public Land Law*, p. 500; see also Addison E. Sheldon, *Land Systems and Land Policies in Nebraska* (Lincoln: University of Nebraska Press, 1936).

39. Quoted in Robbins, *Our Landed Heritage*, p. 375.

40. Bradley H. Baltensperger, "Agricultural Adjustments to Great Plains Drought: The Republican Valley, 1870–1900," in *The Great Plains: Environment and Culture*, ed. Brian W. Blouet and Frederick C. Luebke (Lincoln: University of Nebraska Press, 1979), pp. 43–60.

41. *Oklahoma Comprehensive Water Plan*, Publication 94 (Oklahoma City: Oklahoma Water Resources Board, 1980), pp. 8–9.

42. See Morton W. Bittinger and Elizabeth B. Green, *You Never Miss the Water till . . . (The Ogallala Story)* (Littleton, Colo.: Water Resource Publications, 1980).

43. A useful compendium of definitions and classifications of water is included in the *Oklahoma Comprehensive Water Plan*, pp. 18–22.

44. The best recent study of historical and current legislation and policies is Robert G. Dunbar, *Forging New Rights in Western Waters* (Lincoln: University of Nebraska Press, 1983).

45. Dunbar, *Forging New Rights*, p. 61.

46. *Oklahoma Comprehensive Water Plan*, p. 23.

47. Dunbar, *Forging New Rights*, pp. 79–81.

48. Dunbar, *Forging New Rights*, p. 82.

49. Powell, *Lands of the Arid Region*, pp. 4–8.

50. Powell, *Lands of the Arid Region*, pp. iii–vii.

51. Powell, *Lands of the Arid Region*, pp. 37–38.

52. Powell, *Lands of the Arid Region*, pp. 22–40.

53. This section is indebted to the excellent essay by Timothy J. Rickard, "The Great Plains as Part of an Irrigated Western Empire," in *Great Plains*, ed. Blouet and Luebke, esp. pp. 82–91.

54. John Wesley Powell, "The Irrigable Lands of the Arid Region," *Century Magazine* 39 (November 1889–April 1890): 770.

55. Frederick H. Newell, "Irrigation on the Great Plains," in *Yearbook of the United States Department of Agriculture, 1896* (Washington, D.C.: U.S. Government Printing Office, 1897), pp. 168–69.

Chapter 8

1. Powell's views, and the debates they provoked, can be followed in Wallace B. Stegner's sympathetic and thorough account, *Beyond the Hundredth Meridian: John Wesley Powell and the Second Opening of the West* (Boston: Houghton Mifflin, 1953).

2. William E. Smythe, *The Conquest of Arid America* (New York: Harper, 1899; rev. ed., New York: Macmillan, 1905; reprinted Seattle: University of Washington Press, 1970, introduction by Lawrence B. Lee).

3. Space does not allow attention to other major irrigation advocates, particularly Frederick Haynes Newell and Elwood Mead in the twentieth century. See the indispensable bibliographical study by Lawrence B. Lee, *Reclaiming the American West: An Historiography and Guide* (Santa Barbara: ABC-Clio, 1980), pp. 17–21, 26–28, 31–33.

4. See the discussion in Timothy J. Rickard, "The Great Plains as Part of an Irrigated Western Empire," in *The Great Plains: Environment and Culture*, ed. Brian W. Blouet and Frederick C. Luebke (Lincoln: University of Nebraska Press, 1979), p. 87.

5. Frederick H. Newell, "Water," in *Conservation of Our Natural Resources*, ed. Loomis Havemeyer (New York: Macmillan, 1930), p. 173.

6. See Rickard, "Great Plains," pp. 88–89.

7. Quoted in Rickard, "Great Plains," p. 90.

8. Quoted in Rickard, "Great Plains," p. 91.

9. Dorothy Lampen, *Economic and Social Aspects of Federal Reclamation* (Baltimore: Johns Hopkins University Press, 1930), pp. 66–68.

10. Norris Hundley, Jr., *Water and the West* (Berkeley: University of California Press, 1975); Alfred R. Golze, *Reclamation in the United States* (New York: McGraw-Hill, 1952).

11. Philip E. LeVeen, "Reclamation Policy at a Crossroads," *Public Affairs Report* 19 (October 1978): 2–3. Similar data, released by the National

Wildlife Federation in May 1984, have been publicly questioned by Reclamation officials.

12. Kenneth Frederick and James C. Hanson, *Water for Western Agriculture* (Washington, D.C.: Resources for the Future, 1982), pp. 116–21.

13. See the data gathered in Frederick and Hanson, *Water for Western Agriculture.*

14. Quoted, with other useful sources, by Peter Rogers, "The Future of Water," *Atlantic Monthly* 252, no. 1 (July 1983): 80–92.

15. See the important summary provided by Charles Coate, "Seventy-five Years of Reclamation: An Assessment," paper presented at the 1977 Western History Association, p. 8 and passim.

16. *Federal Charges for Irrigation Projects Reviewed Do Not Cover Costs* (Washington, D.C.: U.S. Government Accounting Office, 1981).

17. Randal R. Rucker and Price V. Fishback, "The Federal Reclamation Program: An Analysis of Rent-Seeking Behavior," in *Water Rights: Scarce Resource Allocation, Bureaucracy, and the Environment,* ed. Terry L. Anderson (Cambridge, Mass.: Pacific Institute for Public Policy Research/Ballinger, 1983), pp. 63–81.

18. The major exception to large-scale exemptions was the Columbia basin project in the 1940s, where tract limitations were largely enforced. See Donald C. Swain, "The Bureau of Reclamation and the New Deal, 1933–1940," *Pacific Northwest Quarterly* 61, no. 3 (July 1970): 144–46.

19. *Oklahoma Comprehensive Water Plan,* Publication 94 (Oklahoma City: Oklahoma Water Resources Board, 1980), pp. 11–12.

20. See Earl O. Heady et al., *Roots of the Farm Problem* (Ames: Iowa State University Press, 1965), who praised the capacity of new capital inputs (irrigation, fertilizers, equipment, etc.) to create more production on less land but wondered whether new conditions would bring about the demise of the family farm. And see Frederick and Hanson, *Water for Western Agriculture,* p. xv; "Public Works for Water and Power and Energy Research," document presented at subcommittee hearings, Committee on Appropriations. U.S. House of Representatives, 95th Cong., 1st sess., 1982, pp. 225–26.

21. "Changes Are Confronting U.S. on Water Projects," *New York Times,* 17 March 1985, p. 14.

22. E. Louise Peffer, *The Closing of the Public Domain: Disposal and Reservation Policies, 1900–1950* (Stanford: Stanford University Press, 1951); Alfred G. Cuzan, "Appropriators versus Expropriators: The Political Economy of Water in the West," in *Water Rights,* ed. Anderson, pp. 20–21.

23. Lee, *Reclaiming the American West,* p. 43; see also pp. 16, 28–29, 43–44, 59.

24. The most balanced and historically accurate recent study is Robert G. Dunbar, *Forging New Rights in Western Waters* (Lincoln: University of Nebraska Press, 1983).

25. Oklahoma Supreme Court, *Canada v. Shawnee,* 179 OKL. 53, 64 P.2d 694 (1936, 1937).

26. New Mexico law professor Charles DuMars, quoted in *Wall Street Journal,* 19 November 1984.

27. *New York Times*, 17 June 1985.

28. B. Delworth Gardner, "Water Pricing and Rent Seeking in California Agriculture," in *Water Rights*, ed. Anderson, pp. 86–112.

29. *Six-State High Plains—Ogallala Aquifer Regional Resources Study* (Washington, D.C.: Department of Commerce, 1982), pp. 6–77.

30. *Oklahoma Comprehensive Water Plan*, p. 15; see also p. 39.

31. Anderson, *Water Rights*, pp. 242–48.

32. "Cost of Irrigating California Farms to Rise Steeply," *New York Times*, 17 November 1984.

33. K. W. Easter, J. A. Leitch, and D. F. Scott, "Competition for Water, a Capricious Resource," in *Water Resources Research*, ed. Ted L. Napier et al. (Ankeney, Iowa: North Central Committee 111, Natural Resource Use and Environmental Policy/Soil Conservation Society of America, 1983), pp. 135–53.

34. "Day of Reckoning for the Garrison Project," *Science* 225 (31 August 1984): 904–6; "Dakota Water Project Is Cut by Reagan Panel," *New York Times*, 16 December 1984, p. 14.

35. Kenneth D. Frederick, "Water Supplies," in *Current Issues in Natural Resource Policy*, ed. Paul Portney (Washington, D.C.: Resources for the Future, 1982), pp. 216 ff.

36. Quoted in "Arizona Aims to Cut per Capita Water Use in Half," *New York Times*, 30 January 1984.

37. "Thirsty Arizona Debates Water Plan," *New York Times*, 9 April 1984.

38. Frederick and Hanson, *Water for Western Agriculture*, pp. 131–33; Micha Gisser and Ronald N. Johnson, "Institutional Restrictions on the Transfer of Water Rights and the Survival of an Agency," in *Water Rights*, ed. Anderson, pp. 137–52.

39. Frederick and Hanson, *Water for Western Agriculture*, pp. 137–39.

40. Frederick and Hanson, *Water for Western Agriculture*, pp. 81–84, 120.

41. *Appraisal 1980: Soil and Water Resources Conservation Act, Review Draft* (Washington, D.C.: USDA, 1980); William E. Larson et al., *Soil and Water Resources: Resource Priorities for the Nation* (Madison, Wisc.: Soil Science Society of America, 1981), pp. 198 ff.

42. Frederick and Hanson, *Water for Western Agriculture*, pp. 165–84. Arlo Biere and Frederick Worman, "Irrigation Management: Current and Prospective Issues," in *Water Resources Research*, ed. Napier et al., pp. 99–116.

43. Frederick and Hanson, *Water for Western Agriculture*, pp. 13–22, 72; J. R. Gilley and M. E. Jensen, "Irrigation Management: Contributions to Agricultural Productivity," in Napier, *Water Resources Research*, pp. 22–35.

44. *Oklahoma Comprehensive Water Plan*, p. 150 and passim.

45. *Water Spectrum* 13, no. 4 (Fall 1981): 51.

46. Frederick and Hanson, *Water for Western Agriculture*, pp. 86–91.

47. Howard W. Ottoson, William L. Powers, and Susan M. Miller, "Water Research in the North Central Region . . . 1950–1980," in *Water Resources Research*, ed. Napier, pp. 3–21; *Ogallala Aquifer Study in Kansas* (Topeka:

Kansas Water Office, 1982); *Summary of the Nebraska Research . . . Six-State . . . Study* (Lincoln: Nebraska Natural Resources Commission, 1981).

48. *Water-Related Technologies for Sustaining Agriculture in U.S. Arid and Semiarid Lands* (Washington, D.C.: U.S. Office of Technology Assessment, 1982).

49. *The Nation's Water Resources, 1975–2000: Second National Water Assessment*, vol. 1 (Washington, D.C.: U.S. Water Resources Council, 1978); Earl R. Swanson and Earl O. Heady, "The Future of Agriculture in the North Central Region," in *Water Resources Research*, ed. Napier, pp. 85–87.

50. Interview in *Dallas Morning News*, 19 August 1984.

Chapter 9

1. Gilbert C. Fite, *The Farmers' Frontier, 1865–1900* (New York: Holt, Rinehart and Winston, 1966), p. 158.

2. Paul W. Gates, *History of Public Land Law Development* (Washington, D.C.: Public Land Law Commission, 1968), pp. 115, 301–3; see also W. W. Robinson, *Land in California* (Berkeley: University of California Press, 1948).

3. *Transactions of the California State Agricultural Society* (Sacramento, 1859), pp. 361 ff.

4. See Fite, *Farmers' Frontier*, pp. 162 ff.

5. See Gerald D. Nash, *State Government and Economic Development: A History of Administrative Policies in California, 1849–1933* (Berkeley: University of California Press, 1964).

6. See Gates, *History of Public Land Law*, pp. 116–17, 117n.

7. Calculated by Gates, *History of Public Land Law*, p. 413n.

8. The following uses documentation in Gerald D. Nash, "Henry George Reexamined: William S. Chapman's Views on Land Speculation in Nineteenth Century California," *Agricultural History* 35, no. 3 (July 1959): 133–37.

9. Nash, *State Government and Economic Development*, p. 135.

10. See Fite, *Farmers' Frontier*, pp. 166–67.

11. See Donald Worster's pathbreaking article "Hydraulic Society in California: An Ecological Interpretation," *Agricultural History* 56, no. 3 (July 1982): 508–10; and also Fite, *Farmers' Frontier*, pp. 171–72.

12. Fite, *Farmers' Frontier*, pp. 166–69.

13. Quoted in Worster, "Hydraulic Society," p. 509.

14. See William E. Smythe, *The Conquest of Arid America* (New York: Harper, 1899; rev. ed., New York: Macmillan, 1905; reprinted Seattle: University of Washington Press, 1970), which includes an important essay about Smythe's career by Lawrence B. Lee. See also Donald J. Pisani, "Reclamation and Social Engineering in the Progressive Era," *Agricultural History* 57, no. 1 (January 1983): 49–51. For Mead see Paul G. Conkin, "The Vision

of Elwood Mead," *Agricultural History* 34, no. 2 (April 1960): 88–97; and Elwood Mead, *Irrigation Institutions* (New York: Macmillan, 1903).

15. Told to the *New York World*, 3 March 1895.

16. Elwood Mead, *Helping Men Own Farms* (New York: Macmillan, 1928), pp. 201–8.

17. See R. Louis Gentilcore, "Ontario, California and the Agricultural Boom of the 1880s," *Agricultural History* 34, no. 2 (April 1960): 77–87; see also Robert G. Dunbar, *Forging New Rights in Western Waters* (Lincoln: University of Nebraska Press, 1984), pp. 31–33.

18. Gentilcore, "Agricultural Boom of the 1880s," p. 85.

19. Quoted in Fite, *Farmers' Frontier*, p. 169.

20. See Dunbar, *Western Waters*, pp. 32–34.

21. See the useful data in Frank Adams, *Irrigation Districts in California* (Sacramento: State Printing Office, 1929).

22. Fite, *Farmers' Frontier*, pp. 170–71.

23. Quoted in Gates, *History of Public Land Law*, pp. 653–54; see also Michael G. Robinson, *Water for the West: The Bureau of Reclamation, 1902–1977* (Chicago: Public Works Historical Society, 1979).

24. But see Clayton Koppes, "Public Water, Private Land: Origins of the Acreage Limitation Controversy, 1933–1953," *Pacific Historical Review* 47 (November 1978): 607–36.

25. Worster, "Hydraulic Society," pp. 507, 512–13.

26. Quoted in Worster, "Hydraulic Society," p. 512. Early boosterism can also be found in George W. James, *Reclaiming the Arid West: The Story of the United States Reclamation Service* (New York: Dodd, Mead, 1917).

27. See Mary Montgomery and Marion Clawson, *History of Legislation and Policy Formation of the Central Valley Project* (Berkeley: University of California Press, 1946); see also Robert de Roos, *The Thirsty Land: The Story of the Central Valley Project* (Palo Alto: Stanford University Press, 1948); Philip L. Fredkin, *A River No More: The Colorado River and the West* (New York: Alfred A. Knopf, 1981).

28. Worster, "Hydraulic Society," p. 504; see also p. 509.

Chapter 10

1. See the discussion in Roy M. Robbins, *Our Landed Heritage: The Public Domain, 1776–1970*, 2d ed. (Lincoln: University of Nebraska Press, 1976), pp. 354–62.

2. Frederick Jackson Turner, "The Significance of the Frontier in American History," in *The Frontier in American History* (New York: Henry Holt, 1920), p. 21. See also John Opie, "Frederick Jackson Turner, the Old West, and the Formation of a National Mythology," *Environmental Review* 5, no. 2 (Fall 1981): 79–91.

3. See the data gathered in Willard W. Cochrane, *The Development of American Agriculture: A Historical Analysis* (Minneapolis: University of Minnesota Press, 1979), p. 175; Robbins, *Our Landed Heritage*, p. 410.

4. Quoted in Leslie Hewes, "Agricultural Risk in the Great Plains," in *The*

Great Plains: Environment and Culture, ed. Brian W. Blouet and Frederick C. Luebke (Lincoln: University of Nebraska Press, 1979), p. 158; and see Gilbert C. Fite, "The Great Plains: Promises, Problems, and Prosepcts," in *Great Plains,* ed. Blouet and Luebke, p. 188.

5. Quoted in Robbins, *Our Landed Heritage,* p. 352; see also pp. 289–90.

6. Robbins, *Our Landed Heritage,* pp. 331–33; Paul W. Gates, *History of Public Land Law Development* (Washington, D.C.: Public Land Law Commission, 1968), p. 511.

7. Quoted in Robbins, *Our Landed Heritage,* p. 347; see also pp. 347–48.

8. Quoted in the Spokane *Spokesman-Review,* 21 June 1910, and in Robbins, *Our Landed Heritage,* pp. 372–73; see also pp. 374–75.

9. *Congressional Record,* 63d Cong., 2d sess., appendix, pp. 683–85.

10. Mary W. M. Hargreaves, "Dry Farming Alias Scientific Farming," *Agricultural History* 22, no. 1 (1948): 39–56.

11. Quoted in Peter Steinhart, "The Edge Gets Thinner," *Audubon Magazine* 85, no. 6 (November 1983): 114.

12. See Fite, "Great Plains," pp. 188–89.

13. For 1928 see H. H. Bennett and W. R. Chapline, *USDA Circular 33* (Washington, D.C., 1928); for post-1933 see the analysis of Stanley W. Trimble, "Perspectives on the History of Soil Erosion Control in the Eastern United States," *Agricultural History* 59, no. 2 (April 1985): 165.

14. See, for example, the classic environmental argument as developed by Paul B. Sears, *Deserts on the March* (Norman: University of Oklahoma Press, 1935); James C. Malin, *The Grassland of North America* (Lawrence, Kans.: privately printed, 1947); and the updated argument developed by Donald Worster in "Grass to Dust: Ecology and the Great Plains in the 1930s," *Environmental Review* 2, no. 4 (1977): 2–12, and his *Dust Bowl: The Southern Plains in the 1930s* (New York: Oxford University Press, 1979). See also R. Douglas Hurt, *The Dust Bowl: An Agricultural and Social History* (Chicago: Nelson-Hall, 1981).

15. James H. Shideler, *Farm Crisis, 1919–1923* (Berkeley: University of California Press, 1957); Clarence A. Wiley, *Agriculture and the Business Cycle since 1920,* Studies in the Social Sciences and History no. 15 (Madison: University of Wisconsin, 1930); Gilbert C. Fite, *American Farmers: The New Minority* (Bloomington: Indiana University Press, 1981), esp. chaps. 2–4.

16. See the clear and revealing interview of Ickes by the leading journalist Marquis James, "The National Domain and the New Deal," *Saturday Evening Post* 206 (23 December 1933): 10–11.

17. The historical policies related to the Soil Conservation Service are analyzed in Sandra S. Batie, "Soil Conservation in the 1980s: A Historical Perspective," paper presented at the Symposium on the History of Soil and Water Conservation, University of Missouri, Columbia, 23–26 May 1984, published in *Agricultural History* 59, no. 2 (April 1985): 107–23; see also Don Paarlberg, "Effects of New Deal Farm Programs on the Agricultural Agenda a Half Century Later and Prospects for the Future," *Journal of Agricultural Economics* 65 (1981): 1163–67; and R. B. Held and M. Clawson, *Soil Conservation in Perspective* (Baltimore: Johns Hopkins Press, 1975).

18. *United States vs. Butler et al., Receivers of Hossac Mills Corp.,* 297 U.S. 1–88 (1936).

19. For a contemporary assessment, see H. R. Tolly, "To Conserve Farm Income and Soil Resources," *Soil Conservation* 4 (July 1938): 11; for a recent review, see Randall A. Kramer and Sandra S. Batie, "Cross Compliance Concepts in Agricultural Programs: The New Deal to the Present," *Agricultural History* 59, no. 2 (April 1985): 308–10.

20. Kramer and Batie, "Cross Compliance Concepts," pp. 311–12.

21. See the public debate reviewed in L. C. Gray, "The Social and Economic Implications of the National Land Program," *Journal of Farm Economics* 18 (May 1936): 260; and Richard S. Kirkendall, *Social Scientists and Farm Politics in the Age of Roosevelt* (Columbia: University of Missouri Press, 1966).

22. See R. Douglas Hurt's important essay, "Agricultural Technology in the Dust Bowl, 1932–1940," in *Great Plains,* ed. Blouet and Luebke, pp. 139–56.

23. R. S. Dallavalle and L. V. Mayer, *Soil Conservation in the United States: The Federal Role, Origins, Evolution, and Current Status,* CRS Report 80-144S (Washington, D.C.: Congressional Research Service, 1980).

24. Richard Barrows et al., *Mapping to Preserve Agricultural Land,* Publication A3037 (Madison: Agricultural Extension Service, 1980); see also R. E. Couglin, John C. Keene, et al., *The Protection of Farmland: A Reference Guidebook for State and Local Governments* (Washington, D.C.: National Agricultural Lands Study, [1982?]).

25. This is a major theme in Fite, *American Farmers,* p. 42 and passim; see also the essays collected in H. G. Halcrow, E. O. Heady, and M. G. Cotner, eds., *Soil Conservation: Policies, Institutions and Incentives* (Ankeny, Iowa: Soil Conservation Society of America, 1982); and see Sandra S. Batie, *Soil Erosion: Crisis in America's Croplands?* (Washington, D.C.: Conservation Foundation, 1981).

26. R. Douglas Hurt, "The National Grasslands: Origin and Development in the Dust Bowl," *Agricultural History* 59, no. 2 (April 1985): 157; and see Stanley Baldwin, *Poverty and Politics* (Chapel Hill: University of North Carolina Press, 1968).

27. See the discussion by Paarlberg, "Effects of New Deal Farm Programs," pp. 1163–67; and Robbins, *Our Landed Heritage,* pp. 421–23.

28. Kramer and Batie, "Cross Compliance Concepts," p. 313.

29. Quoted in Fite, "Great Plains," p. 195.

30. Quoted in Robbins, *Our Landed Heritage,* p. 461.

31. *One Third of the Nation's Land: A Report to the President and to Congress by the Public Land Law Review Commission* (Washington, D.C.: Government Printing Office, 1970), pp. 1–7, 177–82.

32. *One Third of the Nation's Land,* pp. 68–70, 190–91, 224, 266–67.

33. See especially the essays on RCA in Halcrow, Heady, and Cotner, *Soil Conservation,* pp. 47–88, 93–108.

34. See the analysis by Richard H. K. Vietor, *Environmental Politics and the Coal Coalition* (College Station: Texas A & M Press, 1980), pp. 197–226.

35. See the discussion in Kramer and Batie, "Cross Compliance Concepts," pp. 314–16.

36. Batie, *Soil Erosion*, p. 5 and passim.

37. "Soil Erosion Threatens U.S. Farm Output," *New York Times*, 26 October 1980.

38. Don Paarlberg, *Farm and Food Policy: Issues of the 1980s* (Lincoln: University of Nebraska Press, 1980), p. 9.

39. Sara Ebenreck, "Stopping the Raid on Soil: Ethical Reflections on 'Sodbusting' Legislation," *Agriculture and Human Values* 1, no. 3 (Summer 1984): 3–10; and see the comments by agricultural economist Gary Lynne, pp. 10–14 of the same issue.

40. "Cropland Erosion Is a Growing Problem," *Wall Street Journal*, 26 April 1985, p. 6.

Chapter 11

1. This debate is admirably reviewed by Richard H. K. Vietor, *Environmental Politics and the Coal Coalition* (College Station: Texas A&M Press, 1980), pp. 197–226.

2. Aldo Leopold, "The Land Ethic," in *A Sand County Almanac* (New York: Oxford University Press, 1953), pp. 237–63.

3. *The Protection of Farmland: A Reference Guidebook for State and Local Governments*, National Agricultural Lands Study (Washington, D.C.: U.S. Government Printing Office, [1981]), pp. 104 ff., henceforth cited as NALS.

4. See the discussion in NALS, pp. 255–65.

5. This is a major theme covered in Gilbert T. Fite, *American Farmers: The New Minority* (Bloomington: Indiana University Press, 1981).

6. Arizona, Arkansas, Colorado, Delaware, Florida, Idaho, Indiana, Iowa, Louisiana, Mississippi, Missouri, New Mexico, North Dakota, Oklahoma, South Dakota, West Virginia, and Wyoming; see NALS, p. 57.

7. NALS, p. 62.

8. NALS, p. 79.

9. NALS, pp. 76–78.

10. NALS, pp. 87–90.

11. Quoted in NALS, p. 92.

12. Quoted in NALS, p. 93.

13. NALS, pp. 125–26.

14. NALS, p. 99; see also pp. 100–102.

15. NALS, pp. 99, 108–10.

16. NALS, pp. 120–21.

17. See the detailed review of PDRs and related programs in NALS, pp. 148–73.

18. A preliminary study is in NALS, pp. 183–86; see also Robert A. Lemire, *Creative Land Development* (Boston: Houghton Mifflin, 1979), Charles E. Little, *Middleground Approaches to the Preservation of Farmland* (Wash-

ington, D.C.: American Land Forum, 1980), and W. Wendell Fletcher and Charles E. Little, *The American Cropland Crisis* (Bethesda Md.: American Land Forum, 1982).

19. *American Farmland* 5 (March–April 1985): 2.

20. Both reports were received in a promotional mailing in December 1984.

21. "Some Landed Gentry Try to Treat the Land More Gently," *New York Times*, 12 May 1985, "News of the Week in Review," p. 4.

22. NALS, pp. 206 ff.

23. NALS, pp. 208–10.

24. Quoted in NALS, p. 219.

25. NALS, p. 236.

26. NALS, p. 239.

27. NALS, p. 240.

28. NALS, p. 240.

29. NALS, p. 240.

30. NALS, pp. 245–46.

31. Summary report in *American Farmland* 5 (March–April 1985): 2.

32. See the provocative summary of the issues by Charles E. Little, "On Saving Farmland," *American Land Forum* 2, no. 1 (Winter 1981): 8–11, 27–29, and the comments by Richard Layman, *American Land Forum* 2, no. 4 (Fall 1981): 2, 36.

33. See Little, "On Saving Farmland," pp. 11–13, 27.

Chapter 12

1. See Douglas E. Bowers et al., *History of Agricultural Price-Support and Adjustment Programs, 1933–84*, Agricultural Information Bulletin no. 485 (Washington, D.C.: USDA, ERS, 1984), p. 45.

2. See *The Current Financial Condition of Farmers and Farm Lenders*, Agriculture Information Bulletin no. 490 (Washington, D.C.: USDA, ERS, 1984).

3. See the important summary by Sandra S. Batie and Robert G. Healy, "The Future of American Agriculture," *Scientific American* 248 (February 1983): 45–53.

4. Reported in Peter Rogers, "The Future of Water," *Atlantic* 252 (July 1983): 90–91.

5. Batie and Healy, "Future of American Agriculture," pp. 45–47.

6. USDA Economics, Statistics, and Cooperatives Service, compiled in Lester R. Brown, "World Population Growth, Soil Erosion, and Food Security," *Science* 214 (27 November 1981): 995–97.

7. Brown, "World Population Growth," pp. 995–1002.

8. Batie and Healy, "Future of American Agriculture," pp. 47–53.

9. This is the conclusion reached in the background literature for the 1985 congressional farm bill debate. See Bowers et al., *Price-Support and Adjustment*, p. 44.

10. This is a major theme in Gilbert C. Fite, *American Farmers: The New Minority* (Bloomington: Indiana University Press, 1981).

11. Quoted in Peter Steinhart, "The Edge Gets Thinner,"*Audubon* 85 (November 1983): 6.

12. See J. B. Penn, "The Changing Farm Sector and Future Public Policy: An Economic Perspective," in *Agricultural–Food Policy Review: Perspectives for the 1980's* (Washington, D.C.: USDA, ESS AFPR-4, 1981), p. 47.

13. Donald Worster, *Nature's Economy: The Roots of Ecology* (Garden City, N.Y.: Anchor-Doubleday, 1977, 1979), pp. 205 ff.

14. Penn, "Farm Sector and Public Policy," pp. 48 ff.

15. Reported by William Robbins, "How Iowa Farmer Ended up in the Black During Hard Times," *New York Times*, 22 November 1985, including data from Federal Reserve economist Emanuel Melichar.

16. See Brown, "World Population Growth," pp. 996–1002.

17. See Paul Rosenbery et al., "Predicting the Effects of Soil Depletion from Erosion," *Journal of Soil and Water Conservation* 35, no. 3 (May/June, 1980): 131–134; Leon Lyles, "Possible Effects of Wind Erosion on Soil Productivity," *Journal of Soil and Water Conservation* 30, no. 6 (November/December 1975): 279–83.

18. See Penn, "Farm Sector and Public Policy," pp. 31–34.

19. Kenneth Cook, "Surplus Madness," *Journal of Soil and Water Conservation* 38, 1 (January/February 1983): 25–28; see also Lester Brown's conclusions based on information from USDA Agricultural Stabilization and Conservation Service official Randy Weber, in *State of the World 1984* (New York: W. W. Norton, 1984), pp. 186–88.

20. O'Brien, *Agricultural–Food Policy Review*, p. 5.

21. Brown, *State of the World 1984*, p. 188.

22. See *Summary of Appraisal, Parts I and II, Program Report Review Draft 1980: Soil and Water Resources Conservation Act* (Washington, D.C.: USDA, 1980); *Basic Statistics 1977 National Resources Inventory, Statistical Bulletin no. 686* (Washington, D.C.: USDA, SCS, 1982).

23. These withdrawal policies are emphasized in Harold G. Halcrow et al., *Soil Conservation Policies, Institutions and Incentives* (Ankeny, Iowa: Soil Conservation Society of America, 1982).

24. This is the essential conclusion of Avery, "U.S. Farm Dilemma," p. 412.

25. John E. Lee, in *Agricultural–Food Policy Review*, p. 136.

26. Lee, *Agricultural–Food Policy Review*, pp. 138–48.

27. Lee, *Agricultural–Food Policy Review*, p. 139.

28. See Lee, *Agricultural–Food Policy Review*, pp. 138–48.

29. See the summary discussion in Brown, *State of the World*, pp. 182–85.

30. Brown, *State of the World*, pp. 996–97.

31. Brown, *State of the World*, p. 996.

32. Brown, *State of the World*, p. 185.

33. See Penn, "Farm Sector and Public Policy," pp. 50–53, 57.

Index